SALES LAW AND PRODUCT LIABILITY

SALES LAW AND PRODUCT LIABILITY

A Business Guide

Michael Whincup

Gower

This edition supersedes *Product Liability Law* published in 1985.
Published by
Gower Publishing Limited
Gower House
Croft Road
Aldershot
Hampshire GU11 3HR
England

Gower
Old Post Road
Brookfield
Vermont 05036
USA

Michael Whincup has asserted his right under the Copyright, Designs
and Patents Act 1988 to be identified as the author of this work.
British Library Cataloguing in Publication Data

Whincup, Michael, 1929–
Sales law and product liability
1. Product liability – Great Britain   2. Sales – Great Britain
I. Title   II. Product liability law
346.4′1′038

ISBN 0–566–08076–1

Library of Congress Cataloging-in-Publication Data
Whincup, Michael.
Sales law and product liability: a business guide/Michael Whincup.
p.   cm.
Supersedes 1985 ed. published under title: Product liability law.
Includes index.
ISBN 0–566–08076–1
1. Products liability – Great Britain.   2. Sales – Great Britain.
I. Whincup, Michael. Product liability law.   II. Title.
KD1987.W543   1998
346.4103′8 – dc21   98–8750
                                                       CIP

Phototypeset in Century Old Style by Intype London Ltd
and printed in Great Britain by MPG Ltd, Bodmin.

Contents

Statutes

Orders and Regulations

Table of cases

Case References

The many cases given above as examples or illustrations can be read in full in the various series of law reports noted in the Table of Cases. These include the All England Law Reports (All ER), Weekly Law Reports (WLR),

Appeal Cases (AC) and Scottish Law Times (SLT). Canadian cases are reported in the Dominion Law Reports (DLR). Many of the cases cited from American law reports have regional references, for example 'P' for Pacific.

1 Making commercial contracts

1.1 INTRODUCTION

This chapter and the next three chapters set out to explain without technicality the theory and practice of English law affecting everyday commercial contracts. We shall refer also to rules of Scots law (cases marked 'Scot.') and to some helpful Commonwealth examples ('Aust.', 'Can.', 'NZ'). We describe here how and when a contract is made, discuss in Chapters 2 and 3 the effects of some typical terms, and in Chapter 4 consider the possible consequences of breach of contract. In later chapters we look at the responsibilities of manufacturers and distributors to the users of their products – responsibilities which are different from those of seller to buyer. The law in this area has changed fundamentally over the past 10 years or so, as explained in Chapter 6. In Chapter 7 we compare the new rules with American product liability law. In our last chapter we look at a range of important criminal liabilities on suppliers of consumer, commercial, and industrial goods and services.

To begin our discussion of contracts of sale it may be helpful to make these fundamental points about contract law in general. First, commerce would be impossible without contracts, and contracts would be meaningless if they were not enforceable at law. That is not to say, of course, that legal intervention is necessary or desirable in day-to-day commercial relations – and indeed recourse to law should be avoided if at all possible – but only that we should recognise that commercial relations are and must be conducted within a legal framework. Second, the basic principle of English contract law is that of freedom of choice. Within certain very broad limits (see paras. 2.14–23), contracting parties are free to make whatever agreement they please on whatever terms they please. Third, each contract is new and unique, even if made on the most familiar standard forms. In each case the precise words used or the purpose or understanding of the parties or other surrounding circumstances will differ in some way, major or minor, and so make the contract different from any previous contract made between the parties or by anyone else. Each case must therefore be examined on its own merits, in the light of the parties' wishes as far as they are made clear in their contract. It follows that when judgments are given in contract cases they can rarely be more than indications of the possible outcome of future cases, however similar they may seem to be.

When an aggrieved party goes to court in a contract dispute, essentially what he or she wants the judge to do is to give legal effect to the contract as he or she originally intended – usually by making the alleged wrongdoer pay damages for breaking it. If the judge agrees to enforce the contract in this way and makes an order accordingly, then the position is that 'the law is the contract'. In other words, the parties make their own law every time they exercise their freedom of choice and make a contract.

We have to bear in mind, however, that such 'home-made' law is bound to reflect the will of the stronger of the two contracting parties. The only real freedom of choice for an individual or a small business dealing with a big company or a government department is to accept what is offered or do without. Once the terms are accepted, on principle they are binding. Broadly speaking again, English judges do not consider it part of their responsibilities to question the wisdom or fairness of the transaction, or to try to help one side or the other to get a better deal.

Our last introductory point, therefore, is that when contracting parties go to law and ask the judge to enforce what they have agreed, the judge looks only at what they *seem* to want in the contract. Unless there is evidence of fraud, duress, misrepresentation or fundamental mistake, the judge is bound by the outward manifestations of their agreement – by what the parties said or wrote at the time in question – and cannot take account of their private and unspoken hopes or fears. The result may sometimes be that the agreement he enforces is not in all respects what one or both parties actually intended.

1.2 WHAT IS A CONTRACT?

We begin our inquiry by trying to define our terms – by no means an easy task. English contract law is largely judge-made; that is to say, the principles are to be found among thousands of cases decided by our judges over the past two hundred or more years. These common law rules and examples are overlaid by several major Acts of Parliament such as the Sale of Goods Act 1979, and increasingly by rules resulting from membership of the European Union. But despite all the cases and Acts and regulations, and tons of books, there is still no clear and comprehensive definition of a contract under English law, nor, therefore, of what must be done to make one.

For present introductory purposes, however, we might very tentatively suggest that *a contract is an agreement* (to use a 'neutral' word) *which is intended to have legal consequences and which imposes obligations on both sides*. Typically it is made when one party pays or promises to pay for goods or services delivered or promised by the other. English contract law is concerned therefore with the enforcement of *bargains*; not merely with promises by one side only which do not then or in the future require any action or promise (see 'consideration', below) by the other.

Since the crucial question is whether or not a bargain has been made, it does not usually matter whether or not it has been made in writing. Many people think that only a written agreement can properly be called a contract, but that is not so. A bargain can be made by word of mouth, and in fact most contracts are made in this way – even if they are not usually the most significant in commercial terms. As a general rule (see para. 1.21), writing is important only because and insofar as it helps to prove what has been agreed, which is otherwise just 'your word against mine'. As a matter of common sense, therefore, it is extremely useful.

1.3 THE FOUR ESSENTIALS

Case law tells us that there are four main elements or 'ingredients' needed to make an agreement into a contract, that is, to make it legally binding. These four elements, and one or two others which may be important in certain specific or exceptional circumstances, are the subject of this chapter. They are (i) proof of the parties' intention to be legally bound by their agreement; (ii) terms which are clear enough and certain enough to be capable of enforcement; (iii) an offer by one side and an acceptance by the other; and (iv) the existence of 'valuable consideration'. The first three elements are largely matters of common sense, while the fourth is essentially a matter of law.

1.4 INTENTION

Generally speaking, the object of contract law is to give effect to the parties' wishes, as expressed in their words and deeds. There are nonetheless many reasons why this objective might not be fulfilled. It is not enough simply to ask 'What did the parties intend?' In the first place, if the agreement is of a social, domestic or friendly nature, it will almost certainly be presumed on their behalf that they did not intend it to be enforceable by law. If made in a commercial context, each party may have had different and conflicting intentions, otherwise the case would not have gone to court. And even if they are notionally agreed, then, as we said above, the weaker party contracting on disadvantageous terms with a monopoly supplier hardly 'intends' to do so to his own detriment.

Doubts may arise over the meaning and effect of an agreement for many different reasons, and the law's response varies accordingly. The judge may refuse to enforce an agreement, for example, because the parties have expressly said that their bargain was 'binding in honour only' or was a 'gentlemen's agreement', or used other such optimistic phraseology to show they do not intend their agreement to be subject to the scrutiny of the courts. They are free to make agreements of that kind, and to avoid liability accordingly – *Rose & Frank* v *Crompton*, 1925 – though they would not thereby be allowed to defraud each other, for example by accepting payment but refusing to deliver goods. Nor are they free to say at one and the same time that while their agreement is not to be enforced by the law it can be enforced by one side only, for example 'our decision is final', or by some specified third party such as a trade association: *Baker* v *Jones*, 1954. Even where there is no 'honour clause', an otherwise clear commitment may still possibly be invalidated because of its informality. So the absence of written evidence in circumstances where writing would normally be expected, for example in the minutes of a board meeting, might suggest that the parties did not regard their agreement as final or binding, as illustrated in *Licences Insurance Corp* v *Lawson*, 1896.

1.5 Advertisements, sales literature and price lists

One particular aspect of the question of contractual intention which is important in sales law is whether advertisements or other pre-contract statements are intended to be binding, or should be so in any event. It would not be right, of course, to give legal effect to everything said or written before agreement was reached. If a dealer says in the course of negotiations that he thinks he can meet his customer's requirements, for example, that is not necessarily put forward as a binding promise: *IBA* v *EMI*, 1980. The same could well be true of many minor post-contractual commitments. So in *Sim* v *Rotherham BC*, 1986, it was held that a school timetable was not in itself a term of a teacher's contract of employment.

Advertisements cannot usually be enforced because more often than not they are merely 'puffs' or expressions of opinion, as when goods are said to be 'bigger' or 'better' or 'whiter' or 'faster', without any standards by which such claims could be tested. But if advertisements state *facts* which can be tested and relied upon, they may in appropriate circumstances be regarded as contractual promises. So in the famous case of *Carlill* v *Carbolic Smoke Ball Co.*, 1893, the defendant manufacturers were held bound by an express promise in their advertisement to pay £100 to anyone who used their product but nevertheless caught flu, both of which were provable facts. In *Anthony* v *Norwich Building Society*, 1997, the Society's promise to pay 'very competitive rates of interest' was found sufficiently factual to be enforceable by the plaintiff who invested on the strength of that promise.

We bear in mind that a statement may be factual in one context, but not in another. A dealer's glowing description of a new car, for instance, might be mere puff because he clearly could not say whether this model was more reliable or effective than any other, but if he said the same thing about a used car he could be liable for breach of contract because he has examined that car himself and should know about its quality or condition: *Andrews* v *Hopkinson*, 1957, below.

Sales literature, price lists and the like often state that they are not to be regarded as contractually binding. This is probably because the seller or manufacturer wants to reserve the right to change his materials or specifications over a period of time, or wishes to protect himself against unauthorised promises made by his sales representatives. Alternatively, the conditions of sale themselves may make it clear that the parties are contracting only on the basis of what is agreed there and then, and provide that nothing said previously in advertisements or sales literature is of any significance at all. This may seem like sharp practice, since the customer may have bought the goods in reliance on the advertisement, but the law permits exclusion of liability for pre-contractual statements if it is reasonable in the circumstances. We shall see what that involves when we look at the Unfair Contract Terms Act in Chapter 2. In any case a strong buyer may simply insist in his contract that the goods conform with any pre-contractual statement made by the seller.

1.6 Representations

Another possibility is that advertisements or other sales talk may be classed as 'representations', a kind of half-way house between puffs which have no legal effect and the binding terms of the contract itself. The law defines a representation as a statement of *fact* which encourages or induces a person to make a contract, but which is not necessarily intended as binding and does not necessarily form part of that contract. It follows that unless there is a duty to disclose information, as, for example, in insurance contracts, mere silent acquiescence in another person's mistaken belief is not a representation. It would probably be a representation to say in the course of negotiations, for example, that a car has had only one previous owner or has done such and such a mileage, or that a boat has a certain capacity: *Howard Marine* v *Ogden*, 1978. Such statements would not usually be made terms of the contract but may still be quite important from the buyer's point of view. If the statement is subsequently proved wrong, the buyer's remedy depends on whether the misrepresentation was made fraudulently, negligently, or innocently. He is entitled to repudiate the contract and/or claim damages for fraudulent misrepresentation. The Misrepresentation Act 1967 allows a claim for damages for both negligent and innocent misrepresentation. Independently of any contractual relationship, a claim for damages for negligent statements may also be made at common law under the rule in *Hedley Byrne* v *Heller*, 1964 (para. 5.18), but in claims brought under the Act the onus of *disproving* negligence is upon the person making the statement. If the representation is negligent or innocent the Act might enable the buyer to rescind the contract, that is to give back the goods and recover his money. But if he has used the goods to any extent or resold them, or otherwise seems to have accepted them, that cannot be done. *Long* v *Lloyd*, 1958, was a particularly hard case of a buyer of a vehicle advertised as 'in exceptional condition', which in a way it was, who lost his money simply because he drove the defective vehicle for a few days and let the seller do some repairs.

1.7 CERTAINTY OF TERMS

The parties' intention to be bound by their agreement and the clarity with which they express their wishes are overlapping elements of enforceability. We examine here some typical commercial contract phrases, and consider their possible effects. It is important to remember, however, that the meanings of words may depend very largely on their context.

Contract terms such as a 'reasonable price', or 'at a price to be agreed', or 'on the usual h.p. terms', usually invite disaster because of their uncertainty. But judges have sometimes found agreements requiring payment 'at current market value' or the like sufficiently clear or ascertainable to be enforced: *Brown* v *Gould*, 1971; *Scottish Wholefoods* v *Raye*, 1994 (Scot.). The solution to problems of uncertainty such as these may depend on whether goods have actually been delivered and accepted, or services performed. They must then be paid for, even though no definite price has yet been agreed. Under s. 8 of the Sale of Goods Act and s. 5 of the Supply of Goods and Services Act, the judge has to decide what is a reasonable price in the circumstances, relying on the available evidence of market prices or valuation: *Foley* v *Classique Coaches*, 1934; *Avintair* v *Ryder Airline Services*, 1994 (Scot.).

A 'quotation' is usually enforceable, and exceptionally even an 'estimate' may be, but it is more a matter of the sense of the contract than the precise wording: *Croshaw* v *Pritchard*, 1889. An estimate which is much lower than the final price might suggest that the contractor should be liable for negligence or misrepresentation: *Kidd* v *Mississauga Commission*, 1979 (Can.). We note that normally the contractor must bear the expense involved in preparing estimates and quotations if no contract is then made, but the proposed buyer may have to pay if he asked for exceptionally detailed costing and then abandoned the project: *Lacey* v *Davis*, 1957.

Promises to use one's 'best endeavours' seem very vague, but may depend on whether they are past or future obligations. They could be tested and enforced in the light of what a party has actually done or failed to do, but as obligations for the future they are probably unenforceable: *Walford* v *Miles*, 1992; *Lambert* v *HTV Cymru*, 1998. *Walford* also decided that promises to 'continue negotiating' were inconsistent with a party's freedom to withdraw from fruitless bargaining, and therefore meaningless. A 'letter of comfort' usually seeks to reassure another party that a debt or other obligation will be paid or honoured, but stops short of an express promise to do so – probably in order to avoid a formal statement of debt in the accounts. On that basis it may be only a moral and not a legal obligation, regrettable though that may be: *Kleinwort Benson* v *Malaysia Mining Corp.*, 1989. The Australian case of *Banque Bruxelles* v *Australian National Industries*, 1989, is to the contrary, however, on very similar facts. Promises made in 'letters of intent' are generally unenforceable, unless perhaps acted on by one party at the request and for the benefit of the other. The first party's costs may then have to be reimbursed and benefits paid for: *Turiff* v *Regalia Mills*, 1971; *British Steel Corp.* v *Cleveland Bridge Co.*, 1984. The phrase 'subject to contract' usually means that no contract has yet been made and that the details will be settled later by legal advisers, but sometimes – depending on the circumstances of the case – it may mean only that the parties intend to put their spoken agreement into writing. If that is so, the writing adds nothing to the spoken agreement, whose validity is not affected. In other cases again, commercial parties might take it for granted that their oral agreement would be supplemented (but not contradicted: *Jayaar* v *Toaken*, 1996) by further written provisions: *British Crane Hire* v *Ipswich Plant Hire*, 1975.

It is quite common to reach an 'agreement in principle', or to state 'heads of agreement', or suchlike expressions, and leave the details to be decided later. These outline agreements may sometimes be clear enough to be enforceable, but there can be no definite rule. The judge put the point very aptly in *Clifton* v *Palumbo*, 1944:

> It is quite possible for persons on a half sheet of notepaper, in the most informal and unorthodox language, to contract to sell the most extensive and most complicated establishment that can be imagined... but having regard to the habits of the people in this country it is very unlikely.

In *Malcolm* v *University of Oxford*, 1990, a 'firm commitment' to publish was held enforceable despite the absence of any agreement on presentation, price, royalties, etc. These were regarded as minor details which could be settled at a later date. But if the judge can find only a promise to reach an agreement in the future, that cannot be a contract. Common sense tells us that reasonable certainty as to prices, dates, quality and quantity is usually necessary: *Australian Banking Group* v *Frost*, 1989 (Aust.).

A contract which is otherwise clear and self-sufficient should not be invalidated just because some incidental part has no apparent meaning. This was the conclusion in *Nicolene* v *Simmonds*, 1953, where a contract in all other respects complete and clear stated that it was subject to 'the usual conditions of acceptance'. Neither side could explain what these were, and so the phrase was struck out. 'It would be strange indeed', said the judge, 'if a party could escape from every one of his obligations by inserting a meaningless exception from some of them... The parties treated the contract as subsisting... It would be most unfortunate if the law should say otherwise. You would find defaulters scanning their contracts to find some meaningless clause on which to ride free.'

We should note nonetheless that the mere fact that contracting parties believe themselves bound does not of itself make them so, if subsequently some basic omission is discovered such as a failure to provide written confirmation required by the contract, or a mistake appears which nullifies their agreement: *Bishops & Baxter Ltd* v *Anglo Eastern Trading Co.*, 1943;

Compagnie de Commerce v *Parkinson*, 1953. Payment for goods or services supplied may then have to be made on a 'quantum meruit' ('as much as it is worth'; i.e. non-profit making) basis: *Lachhani* v *Destination Canada*, 1997.

1.8 Judicial policy

It may be of interest to record here some statements of the judges' policy when faced with inadequate or ambiguous or otherwise obscure or contradictory contracts. At least in theory – though not, it must be said, always in practice – the judges wish to be helpful and constructive. In *Hillas* v *Arcos*, 1932, for example, one of their Lordships said:

> The problem . . . must always be so to balance matters that, without violation of essential principles, the dealings of men may so far as possible be treated as effective and the law may not incur the reproach of being the destroyer of bargains.

In *Antaios Compania Naviera* v *Salen Rederierna*, 1985, Lord Diplock said firmly:

> I take this opportunity of restating that if detailed semantic and syntactical analysis of words in a commercial contract is going to lead to a conclusion that flouts business common sense, it must be made to yield to business common sense.

And from the Scottish Court of Session came the view that 'If parties have apparently intended to bind themselves, the court should be slow to abort that intention on the basis that there is some inadequacy on a particular aspect': *British Coal* v *S. Scotland Electricity Board*, 1988. The court should be particularly reluctant to upset contracts between lay people: *Clement* v *Gibbs*, 1996.

1.9 OFFER AND ACCEPTANCE

The next question, overlapping the issues we have just discussed, is whether the legal and common-sense requisites of an offer and an acceptance can be established. Do the apparent intentions of buyer and seller coincide, or are they at cross-purposes in some fundamental respect, in which case there can be no contract between them? It is not necessary to prove a formal offer and acceptance, nor is use of the words 'offer' or 'acceptance' conclusive. Acceptance may sometimes be inferred from conduct, though probably not merely from silence. In *Trentham* v *Archital*, 1993, the court accepted that the continued dealings between the parties established that there must have been an offer and acceptance at some earlier date, though it was not possible to say exactly when.

An offer must be distinguished from a mere 'invitation to treat', that is an invitation to make an offer or tender. Advertisements, price lists, and the like are usually seen only as invitations to treat (but see *Carlill*'s case, para. 1.5), and therefore not in themselves binding. In legal theory it is for the buyer to respond to the invitation if he wishes, and offer to buy at the stated price. The seller then has the right to accept or refuse the offer. This is still so in self-service stores – *Pharmaceutical Society* v *Boots*, 1953 – but not at petrol stations, where the buyer must be taken to have accepted the seller's offer by putting the petrol in his car.

Offers are valid only if offerees are free to accept or refuse them. So a contractor cannot demand payment for doing more work than was agreed, unless perhaps on an emergency basis. The Unsolicited Goods and Services Act 1971 makes it illegal to demand payment for unsolicited goods or services. Such goods belong to the recipient after six months, or within one month of his or her giving the sender notice to collect them, whichever is sooner. There is no special duty to take care of the goods in the meantime.

The basic rule is that an offer, for example to buy certain goods, must be accepted as it stands. If, then, after agreement seems to have been reached, the buyer says: 'I'll take the goods but only if you can deliver them within a week', that may well be a new term, in effect a counter-offer, which effectively nullifies the original offer. If the seller rejects the counter-offer, then at least in theory the whole agreement must be re-negotiated: *Northland Airlines* v *Ferranti*, 1970. Or, of course, the buyer might say: 'I'll take the goods. Can you deliver them within a week?' If that is merely a request for information or for a service the buyer would like but does not insist on, the original contract is not affected: *Stevenson* v *McLean*, 1880.

If an offer specifies a time limit for acceptance, it lapses if not accepted within that time. When no time is specified, an offer lapses after a reasonable time. Reasonableness in this context depends on the nature of the offer and the subject matter. An offer to sell shares, for example, is to be accepted much more quickly than an offer to sell land. Under English (but not Scottish or continental European) law, a promise to hold an offer open for a certain length of time is not binding unless accepted by the promisee by giving consideration (below) for it – *Routledge* v *Grant*, 1828 – or indirectly by both parties agreeing not to deal with anyone else during that time: a 'lock-out' agreement.

Acceptance made by post is usually complete and binding as soon as the letter is posted. So in *Household Insurance* v *Grant*, 1879, a company posted a letter accepting an application for shares. The applicant never received the letter, but was nonetheless held liable to pay for the shares. But the general principle can be set aside when the offer states expressly that acceptance is only effective when received, or on other reasonable grounds: *Holwell* v *Hughes*, 1974. Many continental countries, including Holland, Germany and Italy, consider postal acceptances complete only when received.

1.10 The battle of the forms

When businessmen contract with each other on their own standard conditions of sale and purchase it is quite likely that some of the terms will be contradictory and irreconcilable. If so, whose terms prevail? Doubt and confusion often arise because neither side reads the other's terms – nor even, it sometimes seems, its own. Each side's form is designed to secure significant bargaining advantages. Sellers seek to escape liability for defects in their goods while buyers draft clauses designed to hold sellers tightly to agreed specifications. A seller might include a price escalation clause while the buyer's form contemplates a fixed price. Or again the forms might make entirely different provision as to risk of accidental loss or damage – the seller seeking to relieve himself of liability at the earliest possible moment, and the buyer accepting it only at the latest. In all these cases the two sets of provisions are fundamentally irreconcilable. If neither side proceeds any further, there should be no question of liability for breach of contract since on the face of it there is no contract. But if one side or other believes a contract exists and acts according, disputes are more than likely.

The law's solutions to these particular conflicts of interest are not always as clear as business people might wish them to be, but that may be unavoidable. The possibilities were explored by Lord Denning in *Butler* v *Ex-Cell-O*, 1979:

> In most cases where there is a battle of the forms there is a contract as soon as the last of the forms is sent and received without objection being taken to it ... The difficulty is to decide which form, or which part of which form, is a term or condition of the contract. In some cases the battle is won by the man who fires the last shot. He is the man who puts forward the latest terms and conditions and, if they are not objected to by the other party, he may be taken to have agreed to them ... In some cases however the battle is won by the man who gets the blow in first. If he offers to sell at a named price on the terms stated on the back and the buyer orders the goods purporting to accept the offer on an order form with his own different terms on the back, then, if the difference is so material that it would affect the price, the buyer ought not

to be allowed to take advantage of the difference unless he draws it specifically to the attention of the seller. There are yet other cases where the battle
depends on the shots fired on both sides. There is a concluded contract but
the forms vary. The terms and conditions of both parties are to be construed
together. If they can be reconciled so as to give a harmonious result, all
well and good. If the differences are irreconcilable, so that they are mutually
contradictory, then the offending terms may have to be scrapped and replaced
by a reasonable implication.

The only weakness in this otherwise admirable statement is that it does
not tell us when or why any one of these various divergent answers may
be given. The most the law can offer is a set of general principles as to
what constitutes a valid contract – in particular, here, the requirements of
offer and acceptance. How those principles will apply to a given set of facts
depends entirely on those facts, and the possible complications and variations from one case to the next are, of course, infinite.

Before we consider the facts of *Butler*, perhaps the foremost English
authority on the subject, let us look at the earlier and simpler issue posed
in *British Road Services* v *Crutchley*, 1968. BRS delivered a consignment of
goods to Crutchley's warehouse. The BRS driver handed over a delivery
note stating that the goods were left on BRS's terms. Crutchley's ware-
houseman overstamped the note to the effect that they were received
on Crutchley's terms. The driver made no objection, and nor did BRS.
Subsequently a dispute arose between the parties, and the question was,
whose terms prevailed?

The court decided that BRS's delivery note was an offer and Crutchley's
stamp a counter-offer. By its silence BRS was deemed then to have accepted
the counter-offer, and so Crutchley's terms carried the day. The case
therefore represents a straightforward example of the first of Lord
Denning's answers, and in practice the one most commonly applied, that
of victory for the man who fires the last shot.

Butler v *Ex-Cell-O* was more complicated, however. Machinery sellers
quoted a price to the buyers. On the back of the sellers' quotations were
various provisions including a price variation clause and the following
statement: 'These terms shall prevail over any terms in the buyer's order.'
The buyers placed an order using their own form. This contained no price
variation clause but included a tear-off acknowledgment slip requiring the
sellers to agree: 'We accept your order on the terms and conditions stated
thereon.' The sellers signed and returned the acknowledgment but sent
with it a letter saying they were fulfilling the order in accordance with
their own original quotation. Costs increased after lengthy delays, and in

due course the sellers charged some £3000 more than had been agreed, which they said they were entitled to do under the price variation clause.

Several important issues arose. The sellers fired the first shot. They said that the contract was to be made on their terms alone. Lord Denning seems to suggest that in that event they should win the day, but what significance should be attached to their returning the acknowledgment slip? Should compliance with such clear wording have no effect at all? Against that in turn is the fact that by their accompanying letter the sellers simultaneously seemed to reintroduce, if they ever lost, the advantage of their own original terms.

At the trial the judge thought the sellers should win because the terms of their quotation made the price variation clause the basis of all subsequent dealings. In the Court of Appeal this view was unanimously rejected. With the exception of Lord Denning, who agreed but on other grounds, the judges thought that the issue could be resolved by asking simply 'Who offered?' and 'Who accepted?' The sellers offered, but by returning the acknowledgment form they then accepted the buyers' counter-offer. The wording of their accompanying letter was held only to identify the machinery and refer to the price first quoted, and not to reintroduce all their terms, so in the event it was no help to them. We note again the benefit of using acknowledgment forms to resolve such problems: *Chichester Joinery* v *Mowlem*, 1987.

But what would the decision have been if the sellers' letter had in fact invoked all their original terms of supply, and in particular the provision overriding the buyers' terms? Presumably the letter would then at the same moment both have cancelled and been cancelled by the acknowledgment slip, leaving the buyers' and sellers' original forms irreconcilably opposed. One side or the other might then withdraw without fear of breach of contract, since there could be no contract in existence at that point. But if the sellers went on to deliver the goods, clearly it would be difficult to deny the existence of a contract. The buyers would have to pay for the goods, but it is very doubtful whether they could be said to have accepted or would be bound by the price variation clause.

1.11 **Delivery** Typically then, the kind of conduct proving acceptance of the other's terms is delivery of goods by the seller or payment for them by the buyer. But such actions do not always have that effect. The need for caution is well illustrated in the Canadian case of *Tywood* v *St Anne Co.*, 1980. Tenders were invited by a buyer. The seller offered a quotation on his own standard form. The buyer accepted the quotation on his own form which for the first time required the parties to the contract to submit any dispute to arbitration. The seller did not note or appreciate the significance of this new provision but in reliance on the buyer's acceptance went ahead and delivered the goods.

Later on a dispute arose over the goods and the question was whether the seller was bound by the arbitration clause. The fact that he had delivered the goods might suggest he had accepted this particular counter-offer, but equally his conduct was consistent with the view that since the original forms made no reference to this issue he was entitled to assume the terms would not be changed at a later stage. The court held that delivery of the goods did not establish beyond doubt that he knew of or agreed to the new provision, and therefore that he was not bound by it.

This Canadian decision seems a very sensible one, though not binding on UK courts. Mechanical application of the 'last in time' rule could obviously cause injustice. It would be all too easy for one of the contracting parties to take advantage of the other by adding another clause at a late stage to what had already been agreed and hoping it would not be noticed. So when we ask whether there has been an acceptance of an offer or counter-offer, we must judge the conduct in question according to what was actually known or in the circumstances ought realistically to have been known by the party who is said to have accepted.

It should be understood in any case that the 'last in time' rule can only apply up to the time the parties appear to reach final agreement. Once agreement is reached it cannot be varied by one side's attempt to add in some new provision without the consent of the other (but see *British Crane Hire*, para. 1.7). In *Evans* v *Merzario*, 1976, for example, certain longstanding shipping arrangements were to be changed by putting the goods in containers. The owner of the goods agreed to the change only on condition that his goods would be shipped in containers between decks. By an oversight one consignment was put on deck, and then washed overboard in a storm. When the owner sued he was referred to the standard form of shipment which he had earlier received, which entitled the shippers to put the goods where they thought fit and disclaimed any liability for loss. The court held that this standard form had no effect in the light of the express agreement to the contrary.

A similar point is that if the terms of a standard form are misrepresented in any way by the person putting them forward, or if the customer does not read them because he is advised not to worry about them, then again the form will probably be nullified: *Curtis* v *Chemical Cleaning Contractors*, 1951. That should be so even if the customer signs the form, though normally of course signature is binding: *L'Estrange* v *Graucob*, 1934. And if the terms in question are really exclusion clauses they must in any case be read subject to the Unfair Contract Terms Act (see Chapter 2).

We must add that these conclusions are not all equally acceptable elsewhere. Trading overseas brings further uncertainties. In America, for example, the basic rule in the Uniform Commercial Code is that a definite expression of acceptance of an offer constitutes acceptance of that offer *even though* the acceptor seeks thereby to introduce new or different terms. This rule applies unless his acceptance was clearly stated to depend upon the other's agreement to the new terms. Otherwise the new terms become part of the contract, subject to these three vital provisions. First, the offeror's original terms may make it clear that any subsequent amendment is of no effect (thus reaching the opposite conclusion to that in *Butler* v *Ex-Cell-O*); second, if the new terms 'materially alter' those proposed, that of itself ensures they are not binding (thus contradicting the *BRS* conclusion); and third, the offeror's express objection within a reasonable time of receipt of the new terms will likewise nullify them. It should follow that under the American system, unlike ours, the man who fires the *first* shot should win. A German solution, on the other hand, is to give effect only to those terms which have been agreed.

The American answer may have more to commend it than ours. It recognises that a person who opens negotiations on the basis that his terms of sale or purchase alone will govern the transaction probably means what he says and ought to be allowed to rely on his foresight in making that provision, rather than be deemed by subsequent silence, nothing if not understandable in the circumstances, to have agreed to precisely the opposite. Whether or not such prior provision is made, the idea of implied assent to terms incompatible with one's own is difficult to accept.

1.12   VALUABLE CONSIDERATION

We have looked now at three of the four main elements which go to make up a contract in English law. The fourth, valuable consideration, is more strictly a matter of law and more complex than the other three. It is in fact a feature of contract law unique to the English system (and so to all the systems based upon it, from America to New Zealand). While Scottish law and continental European systems would probably accept our first three elements – intention to be bound by a promise, certainty, and offer and acceptance – as sufficient to constitute a contract, English law by the requirement of consideration demands also proof of *reciprocal obligation*. In effect, in the terms of their offer and acceptance the parties must agree:

15

'I will do this for you if in return you will do that for me.' Consideration represents, in other words, the idea of 'buying' the other's promise in order to make it binding.

The 'price' which must be paid to 'buy' another party's promise need not be in money, nor equivalent or even similar in value, nor directly for the promisor's benefit. It can be anything of economic value – goods or services, or other benefits or detriments such as an agreement not to sue on a potentially valid claim, as required by and agreed with the promisor. The commonest form is probably an exchange of promises: 'I promise to pay £X in return for your promise to deliver Y.' It may also be sufficient if the promisor derives some benefit *as a result of* his promise, though not directly *in return for* it, as is the usual rule. So in *Williams* v *Roffey*, 1990, the Court of Appeal held a building contractor's voluntary promise to pay more to his sub-contractor than originally agreed was binding upon him, because he thereby ensured that the work would be done on time and thus escaped liability to his employer for delay.

Once promises of economic significance have been exchanged or acts undertaken in return, as the case may be, proving in turn the existence of offer and acceptance, there is a contract for the purposes of English law. Conversely, a 'bare' promise – one for which the promisee gives or does nothing in return – is unenforceable. It follows, as a point of passing interest, that when Englishmen have gone round the world proclaiming that 'an Englishman's word is his bond', our legal system has always denied it. The only overall exception to the consideration rule is where the promise is in a deed, a signed and witnessed document whose formality makes it binding, but which is rarely used in commerce.

The consideration rule may seem very technical and likely to upset ordinary commercial dealings. In practice it affects only a very small minority of cases. It is, after all, of the essence of commerce that one party promises to pay for the goods or services which the other promises to deliver. In the business context it is probably fair to say that relatively few people promise to do something for nothing.

1.13 Exceptions to the rule

Nonetheless, problems do occasionally arise; some practical, others theoretical. Given the basic rule that one cannot enforce another's promise unless one has given consideration in return, it is clear that where A and B make a contract to benefit C, C may have great difficulty in enforcing it. C is not a party ('privy') to the contract because the promise was not made to him, nor did he give consideration for it. On principle, therefore, he cannot enforce it: *Beswick* v *Beswick*, 1967. Other legal systems which do not have the consideration rule would have little difficulty in allowing C to enforce the contract. Reform of English law to the same effect may be expected in the not too distant future, following the example of American common law and statutory developments in the Commonwealth such as New Zealand's Contracts (Privity) Act 1982.

Pending more general reform, difficulties over third party rights have led both Parliament and the judges to make several exceptions to the privity of contract rule. A familiar example is the Married Women's Property Act 1882, which among other matters made life insurance contracts enforceable by the beneficiary. Other insurance policies expressed to be for the benefit of third parties should be similarly enforced – *Trident Insurance* v *McNeice*, 1988 (Aust.) – but there is still an element of doubt here. Other exceptions are in the Consumer Credit Act 1974, making creditors liable for dealers' defaults: para. 3.18. In another context, the Carriage of Goods by Sea Act 1992 entitles sub-purchasers of goods who hold bills of lading to enforce the terms of the original contracts of carriage and insurance against the carrier.

When UK sellers of goods seek to ensure payment by foreign buyers they often rely on bankers' confirmed credits. The seller requires the foreign buyer to contract with his bank that the bank's correspondent bank in the UK will pay the seller when he transfers to it the documents of title to the goods. In theory the seller could not enforce the buyer's bank's promise because he is not a party to it. In practice the courts accept that this is how business is done and that they should uphold commercial custom and convenience: *Malas* v *British Imex*, 1958. They seem also to have decided on grounds of business efficacy that third party carriers and other agents can take the benefit of limitations of liability agreed on their behalf between buyers and sellers: *New Zealand Shipping* v *Satterthwaite*, 1975.

1.14 **Manufacturers' guarantees**   Another controversial question arising from the consideration rule concerns enforcement of manufacturers' guarantees. Although so many thousands of guarantees are given every day, their legal status (pending proposed EU reform, which will affect only consumer guarantees) remains surprisingly unclear. The problem is that on the face of it, a buyer's contract is only with the seller. If a buyer tries to enforce a manufacturer's promise, he or she is trying to enforce a promise for which he or she has not (usually) given consideration.

The best known case is still *Carlill* v *Carbolic Smoke Ball Co.*, para. 1.5. The plaintiff here succeeded in enforcing the guarantee because she proved she used the product in response to – in effect, in return for – the promise to pay her if the product did not work. It follows that a buyer who can show he bought or used goods knowing they were guaranteed might persuade the court he bought or used them at least partly because of and in return for that promise. Or he might stamp the guarantee card and return it, and give consideration that way. Or, as is now the common practice, he might buy the guarantee separately at the time of purchase (a practice which sometimes proves to be a waste of money because of the guarantor's subsequent insolvency). But if, as often happens, the guarantee is given only after the sale is completed, and does not have to be returned to the manufacturer, or the buyer becomes aware of it only at that time, the problem of enforceability remains. Currently, therefore, it is perhaps best to regard manufacturers' guarantees merely as expressions of good public relations.

1.15 **Collateral contracts** A collateral contract is subsidiary to and dependent upon another, main contract. The consideration for the promise given in the collateral contract is the making of the main contract. The enforceability of a manufacturer's guarantee may depend on the existence of such a collateral contract, as illustrated by the case of *Andrews* v *Hopkinson*, 1957. The used car dealer here told a prospective customer that a particular car was 'a good little bus' and that he would 'stake (his) life on it'. Thus encouraged, the customer decided to take the car on hire purchase. The h.p. contract itself was then made between the customer and a finance company to which the dealer sold the car. The car turned out to be dangerously defective. The customer's rights against the finance company were not clear and so he sued the dealer instead for breach of his glowing promise. His claim was successful. The court held that the customer had given consideration for the dealer's promises by entering into the h.p. agreement with the finance company. It was as if the dealer had said: 'If you make a contract with the finance company I promise the car is in good condition.' Once the customer had acted on the dealer's promise it was then enforceable as a collateral contract, that is one 'alongside' the main h.p. contract. The judge in this case went on to suggest that whenever dealers introduce customers to h.p. companies they should be deemed to enter into *implied* collateral contracts as to the fitness of the goods in question. This suggestion has not had much support, but was adopted in *Robotics* v *First Co-operative Finance*, 1983.

It will be seen that the interpretation and enforcement of manufacturers' guarantees might turn on this collateral contract theory. If essentially the guarantee says 'If you buy our goods from a retailer we promise to provide such and such services' then the courts will enforce it as long as the customer can prove he or she responded by making the purchase. Notable cases showing how far this principle can be taken include *Shanklin Pier* v *Detel Products*, 1951, and *Wells* v *Buckland Sand*, 1964. In *Shanklin* the owners of the pier made inquiries as to the most suitable paint for restoration work. The defendants, paint manufacturers, assured them that their paint was best. Relying on this assurance the owners required their contractor to use the defendants' paint. The paint proved unsuitable and the work had to be done again. The owners could not sue the contractor, who had only done what they had told him to do, and so they turned to the manufacturers. The court held that in recommending their paint the manufacturers had not merely made a bare or unenforceable promise but had entered into a binding contract with the owners. In effect the contract said: 'If you require your contractor to use our paint, we promise it is the best for the job', and it became enforceable once the promisees, the pier owners, acted on it in the way expected of them.

Similarly, in *Wells* a flower grower inquired as to the best sand for his chrysanthemums, and the defendants assured him theirs was the most suitable. He then bought some from a retailer, only to find it unsatisfactory. The retailer could not be liable, since he supplied only what he was asked for, but the plaintiff succeeded in his claim against the producers. Once again the court accepted that their sales talk was meant to encourage him to buy their goods and had contractual effect when he did so.

1.16 **What does the guarantee promise?** It goes almost without saying that a guarantee cannot be enforced unless its terms are reasonably certain. So in *Carlill* the company tried to avoid liability by pointing to the fact that their alleged guarantee did not say how long might elapse between taking the medicine and catching flu. Nor did it say how long the offer itself was open, and obviously such an offer must lapse sooner or later. But as we have seen the judge found that the basic promise to pay was quite unambiguous, and so felt able to resolve the doubts by the standard of 'a reasonable time'.

A similarly strong line was taken in the Canadian case of *Hallmark Pool* v *Story*, 1983. A householder was contemplating purchase of a garden pool. He saw an advert for one particular pool which showed a reproduction of the company's guarantee. The reproduction prominently displayed a 15-year durability guarantee, but the rest was unreadable without a magnifying glass. Duly impressed by the 15-year commitment, the householder bought the pool. Eventually it became unusable and the householder tried to enforce the guarantee. In reply the company pointed to the small print which excluded liability for the defects in question. The judge said that since the details could not be read the 15-year commitment was clear and apparently unqualified and therefore binding. Since the householder bought the pool in response to this promise the company would still have been liable even if he had received the guarantee after the sale and read the details then. On the other hand if the details had been clear beforehand they would have been binding even though unread, and however limited their terms. In *Adams* v *Richardson*, 1969, prior promises as to after-sale dry rot treatment which Lord Denning thought better described as a 'non-guarantee' were nonetheless enforceable.

Lambert v *Lewis*, 1981, is a further example of the possible weaknesses of guarantees. The facts are complicated, but very briefly the Court of Appeal held that a manufacturer's advertisements that his goods – caravan hitches – were completely safe and 'foolproof' did not amount to a promise to reimburse any retailer who might sell the hitches and then be held liable if they caused an accident. This conclusion may be acceptable on its own facts, but surely not if it means that manufacturers can make quite unfounded claims as to the safety of their products and yet escape liability for the consequences.

1.17 Statutory regulation of guarantees In the light of what we have said, it is not surprising that consumer guarantees have been the cause of a great many complaints. The Office of Fair Trading noted some years ago complaints where the guarantee was in the name of the purchaser and could not be transferred; others where the guarantee had expired before the goods could be repaired, and others subject to unreasonable conditions such as return of the goods in the original packaging or instant return of the guarantee card.

Parliament has made one or two attempts to stop specific abuses. We note the rule in s. 5 of the Unfair Contract Terms Act, para. 2.16, nullifying any term in a guarantee which excludes liability for death or injury caused by negligence. The Consumer Transactions (Restrictions on Statements) Order 1978 is also important. It forbids sales of goods which are accompanied by written statements as to buyers' rights unless 'in close proximity' there is also a 'clear and conspicuous' statement that consumers' rights are not affected thereby. Because of the 1978 Order, manufacturers' guarantees now always say that 'These rights are in addition to the buyer's rights under the Sale of Goods Act', or words to that effect. So, for example, a new car warranty does not oblige the buyer to tolerate faults which would not otherwise be acceptable: *Rogers* v *Parish*, 1987, para. 3.12. And a guarantee cannot itself reduce the length of time a product can be expected to last: *Hunter* v *Syncrude*, 1989 (Can.). Guarantees which fall within the Unfair Terms in Consumer Contract Regulations 1994 (para. 2.21) are subject to overall tests of fairness and good faith.

The most far-reaching reform, however, is that currently proposed by the EU draft Consumer Guarantees Directive. The primary purpose of the Directive is to harmonise Member States' widely varying rules on consumers' rights against retailers – in effect underwriting the Sale of Goods Act (Chapter 3) so far as UK consumers are concerned. But the Directive seeks also to ensure that guarantees of consumer goods given voluntarily by producers shall be legally enforceable – on condition that they provide real benefits over and above rights against retailers. Such guarantees must be available in writing before purchase, and state details of application, duration, etc. So far as it goes, therefore, the Directive should resolve some of English Law's problems of enforceability discussed above, but it does not affect the position as regards non-consumer guarantees.

1.18 CONSIDERATION AND ESTOPPEL

Our discussion of the uses and abuses of guarantees arose from our explanation of the consideration rule. We suggested that this rule – that a promise can be enforced only by someone who has given or promised something of value in return for it – might very occasionally cause hardship, and we have noted various exceptions to the rule. The topic of estoppel to which we now turn may be seen as a postscript to the consideration rule; not as a further exception to it, but as a way of avoiding certain possibly unjust consequences of it.

Estoppel deals with problems arising when a person relies on another's promise, but has not given consideration in return for it. Since the promise is therefore unenforceable, it should follow that the promisor can break it at any time, or act in a way completely contrary to it. But clearly that could be very unfair to the promisee, if by relying upon the promise he or she has suffered some loss or detriment.

The judges have accordingly formulated a rule known as 'equitable estoppel', deriving from the leading case of *Central London Property Trust* v *High Trees House*, 1947. We can put the rule this way: *Where a person makes a promise (or other statement or representation) intending another person to act on it, and that other person does act on it as intended, the promisor cannot then deny* – is 'estopped' from denying – *the validity of his promise or statement, even though the promisee gave no consideration for it.*

The case of *Lombard* v *Stobart*, 1990, is a straightforward example of the working of the rule. A debtor asked the finance company how much he still owed on his car. He was very surprised to hear from the company that he owed only £1000, since he thought the debt was much greater. He questioned the company's answer, but the company assured him in writing and by word of mouth that £1000 was the correct sum. Relying on this assurance the debtor sold the car. The company then discovered its mistake, and claimed the £6000 which he actually owed. The court rejected the company's claim, because the company had in effect made the debtor a promise which he had acted on as might have been expected, even though he had done nothing *in return for* that promise.

We see from this example that the estoppel rule still applies where the promise is made by mistake, as long as the promisee reasonably believes the promise is genuine. Conversely, promises induced by the promisee's fraud or duress are not binding, as shown by *D & C Builders* v *Rees*, 1965. Here a dissatisfied customer promised to pay half of what he owed to the builders, on condition that they would accept that sum in full settlement. The builders were in financial difficulties, as the customer knew. Under protest – but on a 'bird in the hand' basis – they agreed to the customer's terms. After he had paid them the money, the builders repudiated their promise and sued for the remainder. The Court of Appeal held them free to do so, partly (see below) because their promise had not been a voluntary one. Payment into a bank account of a cheque received under protest does not prove acceptance of the debtor's terms: *Stour Valley Builders* v *Stuart*, 1993.

A curious complication of the law, arising from the House of Lords decision in *Foakes* v *Beer*, 1884, is that even if the builders' promise in *D & C Builders* had been voluntary they could still have gone back on it, because the doctrine of estoppel does not apply to promises to accept part payment in full settlement. So in *Re Selectmove*, 1995, a creditor was able to renege on his promise to accept repayment in instalments of a debt which was already due in full. A creditor's promise to accept less than he is owed could only be made binding if the debtor gave consideration for it, for example by paying before the debt is due, or by paying with goods instead of money, or by agreement with other creditors.

1.19 **Purpose and limits of estoppel** The basic question in estoppel cases is whether it would cause injustice to allow a person to break his or her promise despite the absence of consideration to make it binding. Generally speaking, one should not be able to 'blow hot and cold', particularly in a commercial context, even where no definite contractual commitments have been made. But no injustice could be done unless some reasonably clear promise has been given, expressly or by implication, in the first place. So in *Banning* v *Wright*, 1972, a creditor's initial willingness to give his debtor more time to pay did not estop him from demanding immediate repayment in full when the debtor continued in default. The creditor's conduct did not amount to a promise or representation that he would tolerate delays indefinitely. To be on the safe side, many buyers include 'no waiver' clauses in their standard forms. These are intended to avoid the possible application of the estoppel rule by making it clear that failure to complain immediately after delivery of defective goods, or even payment for such goods, is not to be regarded as acceptance of the goods.

Our last but perhaps most important point about estoppel is that it usually serves only as 'a shield but not a sword': *Combe* v *Combe*, 1951. As we see in the cases above, the rule is essentially defensive. It is intended to benefit promisees who have relied on promises but not given consideration for them. In theory such promises are not binding, but the estoppel rule nonetheless enables a promisee in this situation *to stop a promisor from suing him*, when and if the promisor seeks to do so in breach of his own previous promise. What the estoppel rule does *not* do is to enable the promisee to sue the promisor for breach of that promise (or other statement or assurance: *Russell* v *Elliott*, 1995). We come back to the basic rule of English contract law that a person who wants to sue another for breach of a promise must have given consideration in return for that promise.

1.20 **Proprietary estoppel** As always, there is an exception; this time in the principle of 'proprietary estoppel'. Where A encourages B to spend money on his own or A's land in the belief that he, B, has or will get an interest in or right over that land, B can sue to enforce that interest or right even though he gave no consideration for it: *Crabb* v *Arun District Council*, 1975. Why the right to sue on estoppel should be confined to land, and whether in practice it is desirable to do so, is far from clear. Continental countries see acting in reliance on a promise as just as good a reason, other things being equal, for enforcing the promise as acting in return for it. Among common law countries, America and Australia have taken the same view, as illustrated in s. 90 of the US Restatement of the Law of Contract. In *Drennan* v *Star Paving*, 1958, for instance, a main contractor relied on terms offered by a sub-contractor in order to tender for a contract. The American court held that the main contractor could sue to stop the subcontractor from withdrawing his offer, even though he had not formally accepted it. As it stands at the moment, English law would seem unable to protect the main contractor in this way. In the leading Australian case of *Waltons* v *Maher*, 1988, the defendant had led the plaintiff to believe that he would agree a lease with him. Relying on the defendant's assurance, and to the defendant's knowledge, the plaintiff incurred considerable expenditure in demolishing and rebuilding his property. The defendant then decided not to go ahead with the lease. The plaintiff successfully recovered his expenditure on the basis of estoppel, aimed at preventing loss caused by unconscionable behaviour. Again, it is very difficult to say whether an English court would reach the same conclusion.

1.21 WRITING

We have now examined the four main elements needed to make an agreement into a contract enforceable under English law. Two other issues remain to be briefly noted, which may in certain circumstances affect enforceability. The first is the question of writing.

The general rule, as we have seen, is that the absence of writing does not of itself affect the validity of a contract whose existence and terms can be satisfactorily proved by other means, for example the word of witnesses. But there are several statutory exceptions to that rule, introduced because of the complexity or importance of the transaction and the greater need for certainty as to the terms.

So, for example, the Consumer Credit Act 1974 says that where an individual – whether or not in business – is given credit up to £25 000, he or she and the business creditor must sign the agreement, which must set out details of payments and record the debtor's various rights. These include the right to cancel certain 'doorstep' agreements. Credit contracts which are not in proper form and duly signed are enforceable, if at all, only by court order. Written notice of cancellation rights is required also in doorstep contracts regulated by the Consumer Protection (Cancellation of Contracts Concluded Away From Business Premises) Regulations 1987 and by the Timeshare Act 1992.

The Commercial Agents Regulations 1993 entitle independent intermediaries authorised to buy or sell goods on their principals' behalf to written and signed statements of the terms of the agency, on request. Employees as such are entitled as of right to written statements of pay, hours, holidays, etc. within 8 weeks of starting work. Failure to give a written statement does not affect the validity of the contract, but clearly any resulting difficulty in proving the terms will be the fault of the principal or employer.

Apart from these and miscellaneous other statutory provisions, there may be problems of a more practical kind when contracts are put into writing. If, for instance, the written terms seem to be a comprehensive record of what has been agreed, it may be very difficult to persuade a judge that other terms were agreed orally and should be taken into account. On principle, the so-called 'parol evidence' rule forbids such additions. But the rule begs the question whether the written terms are in fact a complete record. In practice, evidence may be admitted to show that the contract was partly written and partly spoken. Evidence of a collateral contract, written or spoken, or of fraud, duress, misrepresentation or fundamental mistake, is in any case admissible: *Evans* v *Merzario*, 1976, para. 1.11. A common mistake in recording the terms of an agreement may be rectified by the court.

On the other hand, where the meaning of the terms seems clear, evidence of the parties' preliminary negotiations, or their general intentions, or their conduct after the contract was made, is not acceptable, if and insofar as it seeks to contradict or vary that meaning: *Scottish Power* v *Britoil*, 1997. Continental courts, however, would usually accept such evidence.

1.22 CAPACITY

With very limited exceptions, English law considers everyone over 18 able to make and be bound by a contract. A person acting as agent may be authorised to make only certain specific kinds of contract. If he or she exceeds that authority the principal is not liable, but the agent may be sued for breach of warranty of authority. People who are mentally disordered or drunk at the time of making contracts are not bound if the other party knew of their disability. They must, however, pay a reasonable price (which may not be the agreed price) for any necessary goods or services ordered.

The Minors' Contracts Act 1987 regulates the position in England and Wales as regards contracts made by people under 18. Broadly, they must pay a reasonable price for goods or services suitable to their situations and actual needs, but other contracts are unenforceable. Traders concerned not to lose money when dealing with young people normally require an adult to give a written guarantee of payment. The guarantee is enforceable if given in return for future credit facilities for the young person. The 1987 Act enables courts to order the return of property received by minors under unenforceable contracts. In Scotland the rule is that children over 16 have full contractual capacity, but courts may set aside contracts made by those between 16 and 18 if proved detrimental to the young person.

1.23 SUMMARY

Commerce depends on buyers and sellers keeping their promises. Their agreements are enforceable as contracts under English law if they meet four main requirements. First, the parties must show they intended their agreement to be legally binding. But their intentions can be found only by what they say or write when making their agreement, not by unexpressed hopes or fears or beliefs. They will be judged by what they *appear* to want; not necessarily by what one or both of them actually want. The usual result is that the weaker party is bound by the terms imposed by the stronger party.

The second prerequisite of enforceability is that the terms of the agreement are reasonably clear or at least ascertainable. Generally it is necessary to show agreement on price and quantity. There is no single answer to problems arising when contradictory sales and purchase forms are used, but in practice the form which is last in time often prevails. The third requirement is proof of offer and acceptance. Offers must be distinguished from mere 'invitations to treat' – invitations to make an offer, as in most advertisements, price lists, etc. – which have no effect in law. An acceptance involves a reciprocal promise or act, as required by the fourth element – valuable consideration, below.

Valuable consideration may be understood as the 'price' which English (but not Scottish) law requires to be paid *in return* for another person's promise in order to make that person's promise enforceable. Without it, the promise is unenforceable unless made in a deed. Consideration is usually in the form of a promise to pay for or to provide goods or services. It does not have to be of equivalent or similar value to the promise it 'buys'. A person who makes a promise which another person relies on, but does not give consideration in return, may be 'estopped' from denying the validity of his promise.

In general, agreements are equally enforceable whether made orally or in writing. In practice, written evidence often provides the necessary means of proving the terms of the agreement. Certain Acts of Parliament require written evidence of the contracts in question.

2 Express terms of contracts of sale

2.1 PUFFS, REPRESENTATIONS AND TERMS

In this chapter and the next we examine some typical commercial contract terms and their likely effects. The present chapter concerns terms expressly agreed between the parties, in writing or by word of mouth, while Chapter 3 looks at the terms which may be added into the contract by the law – the implied terms of the contract.

We begin with a reminder that not everything a contracting party says or writes in the course of negotiations is necessarily a term of the contract. Many promises fail because of their uncertainty, as we saw in Chapter 1. Mere praise of a product – sales talk or 'puff' – is of no legal effect. Statements of opinion are generally unenforceable, but if it is clear that the person making the statement did not in fact hold that opinion there may well be liability for fraud. Statements of fact made before or at the time of the contract that influence the other party in making the contract are called representations, unless sufficiently important to be regarded as terms of the contract. The remedies for misrepresentation, noted in para. 1.6, are different from but overlap with those for breach of contract, as set out in Chapter 4.

2.2 CONDITIONS AND WARRANTIES

Contract terms, express or implied, are very often classified by English law as 'conditions' and 'warranties'. The usual – though by no means uniform – meaning of these words is that a condition is a basic or vital term of the contract, and a warranty is only a minor or incidental term.

The importance of this division is in the remedies given to the innocent party when one or other kind of term is broken. On breach of condition, the innocent party is entitled to repudiate the contract altogether (unless as buyer he has 'accepted' the goods: para. 3.16) and/or to claim damages, on the basis that he has not received anything like the benefit he was promised. If a contract is to take effect only in certain specified circumstances, for example on securing a loan, the occurrence of those circumstances is a condition precedent. If it is to end when a certain situation arises, that is a condition subsequent.

If he can show only a breach of warranty, then the innocent party cannot give up the contract, because he has received more or less what he asked for, and so is limited to a claim for damages for the difference in value. These definitions, adopted for example by the Sale of Goods Act, are not hard and fast. In commercial practice, 'condition' and 'warranty' are often used interchangeably (and confusingly), and in insurance contracts the insured's answers as to the risk to be insured are generally called warranties even though any mistake in them might nullify the contract. Scottish sales law does not depend to the same extent on the use of these words. In Scotland repudiation is justified for any 'material breach'.

From day to day, of course, contracting parties do not immediately exercise any rights they may have to repudiate their contracts or to claim damages. Aggrieved buyers are more likely to demand replacement or repair of defective parts (but cannot be compelled to accept these alternatives, nor to take credit notes). Replacement or repair are not yet (see para. 3.10) rights recognised as such by the law, but if agreeable to both parties they represent settlements or compromises in lieu of the exercise of legal rights, and as a rule are binding.

2.3 INNOMINATE TERMS

The classification of terms into major and minor, with remedies accordingly, may seem clear and comprehensive, but it can create problems. The judges have therefore moved away from this relatively rigid approach and prefer now to decide the appropriate remedy by reference not to any prior classification but to the seriousness or otherwise of the consequences of breach of contract. The leading case here is *Hong Kong Shipping* v *Kawasaki*, 1962. It involved a 24-month hire of a ship. One of the terms of hire was that the ship should be seaworthy. On the face of it this requirement was fundamental and therefore a condition, so that in theory any breach would justify the hirers in repudiating the agreement. But the Court of Appeal observed that there were many very different reasons why a ship might not be seaworthy, some serious, some trivial; some taking months to put right, others curable almost immediately. That being so, said the Court, it would be absurd to give one and the same remedy in all cases. If the consequences of the breach were trivial then damages would suffice. If they were serious, or potentially so, repudiation would be justified. In this particular case the hirers' grievance concerned structural faults in the ship which kept it out of use for nearly four months, but the Court decided the hirers could not repudiate because they still got 20 months' use out of 24, which was nearly what they had asked for. Damages were therefore the appropriate remedy. The actual decision is debateable, but depends, of course, on the hirers' needs as laid down in the contract.

When as in the *Hong Kong* case it is impossible to say beforehand whether a term in a contract is a condition or a warranty it is called an 'innominate' or 'intermediate' term. Although this approach has much to commend it, in the sense that the law's remedies are or ought to be tailored to what actually went wrong, the effect may be to leave the parties in some doubt as to the precise significance of the terms they have agreed on.

If the parties wish to avoid this kind of uncertainty they are free to adopt for themselves the kind of approach exemplified by the Sale of Goods Act and specify in advance which terms are important and which less so, and what the remedies shall be if they are broken. The only remaining question then is whether the judge will accept that the parties meant what they said. If they seem to have agreed that one side or the other can bring the contract to an end on some essentially trivial ground, the judge would have to be quite satisfied that that was indeed what the parties intended and not the result of inadvertence, for example by using the words 'condition' and 'warranty' in their ordinary non-legal sense.

Schuler v *Wickman*, 1974, was a case of this kind, in which a German machine tool manufacturer agreed with an English agent that the agent should call on a specified number of clients at least once every week. This requirement was stated to be a condition of the contract, and it was provided that any 'material breach' of the contract entitled the manufacturer to end it forthwith. The agent failed to call as agreed and so the manufacturer repudiated the contract. The judge said that the parties could not have intended a right to repudiate for any and every failure, however small or unavoidable or unintentional, and so awarded damages to the English agent on grounds of the manufacturer's wrongful repudiation of the contract. Not all breaches of 'condition', in other words, are necessarily 'material'. Alternatively or additionally the parties may use anti-technicality clauses to ensure that claims are not made too readily, for example, by requiring the buyer of goods to give the seller the opportunity to remedy defects before exercising his right to repudiate, or by the buyer claiming the right to test the goods after delivery without losing his right to repudiate.

2.4 EXPRESS TERMS

In the following pages we look at a wide variety of business contract terms. Some of these terms raise complex issues of law which we discuss at some length; others can be dealt with much more briefly. It is very important to remember that the meaning and effect of any particular term depends not only on rules of law but on the context in which it appears – the contract as a whole, as seen in the light of the apparent intentions and understanding of the parties.

2.5 ENTIRE CONTRACTS

The parties may expressly agree that no payment is due unless and until the contract is completely and properly performed. In these 'entire' (as distinct from 'severable') contracts, any apparently quite minor defect could in theory justify the innocent party in repudiating the contract. But the mere fact that certain works or standards are specified in detail in the contract does not mean that the contract is an entire one, and in any case substantial performance usually prevents repudiation. It may be quite difficult to draw the line. In *Kiely* v *Medcraft*, 1965, it would have cost £200 to remedy faults in a contract for work worth £520, but the customer still had to pay £320. To the contrary was *Bolton* v *Mahadeva*, 1972, where there was a contract to install a central heating system for £560. The work was badly done, with complaints of fumes and some rooms left unheated. Repairs would have cost a further £174. In the circumstances this was more a failure to do the job at all than a substantial but imperfect perform-ance, and so the contractor was not entitled to any pay whatever for his work. Curiously enough, however, if the buyer in *Bolton* had paid in advance he would not be able to recover all his money. At common law a whole sum of money can be recovered only if nothing at all has been received in return – a 'total failure of consideration – which would not be so in this case.

2.6 ENTIRE AGREEMENT OR INTEGRATION CLAUSES

Most standard sales and purchase forms say that the terms they set out are the sole basis and content of the contract, and that they cannot be altered without specific authority. Typical wording is: 'This written agreement constitutes the entire agreement between the customer and the company and no changes of any kind shall alter this agreement unless in writing signed by an authorised signatory of both parties.' One of the purposes of such a clause is to exclude liability for pre-contractual statements made in advertisements or sales literature or by over-enthusiastic sales staff. By s.8 of the Unfair Contract Terms Act, para. 2.17, these provisions are valid if reasonable in the circumstances. It would not be accepted as reasonable to attempt to exclude liability for pre-contractual fraud or for misrepresentation, even though the fraudulent statement or misrepresentation subsequently became a term of the contract: *Witter* v *TBP*, 1996. If an agent or employee who appears to be acting within the course of his employment agrees to a variation in the written terms although not authorised to do so, it seems the variation would override the standard form: *Evans* v *Merzario*, 1976, para. 1.11.

2.7 QUALITY AND FITNESS

Depending on the bargaining power of the parties, any express terms of the contract regarding the quality of the goods in question might either demand complete conformity with agreed descriptions and specifications, or accept imperfections or tolerances within very broad limits. In the absence of express provision, terms as to quality may be implied by the Sale of Goods Act or other legislation, as described in the next chapter. The extent or degree of imperfection which would be a breach of contract, and so give rise to a claim for damages and/or repudiation, depends entirely on the facts of each case. In *Cehave* v *Bremer*, 1975, for example, the contract required that the goods be 'in good condition'. They were in fact imperfect, but nonetheless resaleable and usable as intended. It followed that they could not be rejected, but damages could be claimed. As regards sellers' attempts to limit or exclude their liability for supplying defective goods, see 'Exclusion clauses', below.

2.8 TIME

Buyers' contracts usually insist on prompt delivery; sellers' contracts, on the other hand, are more interested in prompt payment. In either case, what is the legal effect of delay? Section 10 of the Sale of Goods Act says only that the time of payment is not usually to be treated as a condition of the contract, but that the effect of other terms as to time depends on the construction of the contract as a whole and commercial necessity in particular.

So, for example, the effect of delays in delivering instalments of goods, or in making instalment payments, depends upon the length and frequency and likely repetition of the delay. A month's delay in making the first delivery might well justify repudiation of the contract, whereas a day's delay in making the last one could hardly justify more than a token claim for damages: *Maple Flock* v *Universal Furniture*, 1934. In shipping contracts in particular, the courts often regard times and dates as conditions, whether or not expressly described as such and even where the innocent party does not suffer any loss as a result of the delay. In *Bunge* v *Tradax*, 1981, for example, the contract required the buyer to give 15 days' notice of readiness to load, but he gave only 13 days. The House of Lords held the seller could repudiate the contract. A similarly strict decision was given in *Scandinavian Tanker* v *Flota*, 1982, where one day's delay in payment under a charter party was held to justify the owner in withdrawing the ship.

If time limits are not expressly agreed to begin with, they may be imposed later by one party giving the other due notice that he will make time 'of the essence' in the event of further delay. An example is *Rickards* v *Oppenheim*, 1950, where, after repeated delays by the seller in delivering a new car, the buyer was held entitled to say he would not take it unless it was delivered by a certain date. The complainant must give reasonable notice of this date: *Behzadi* v *Shaftesbury Hotels*, 1990. It is doubtful whether one can make time of the essence simply by saying 'delivery dates are material': *Aries Powerplant* v *Ece Systems*, 1996. But if the contract is quite clear, any delay will be fatal. In a case concerning a contract for the sale of land, payment was to be made by 6 p.m. on a particular day, time being of the essence. The buyer came with his money at 6.10 p.m. The court held the seller free to cancel the contract: *Union Eagle* v *Golden Achievement*, 1997.

2.9   OWNERSHIP AND RISK

Where there is any possibility of doubt, as, for example, in construction or instalment contracts, the parties should take care to say exactly when ownership of the goods is to pass from seller to buyer. The issue may be important for several very different reasons. As we see below, whoever owns the goods often bears also the risk of their accidental loss, theft, damage or deterioration, but on the other hand has the right to keep the goods in the event of his own or the other party's insolvency. The question is not simply one of physical possession, because, of course, a person may possess goods without owning them, and vice versa.

So far as the law is concerned, it is for the parties themselves to make whatever arrangements they please regarding both ownership and risk. If they fail to do so, or their wishes are not clear, the issue will then be dealt with by ss. 16–20 of the Sale of Goods Act. Section 16 says that the rights of ownership, which the Act calls 'the property in the goods', cannot in any case pass unless and until the goods are ascertained, that is until a particular article is identified as the subject matter of the sale. Once they have identified 'this car', rather than 'a car of this type', then under s. 17 the contracting parties are free to decide when ownership shall pass. Usually they say that both ownership and risk shall pass on delivery – a convenient and straightforward provision. If the goods have yet to be made, they might prefer to say, for example, that ownership passes when construction begins, or on payment of the first instalment: *Re Blyth*, 1926; *Bank of NSW* v *Palmer*, 1970 (Aust.).

If there is no express term of that kind, the parties' intentions may be inferred from other aspects of the agreement. Thus a clause enabling the seller to retain documents of title may suggest that he is still owner, whereas an obligation on the buyer to insure the goods from a certain point in time might indicate that he becomes owner then. But if there is no clue one way or the other as to the parties' wishes, the Act itself decides the outcome according to the provisions of s. 18.

2.10   Specific goods

Section 18 rule 1 provides that in contracts for the sale of specific goods – goods identified and agreed upon at the time of sale – which are ready to be delivered as per contract, ownership passes *when the contract is made*. Terms delaying payment or delivery do not of themselves affect the rule. This may seem a somewhat surprising provision, though it is the basic rule in certain other countries also, including France and Italy, and it is certainly one the parties should take account of. Its effect would be that where, for example, a buyer left a piece of furniture he had bought in the store pending delivery, and it was destroyed overnight by accident and without negligence on the store's part, he would still have to pay for it though he received nothing in return. But the store would probably be insured against such losses and so might not find it necessary to sue the buyer. And if there were any continuing uncertainty about the terms of the contract, judges nowadays would probably prefer to say that the requirements of rule 1 were not fulfilled and so avoid the possible unfairness of holding the buyer liable. 'In modern times very little is needed to give rise to the inference that the property in specific goods is to pass only on delivery or payment': *Ward* v *Bignell*, 1967.

There is another very practical reason why it may be important to decide whether the buyer has become owner. If he has become owner and as such then refuses to take delivery of the goods, for example because of some alleged defect in them, the seller can sue him for debt, that is, the price of the goods. But if the buyer is not yet owner, following the reasoning in *Ward*, above, the seller's claim is for damages at large for breach of contract. This may result in a much smaller sum being awarded, because of the seller's duty to try to reduce his losses by selling the goods elsewhere (para. 4.5).

We have said that rule 1 only applies to goods ready to be delivered in accordance with the contract; 'in a deliverable state', as the rule puts it. This might seem to suggest that ownership of defective goods can never pass to the buyer, but that is evidently not so. If the buyer accepts delivery, for example, there is no reason why the goods should not be held at his risk until such time as he discovers their faults and rejects them, whereupon ownership reverts to the seller. In effect then 'deliverable' means only that nothing remains to be done to the goods under the contract. An example is *Head* v *Showfronts Ltd*, 1970, which concerned a contract for the sale and laying of a carpet. The carpet was delivered to the buyer's premises but stolen from there before it could be laid. Whoever owned the carpet at the time of theft had to stand the loss. It was held that the carpet still belonged to the seller because it was not yet 'deliverable', that is, it had not been laid.

The next two rules in s. 18 make much the same point. Both refer to contracts for the sale of specific goods. Rule 2 provides that where the seller is bound under the contract to do something to the goods to put them into a deliverable state, ownership does not pass until he has done that thing and he has notified the buyer. Rule 3 says that if the seller has to weigh, measure or test the goods to establish their price, they do not belong to the buyer until that act has been done and he has been told so.

Rule 4 of s. 18 affects goods delivered on approval or on a sale or return basis. They become the buyer's when he 'signifies his approval' to the seller or in some other way 'adopts the transaction', for example resells them or does something else which prevents him returning them. The contract may expressly preserve the seller's title, to protect his rights against third parties, but he may nonetheless lose the goods if he appears to authorise the buyer to dispose of them.

2.11   Unascertained goods

Rule 5 of s. 18 is very important. It concerns goods which are *not* identified and agreed upon at the time of sale, and tries to determine that point in time *after* the contract is made at which they become the buyer's. It says that in the absence of agreement to the contrary the ownership of unascertained or future goods (meaning goods not yet made or not yet in the seller's hands) can only pass to the buyer when goods as described in the contract and in a deliverable state are *unconditionally appropriated* to the contract by either seller or buyer with the other's express or implied agreement.

The crucial question then is as to the meaning of 'unconditional appropriation'. Suppose, for example, that a seller has several identical goods in store, all answering the same contractual description, for instance a particular type of washing machine. What does he have to do in order to appropriate one of the machines unconditionally to the order of a particular buyer, and thereby make that buyer owner? Would it be sufficient to label the machine with the buyer's name and address? Would the buyer necessarily have agreed, expressly or even by implication, to the labelling of that machine, if, for example, it was not in quite such good condition as the others?

As usual it is easier to pose questions than to answer them, but the case of *Federspiel* v *Twigg*, 1957, provides at least a partial answer. An overseas buyer ordered some bicycles from an English manufacturer and paid for them in advance. The manufacturer crated them, addressed them to the buyer, registered them for consignment and ordered shipping space in a named ship. Before they could be sent to the port from which they would be shipped abroad the manufacturer went into liquidation and his receiver refused to deliver them. The problem for the buyer was whether he could claim the cycles as his own at that time. If not, he would have only a worthless claim for damages for breach of contract against the insolvent manufacturer. The court held that the cycles still belonged to the manufacturer. They had been 'appropriated' to the contract, but not 'unconditionally', in the sense that even at that late stage the manufacturer could have changed his mind, readdressed them and sent them elsewhere.

Appropriation must therefore be 'irretrievable' to be effective. When goods are sent by sea that last decisive act usually occurs when they are loaded across the ship's rail, but only if separately addressed and distinct from any other similar goods on board. Delivering goods to an independent carrier or sending them by post is regarded as unconditional appropriation, though that still begs the question whether the buyer agrees to that particular selection of goods. Goods may also be appropriated by 'exhaustion', that is when goods in bulk are reduced to or less than the amount to which the buyer is entitled, and he is the only claimant.

Another question here is as to the buyer's rights when he buys an unascertained part of a whole, for example half of a ship's cargo. We might expect that the whole cargo would remain in the seller's ownership until the buyer had removed half of it. If then the seller became insolvent before the removal, the buyer would lose any claim to the goods and also any money he had paid in advance. That was indeed the law until the Sale of Goods Act was amended in 1995. The new s. 20A affects buyers of specified quantities of unascertained goods forming part of an identified bulk, as in the above example of purchase of half a certain cargo. If and when the buyer pays for part or all of the goods he becomes owner in common of the appropriate proportion of the bulk, unless otherwise agreed. Under s. 20B he is then deemed to have the agreement of the other owners in common to deal in that share of the whole.

2.12 Retention of title

Section 19 of the Sale of Goods Act says that whether a contract is for the sale of specific goods or for goods subsequently appropriated to the contract, the seller may reserve rights of disposal of the goods until certain conditions are fulfilled by the buyer. If the seller does reserve such rights he remains owner of the goods until the conditions are fulfilled. In practice, conditions of sale agreed between businessmen very often provide that despite delivery to the buyer the seller shall remain owner of the goods until the buyer has paid for them, or paid off any other debts he may have to the seller.

These retention of title clauses are known as Romalpa clauses, from the case of *Aluminium Industrie* v *Romalpa Aluminium*, 1976, where the complexities and consequences of these provisions in British law were first examined in detail. Romalpa clauses are not intended to prevent buyers of goods subject to such clauses from dealing with them; indeed the whole purpose of the sale is usually to enable the buyer to carry on business by reselling the goods, as they stand or processed in some way, and so to pay the seller out of his profits. Thus although the buyer does not become owner of the goods until he has paid for them, he nonetheless appears as owner or otherwise authorised to sell, and so as a general rule can pass a good title to his sub-purchaser (as provided by s. 25 of the Sale of Goods Act and s. 9 of the Factors Act, 1889).

The position becomes more complicated, however, if the buyer then imposes his own Romalpa clause on his sub-purchaser. Until the sub-purchaser pays for the goods, ownership cannot pass to him. It follows that the original seller, if still unpaid, can enforce his own Romalpa clause and recover the goods from the sub-purchaser: In *re Highway Foods*, 1994.

Romalpa clauses, which do not have to be registered or publicised in any way, are understandably unpopular among banks and other large lenders and creditors. On balance, they seem also to be disapproved of by the judges. Certainly there are still many difficulties with their possible application. Some of these difficulties arise from the wording of the clauses in particular contracts; others are matters of principle. It seems, however, that a suitably worded clause can successfully retain ownership until all the buyer's debts to the seller are paid, not merely those arising from the sale in question: *Armour* v *Thyssen*, 1991 (Scot.). But where the buyer mixes the goods with other goods, or makes new products out of them (as, for example, in *Re Peachdart*, 1983 – sale of leather, which the buyer made into handbags), the courts have not so far allowed the seller to claim mixed or new products to the value of his original goods.

Where the buyer sub-sells goods subject to the original seller's retention of title clause, it is still doubtful whether the clause could enable the original seller to claim the proceeds of sale in lieu of the goods themselves. To support such a claim, it would seem at least necessary for the seller to have ensured that the proceeds would be paid by the buyer into a separate bank account and held by him on trust for the seller.

If a purported Romalpa clause fails for any reason, the result is, of course, that ownership of the goods passes immediately on sale to the buyer. Once that happens, the seller cannot claim to recover the goods unless within 21 days of the transaction he or the buyer registered his claim in the companies' registry in Cardiff or Edinburgh as a fixed or floating charge over the buyer's assets: s. 395 of the Companies Act 1985.

We refer finally to s. 20 of the Sale of Goods Act. The section explains the vital connection between ownership and risk. Unless otherwise agreed, goods are at the seller's risk until ownership passes. When that happens they are held at the buyer's risk whether or not he has taken delivery. 'Risk' refers only to loss or damage caused by accident for which no one is to blame. If delivery is delayed through the fault of one party the goods are at that party's risk in respect of any accident which might not otherwise have occurred. So where a buyer of apple juice was late in taking delivery and in the meantime the juice went bad, it was held that he had to stand the loss: *Demby Hamilton* v *Barden*, 1949. In any case whichever side has custody of the goods must take reasonable care of them.

2.13 PRICE

Terms as to price should always be expressly agreed and stated in writing. Uncertainty in this area is a common cause of disputes. If everything else is agreed, but the price is left to be settled at a later date, or is understood to be a 'reasonable price', the contract may well be held void because of uncertainty over this vital element – at least if neither side has done anything to carry out the contract: para. 1.7.

Rights to advance payments, or to part-payment or deposit, or payment by instalment, or as to credit, interest, security, price variation, retention money and the like are not given by law. An exception will be the statutory right to interest given to small businesses by the Late Payments of Commercial Debts Bill 1998[1]. Otherwise, these rights can be conferred only by the express terms of the contract. Every effort should therefore be made to ensure that any such terms are clear and unambiguous, setting out precisely the circumstances in which the rights arise.

It is for the buyer to decide whether the price represents good value. In the absence of fraud or misrepresentation, a mistake as to the value of goods or services is not usually sufficiently fundamental to affect the validity of a contract. As a general proposition, if a buyer does not ask the price before he agrees to buy, but it is available to him if he does ask, he is bound to pay that price: *Copthorne Hotel* v *Arup Associates*, 1996. There is no rule of English law requiring agreement only on 'reasonable' prices, nor any rule limiting rates of interest (other than those condemned as 'exorbitant' under the Consumer Credit Act). It seems nonetheless that sellers who are going to charge unusually high prices should ensure that buyers are aware of these prices (and perhaps other exceptionally burdensome terms) before they commit themselves. In *Interfoto* v *Stiletto*, 1988, the invoice accompanying the goods laid down an exceptionally high charge if the goods were kept beyond the agreed period of hire. The hirers did not read the invoice, and subsequently refused to pay the high charge. The court agreed that because it was so high the owners should have drawn the hirers' attention specifically to the charge, and so could not claim more than the usual trade rate. A curious implication of this case seems to be that even business parties are not expected always to read their contracts.

Section 28 of the Sale of Goods Act 1979 states the general rule that payment is due when the goods are delivered or tendered – but the rule applies only in the absence of agreement to the contrary. See also para. 2.8 as to time of payment.

So far as the method of payment is concerned, the basic rule is that it must be by 'legal tender' – current coin and banknotes. In practice, payment by cheque or direct debit is acceptable if the seller agrees. The buyer remains liable for payment even if the cheque is lost or unpaid for reasons beyond his or her control. But if the seller expressly or impliedly authorises payment by cheque through the post, the risk of loss falls on him.

It is important to note that a buyer's failure or inability to pay does not automatically end the contract, nor necessarily excuse the seller from fulfilling his side of the contract. Sellers therefore often protect themselves with express provisions in the contract entitling them to end the contract and claim the money due and damages in the event of the buyer's default or any act of bankruptcy.

2.14 EXCLUSION CLAUSES

Sellers' standard form contracts very often contain clauses seeking to limit or exclude altogether any possible liability for statements made in the course of negotiations, or for delayed delivery or defective goods. Buyers likewise commonly exclude liability for changing the terms of their orders, or postponing the date of delivery, or even for cancelling their orders. How far are these attempted evasions of liability upheld by the law?

The answer is a complicated one. There are three 'layers' of law to be considered. The first is case law – the common law. The second is the Unfair Contract Terms Act 1977, and the third is the Unfair Terms in Consumer Contracts Regulations 1994 – the result of a European Union Directive.

2.15 Common law controls

We can state the common law position quite briefly. It is broadly true to say that the common law failed to respond adequately to the possibilities

of abuse inherent in the use of exclusion clauses. The judges felt themselves unable to introduce any general rule of fairness or reasonableness
which would restrict or prohibit such clauses. They believed that if two
adults voluntarily made a contract, they should be bound by it. It was not
for the judges to rewrite their contracts for them to remedy any possible
economic inequality. The basic difficulty with this view was, of course, that
it begged the question as to the meaning of 'voluntary', for example in
contracts between consumers and monopoly suppliers.

The furthest the judges were prepared to go to regulate exclusion clauses
was to develop various rules of 'construction' or interpretation of disputed
contracts, as distinct from rules of substantive law. They would ask whether
the weaker party – the consumer or small business – had adequate notice
of the existence of the clause, and whether the clause itself was reasonably
clear. If not, the clause was invalid. But these were not always very
demanding requirements. In *Thompson* v *LMS Railway*, 1930, for instance,
a notice on the back of a railway ticket, 'Issued subject to the Company's
rules and regulations', was held sufficient to warn the passenger that the
company might not be liable for any accidental injuries she might suffer
en route. On the other hand, conditions printed in a cheque book were held
unenforceable because the cheque book did not appear as a contractual
document: *Burnett v Westminster Bank*, 1965. Receipts would probably be
treated in the same way: *Chapelton* v *Barry UDC*, 1940.

Ambiguity or uncertainty as to the scope or effect of an exclusion clause
will be interpreted against the interests of the trader who relied on it,
which may make it invalid. 'E. and O.E.' – errors and omissions excepted
– probably applies only to accounting errors, and certainly does not allow
mis-statement of the terms of the contract: *Van Bergh* v *Landauer*, 1925.
Exclusions of liability are presumed to refer only to contractual liability,
and so not to affect liability for the non-contractual wrong of negligence,
unless the clause clearly covers negligence. Where a contract denied the
buyer's right to repudiate defective goods, the court held the buyer was
nonetheless free to claim damages: *Ashington Piggeries* v *Hill*, 1971. And
where there is evidence of misrepresentation or fraud, or the clause varies
or contradicts the agreement already reached, again it will be of no effect.
Examples include *Lowe* v *Lombank*, 1960, where an exclusion clause which
falsely stated that the buyer had examined the goods beforehand was
struck out, and *Curtis* v *Chemical Cleaning Contractors*, 1951, where a
clause was nullified because a shop assistant misrepresented its effect. A
notice in a hotel bedroom could not vary the terms of the contract made
at reception: *Olley* v *Marlborough Court Hotel*, 1949. We have noted already
(para. 1.11) the important case of *Evans* v *Merzario*, 1976, where an express

oral agreement was 'confirmed' by a standard form which contradicted the oral agreement. The court held that the standard form could not override the express agreement – a ruling which represents a significant limitation on the effectiveness of such standard forms.

In the 1950s and 1960s certain judges suggested that the use of exclusion clauses could be controlled by the 'doctrine of fundamental breach'. This declared that an exclusion clause could not in any circumstances enable a party either to perform his contract in an entirely different way from that agreed on, or not to perform it at all. The doctrine was eventually disapproved by the House of Lords in *Photo Productions* v *Securicor*, 1980, on the grounds of commercial freedom of choice and with due regard to the realities of pricing policies and insurance practice, but it lives on in certain Commonwealth countries: *Fraser* v *Dominion Electric Protection*, 1997 (Can.).

Although, as we have said, the common law has had little effect on exclusion clauses, it should not be disregarded altogether. The requirements of reasonable notice and clarity are still the first hurdles which any exclusion clause must overcome if it is to be enforced. If a clause fails at this stage, there is no need to go on to consider its validity or otherwise under the statutory provisions to which we now turn. Nowadays, however, nearly every case is decided according to these provisions. Their importance both to business people and to consumers cannot be overstated.

2.16 The Unfair Contract Terms Act

Part I of the Act, ss. 1 to 14, applies to England; Part II, ss. 15 to 25, applies the same provisions appropriately to the law of Scotland and Part III, ss. 26 to 32, affects the United Kingdom as a whole. Schedules 1 and 2 contain definitions and exceptions. By way of introduction to this far-reaching measure we might note that its title is a little misleading; in some respects too broad and in others too narrow. It does not affect every different kind of unfair clause but only exclusion clauses, while on the other hand it controls also the use of warning notices and the like which seek to avoid liability in non-contractual contexts. Although mainly concerned with contractual liability, therefore, its provisions should be borne in mind when we discuss questions of negligence in Chapter 5.

The method of the Act is to identify certain kinds of exclusion clauses as particularly objectionable and declare them void wherever they are used, while others are permitted if and insofar as the supplier can prove them reasonable in the circumstances. We shall list the various provisions in turn and then consider the guidelines and cases which explain the test of reasonableness.

The Act's first objective is to prevent or restrict avoidance of liability for negligence; ss. 1 and 2. Section 1 defines negligence as breach of any contractual or legal duty to take reasonable care. It says also that the Act applies only to exclusions of *business* liability, with one minor exception noted below. The Act applies whether the breach of duty is deliberate or accidental and whether the fault is personal or vicarious (Chapter 5). 'Business', a troublesome concept as we note in Chapter 3, is defined in s. 14 to include a profession and the activities of any government department or local or public authority.

Section 2(1) declares null and void contract terms or non-contractual notices excluding or limiting liability for death or personal injury caused by negligence. But liability for other forms of loss or damage – economic loss or damage to property – can be excluded if the contractual term or notice is reasonable in the circumstances: s. 2(2). This key concept of reasonableness is enlarged upon in s. 11 and Schedule 2, and discussed below. Section 2(3) says that a person's awareness of or apparent agreement to a term or notice excluding liability for negligence does not of itself prove acceptance of risk. To this extent therefore the Act overrides *L'Estrange* v *Graucob*, 1934, which held that on principle a person must be bound by his or her signature whether or not he or she has read or understood the agreement.

In commenting on these provisions, except with regard to the question of reasonableness which we pursue later, we should observe that not all injury, loss or damage is necessarily caused by negligence. Injuries may be caused by natural hazards and inherent risks. Notices warning of such dangers are clearly not invalidated by the Act; indeed it might well be evidence of negligence if no warning were given. Likewise there can be no objection to notices excluding liability for loss or damage in circumstances where the danger is unavoidable or there is no duty of care in the first place. 'Owners' risk' notices in car parks, for example, are usually unobjectionable because the car owner generally pays only for space, not care: *Ashby* v *Tolhurst*, 1937. Negligence in these circumstances is only likely to become an issue when one person actually takes another's goods into his possession, for example when the key must be left with the attendant: *Mendelssohn* v *Normand*, 1969.

The case of *White* v *Blackmore*, 1972, is an interesting example of problems left unresolved by the Act. A charity sponsored a car race. The organisers displayed a notice at the entrance to the track saying that as occupiers they accepted no liability for injury howsoever caused. Through their negligence a competitor was killed. The notice was held sufficient to relieve the charity of all liability. It seems likely that the same answer would be given today since on the face of it a charity is not a business.

We should observe also that although the Act invalidates terms or notices excluding liability for negligence it does not actually forbid them. An unscrupulous dealer might therefore go on using clauses of this kind, indeed many do, and hope thereby to dissuade injured parties from legal action. The Office of Fair Trading is aware of this practice and is taking steps under the Unfair Terms in Consumer Contracts Regulations, below, to prevent their use.

Section 3 applies as between contracting parties where one of them deals as consumer (s. 12, below), *or* on the other's written standard terms of business. It says that this (stronger) party cannot by reference to any contract term (a) exclude or restrict his own liability for breach of contract, or (b) claim to be entitled to perform the contract in a substantially different way from that reasonably expected, or (c) claim to be entitled not to fulfil the contract or some part of it, except insofar as any such term is reasonable in the circumstances.

The importance of the second situation covered by s. 3, where the buyer must accept the other's written standard terms, is that it protects the small businessman against abuse of bargaining power by larger businesses upon which he is dependent. This in turn means that when a retailer is held strictly liable for selling defective goods contrary to s. 14 of the Sale of Goods Act (see Chapter 3), he has a reasonable prospect of recovering his loss from his own suppliers.

Many different types of exclusion clauses are covered by s. 3. Under subheading (a), for example, are laundry terms which purport to limit liability for loss of or damage to clothing to a certain sum of money. Under (b) are travel agency booking forms, so worded as to enable the agency to provide different accommodation or different forms of transport or other services without any redress by the customer. Subheading (c) covers among other examples contracts for delivery of goods by a certain date, accompanied by a term excluding liability for failure to deliver or late delivery. All these clauses must now be shown to be reasonable if they are to be upheld (s. 11, below). In many cases it may be perfectly reasonable to exclude liability, as for accidents or delays beyond one's control.

The next section, 4, strikes at unreasonable indemnity clauses in consumer contracts and invalidates them accordingly. One might find such a clause, for example, in contracts for hire of a car, under which the hirer is required to indemnify the owner against liability for injury or damage caused by a defect in the car.

Section 5 says that any term in a manufacturer's guarantee of consumer goods which excludes liability for loss or damage caused by the manufacturer's or distributor's negligence is void.

2.17 **Excluding the Sale of Goods Act** The next two sections are probably the most important rules in the whole Act so far as the consumer is concerned. Essentially s. 6 is intended to end or to restrict business sellers' rights to avoid their liabilities under the Sale of Goods Act and hire purchase legislation. We will see in Chapter 3 that s. 12 of the Sale of Goods Act requires sellers to pass a good title, while s. 13 ensures conformity of goods with their description and s. 14 provides that goods must be of satisfactory quality and reasonably fit for purpose. Section 15 requires conformity with sample. Similar obligations are imposed on finance houses supplying goods on hire purchase. With regard to these various implied duties, s. 6 of the Unfair Contract Terms Act first declares void any attempt to exclude or restrict the duty to give a good title. The possibility of excluding the obligations as to description, quality and fitness then depends on whether the transaction in question is between businesses or with someone dealing as consumer (s. 12, below). Any purported exclusion or limitation of ss. 13–15 ('No refund', etc.) in a *consumer* contract is *void*, and is also a punishable offence under the Consumer Transactions (Restrictions on Statements) Order 1978. Between *businesses*, however, terms excluding ss. 13–15 of the Sale of Goods Act are *valid if reasonable* (s. 11 and Schedule 2, below).

The underlying principle is that consumers need more protection than businessmen, but that there may still be abuses in the business context which need to be regulated, albeit less strictly. Although sales by private individuals are otherwise outside the Act, s. 6 also requires a private seller to pass a good title and provide goods conforming with their description. Sale of goods 'as seen' by either business or private seller might possibly prevent the description rule from arising, and 'with all faults' seems to preclude any contractual claim as to unfitness, but both may be illegal under the Consumer Transactions Order: *Hughes* v *Hall*, 1981, and *Cavendish Woodhouse* v *Manley*, 1984; para. 1.17.

Section 7, amended by the Supply of Goods and Services Act 1982, makes the same provision as s. 6 for title and fitness of goods passing under contracts which are not governed by the law of sale or hire purchase but are supplied on lease or under contracts for services, for example repair.

In s. 8 a provision introduced by the Misrepresentation Act 1967 is restated, making terms intended to avoid liability for pre-contractual statements – 'representations', as explained in Chapter 1 – valid only if reasonable. Proof of reasonableness is upon the person relying on the term. As we said in Chapter 1, and noted above with regard to 'entire agreement' clauses, many standard form conditions of sale exclude liability for non-compliance with advertising or other pre-sale statements. The application of s. 8 will depend on the buyer's familiarity with standard forms, the clarity of the term in question, and other aspects noted below with regard to Schedule 2. Wording which seeks to deny the existence of any representation in the first place, for example 'The accuracy of these statements cannot be guaranteed', will not be allowed to defeat the purpose of the Act: *Cremdean Properties* v *Nash*, 1977. Liability for fraud or misrepresentation cannot be excluded: *Witter* v *TBP*, 1996.

Section 9 declares that the reasonableness or otherwise of a contract term may still be decided, and effect given to it accordingly, whether or not the contract as a whole has been broken or repudiated. Conversely if the injured party decides not to exercise his right to repudiate he may still argue that the exclusion clause is unreasonable. Section 10 prevents a person evading liabilities by means of a secondary or collateral contract. The Act applies only to exclusions of future liabilities, not releases of past liabilities: *Tudor Grange* v *Citibank*, 1991.

Guidance as to the meaning of reasonableness in the present context is given partly by s. 11 and partly by Schedule 2, below. Section 11 says that where a person by contract term or notice tries to restrict liability to a specified sum of money, account must be taken of his resources and how far he might be expected to cover himself by insurance. The section also says that the reasonableness of a contract clause depends on the circumstances prevailing at the time the contract is made – not when the breach occurs – and that it is for the party relying on the clause to prove it reasonable.

There can be no clear rule as to the kinds of clauses which will be upheld or condemned under s. 11. The judge decides each case according to the merits of the clause as he or she sees it in its own particular context. *Overland Shoes* v *Schenkers*, 1998, shows the importance of trade association practice. The Court of Appeal upheld here a clause in a contract of carriage which obliged an importer to pay all sums due on demand regardless of any claims he might have against the carrier. The main reason for the decision was that the clause had been negotiated by both parties' trade association, and had been accepted for many years by all sides of the business as fair and reasonable. The clause did not seek to restrict liability, but only the procedure for deciding competing claims. In

Stewart Gill v *Myer*, 1992, on the other hand, the court held void a clause preventing the buyer from witholding payment 'for any reason whatsoever'.

2.18 **Consumer transactions** We have seen that the effect of several of the above sections depends on whether one of the contracting parties is dealing as consumer. Under s. 12, a person deals as consumer if he or she does not act in the way of business while the other party does so act, and if the goods in question are of a kind normally supplied for private use. The definition excludes sales by auction or competitive tender. The onus of proving that a transaction was not for consumer purposes is upon the supplier.

Sometimes goods may be used for both business and domestic purposes, and if so it may be very difficult to predict how the Act will apply, as in *Symmons* v *Cook*, 1981, and *R&B* v *UDT*, 1988. The question neatly posed in *Symmons* was whether a city firm of chartered surveyors who bought a Rolls Royce partly to impress clients and partly for private use did so as consumers. Was the car bought in the course of their business? It was held that the test was whether the goods were 'bought by a business whose integral or necessarily incidental purpose is the buying of such goods'. It followed in this case that no expertise in the buying of these particular goods could necessarily be expected. As a layman *in this respect* it could be said that the buyer was entitled to protection as a consumer. That at all events was the somewhat controversial conclusion reached in *Symmons*, and a term in the contract of sale excluding liability for defects in the car was annulled accordingly. On similar facts, *R&B* was similarly decided.

We should mention also ss. 13 and 27. Section 13 explains that when the Act forbids exclusion or restriction of liability it thereby forbids terms which admit liability but subject to onerous or restrictive conditions, or which restrict any right or remedy or impose any 'prejudice' on a person seeking to enforce his rights. Clauses requiring complaints to be made within a very short time of delivery, or making the supplier's decision final, would fall within this prohibition: *Green* v *Cade*, 1978, below. On the other hand s. 13 makes it clear that a written agreement to submit to (independent) arbitration is permissible. Lastly s. 27 records that the Act does not apply where parties who would not otherwise be bound by the law of the United Kingdom have voluntarily made it the law governing their contract, but that the Act *is* effective where another country's law has been adopted only in order to avoid it.

2.19   Exceptions   These then are the main provisions of the Act, apart from Schedule 2, below. We have seen that the statute has a very extensive coverage, making it as we have said of incalculable benefit to the consumer and even in some respects to the small business. There are, however, several significant exceptions to its scope. First, various important sections, notably ss. 3, 4, 5, 6 and 7, make special provision for consumers and to that extent leave non-consumer transactions less well provided for. Second, s. 29 declares that the Act does not affect contract terms authorised or required, expressly or by implication, by statute or made under an international agreement to which the UK is party. Further, a term satisfies the test of reasonableness, below, if incorporated in a contract or approved by a competent authority exercising any statutory jurisdiction or function and not itself a party to the contract. A competent authority is defined as any court, arbitrator, government department or public authority. Codes of practice approved by the Office of Fair Trading might therefore confer certain limited immunities which would otherwise be forbidden but are seen to be necessary in particular cases. The OFT's powers in this respect were, however, left in doubt by the decision in *Timeload* v *BT*, 1995.

More specific exceptions, all of great commercial significance, are created by Schedule 1 of the Act. Sections 2 to 4 are here stated not to apply to any contract of insurance (now covered by the Unfair Terms in Consumer Contracts Regulations, below), any contract relating to the creation, transfer or ending of an interest in land or a patent, copyright or other intellectual property right, or one relating to the formation or dissolution of a company or partnership or to its constitution or the rights or duties of its members. Contracts of marine salvage or towage, charter parties of ships or hovercraft, and contracts for the carriage of goods by such means are covered by s. 2(1) (avoidance of terms excluding liability for death or injury caused by negligence), but otherwise ss. 2, 3, 4 and 7 only apply to these particular contracts in favour of consumers. Section 2(1) and (2) does not extend to contracts of employment, except in favour of employees.

2.20   Reasonableness   Finally we must take special account of Schedule 2 of the Act, giving guidance as to the reasonableness or otherwise of contract terms within ss. 6 and 7, that is those excluding or restricting liability in business transactions for defective title to goods, non-conformity with description, unsatisfactory quality or unfitness for purpose. The most important factors are the relative bargaining power of the parties; the availability of other sources of supply; whether the customer received an inducement (such as a lower price for a lower quality) to agree to the terms; whether other suppliers offered similar contracts without excluding liability; the customer's knowledge of the existence and/or extent of the exclusion clause; whether any precondition of liability (e.g. notification within seven days) could practicably be complied with, and whether the goods were made or processed to the customer's own requirements (in which case the supplier could properly demand more protection against default). The same or similar factors are clearly relevant to all the other sections in the Act turning on reasonableness.

The test of reasonableness has been illustrated in a number of important cases including *Mitchell* v *Finney Lock*, 1983. The House of Lords held the seedsmen's exclusion clause valid at common law but unreasonable under provisions in the Supply of Goods (Implied Terms) Act 1973, identical to those now in Schedule 2 of the 1977 Act. The evidence was that a similar limitation of liability had been included in the terms of trade between seedsmen and farmers for many years and although the limitation clause had not been negotiated between representative bodies, neither had the National Farmers' Union objected to it. These factors were as one of their Lordships put it 'equivocal'. More significant was the fact that when anything went wrong the seedsmen usually negotiated settlements in excess of their strict contractual liability, apparently recognising that their terms were not fair. Two further pointers were that the supply of the wrong seed was due to negligence, insofar as the seedsmen knew that the kind they delivered could not be grown in the buyer's area, and that seedsmen could insure against the risk of crop failure without materially increasing their prices. In these circumstances the court decided 'without hesitation' that it would not be fair or reasonable to allow them to rely on the contractual limitation of liability.

In *Green* v *Cade*, 1978, another dispute over seeds, terms of sale had been agreed between seed merchants and a farmers' trade association. All complaints were to be made within three days, and damages, if any, were limited to the contract price. The court rejected the three-day limit as plainly unreasonable but upheld the damage limitation clause, partly because it had been collectively agreed and partly because seeds certified free of disease were available at a higher price. Failure to provide such an alternative service, more expensive but more reliable, led to rejection of another exclusion clause in *Woodman* v *Photo Trade*, 1981.

The judge in the Scottish case of *Knight Machinery Ltd* v *Rennie*, 1994, made some pertinent and instructive comments on the reasonableness or otherwise of clauses like that in *Green*, which undertake to accept liability but only for a very short time after delivery. The seller here had sold printing machinery to a printer, under a contract with a clause limiting the buyer's right of rejection. The machinery was unsatisfactory and remained so despite the buyer's attempts to use it. Some months after delivery, the buyer rejected the machinery. The seller then sued for the unpaid balance of the price. The judge found that the goods were indeed in breach of the quality and fitness requirements in s. 14 of the Sale of Goods Act, but then had to deal with the limitation clause in the contract.

Basically the question was whether the clause was fair and reasonable as between the two businesses, as required by s. 20 – the Scottish equivalent of s. 6 – of the 1977 Act. The clause was in standard form, saying that any notice of rejection had to be given by the buyer within seven days of delivery. Unless notice was given, 'the goods shall be conclusively presumed to be complete, in accordance with their description, in good order and condition and fit for the purpose for which they were acquired.'

The judge held the term unreasonable and invalid, largely because it was not clear how the buyer was supposed to fulfil the requirement as to notice. What was he required to say, and when? Should he have tried to reject the machinery when he first encountered what appeared to be

> fairly typical, apparently minor, possibly temporary, probably remedial problems, particularly when he had no means of determining whether they were symptomatic of some defect in the machine or simply of maladroitness in those attempting to operate it or perhaps related to the emulsions, inks, papers or other materials being used?

It would have been unreasonable to try to make him reject at that stage, and any attempt to do so would have been bound to fail. The judge also held that the buyer's right to reject when he eventually did so was safeguarded even though he had dealt with the seller several times before on the same terms. The seller lost his claim accordingly.

It does not follow, of course, that all terms imposing time limits on the right to complain or reject goods are unreasonable. A minor example to the contrary is *Sargant* v *Citalia*, 1994. A package holiday contract said that the tour operator would not accept any complaints unless they were made within 28 days of the end of the holiday. This was held enforceable because of the operator's obvious need to act quickly to investigate the situation.

The dispute in *White Cross Equipment* v *Farrell*, 1983, concerned a waste compactor sold to a salvage disposal operator. There was a six-month guarantee and an exclusion of all liability thereafter. The machine developed defects soon after the guarantee period and the buyer sought redress. The judge rejected his claim on the following grounds, reported here as a clear and helpful statement of the issues.

These parties were very much at arms' length. I have no doubt that the defendant could have bargained away the plaintiff's terms had he so wished. If the plaintiffs had not been willing to give up (this) condition the defendant could undoubtedly have gone elsewhere. It is to be noted, secondly, that the plaintiffs do undertake to replace parts or the entire machine if necessary and, apart from that, to repair or replace parts which are defective, due to workmanship or design, subject to certain safeguards. That undertaking is good for six months which should, in the ordinary course of events, be ample time for any major deficiency to emerge. Thirdly, once a compactor is in use, it can be subjected to an almost infinite variety of conditions of use and abuse, both as to the waste which is fed into it, the operators who are using it, and the conditions under which it is being used. Those considerations, in my view, amply justify the plaintiffs saying to a purchaser: 'After six months you are on your own as far as defects of design or workmanship are concerned.'

I have borne in mind carefully that this is not a case where the parties could easily insure and, indeed, insurance against breaches of the implied condition of suitability or a representation as to performance would not be a practical proposition at all. So I have viewed this matter simply as a question of allocating risks between two commercial parties of equal bargaining power; and having taken into consideration all the circumstances, I find that the requirements of reasonableness are in fact satisfied.

The availability of insurance was again an important factor in the decision in *St Albans District Council* v *International Computers Ltd*, 1996, coupled on this occasion with clear inequality of bargaining power. ICL had contracted to supply the Council with a computer and software which would work out their local tax requirements. A fault in the software led to a miscalculation of the number of taxpayers, as a result of which the Council suffered a shortfall of over £1 million. They claimed this sum from ICL as damages for breach of contract. The company sought to limit its liability to £100 000, relying on a clause in the contract to that effect.

The judge found the limitation clause unreasonable on several grounds. The plaintiffs were a relatively small local authority, acting under intense government pressure, and were 'over a barrel' in negotiating with this multinational company, on whose expertise they were wholly dependent. If they had sought such assistance elsewhere, no doubt they would have been confronted with similar terms. ICL, on the other hand, while limiting its liability to £100 000, was in fact insured for losses up to £50 million. His Lordship asked:

On whom is it better that a loss of this size should fall – a local authority or an international computer company? The latter is well able to insure, and in this case was insured, and pass on the premium cost to the customers. If the loss is to fall the other way it will ultimately be borne by the local population, either by increased taxation or reduced services. I do not think it unreasonable that he who stands to make a profit should carry the risk.

This very convincing reasoning – for why, after all, should the same party pay for both the other side's insurance and the other side's carelessness? – was upheld by the Court of Appeal, and will no doubt influence future interpretation of the Act.

2.21 The Unfair Terms in Consumer Contracts Regulations

In 1993 the European Commission, seeking both to harmonise terms of trade between Member States of the European Union and to improve generally the levels of consumer protection, approved Directive no. 93/13 on unfair contract terms. The Directive came into UK law as the Unfair Terms in Consumer Contracts Regulations 1994. The immediate and far reaching importance of these Regulations for anyone supplying goods or services to the general public cannot be overstated, as will be seen below. The Regulations are reproduced in Appendix 2.

Before we look at the Regulations in detail, we should make two preliminary points about their relationship with the Unfair Contract Terms Act, above. First, within their limits *the Regulations concern both exclusion clauses and any other kind of unfair contract clause*. They therefore overlap with the provisions of the Act. Unfortunately, when the Regulations were introduced the government made no attempt to unify the two sets of rules or to explain how any possible conflicts between them might be resolved. We shall see that where they do in fact overlap, the approaches of the Act and the Regulations are quite different. Second, *the Regulations affect only standard form contracts with consumers*. In contrast, as we have seen, some of the rules in the Unfair Contract Terms Act protect small businesses as well as consumers. And unlike the Regulations, the Act also controls non-contractual notices.

The Regulations apply to terms in contracts between professional sellers or suppliers of goods or services and consumers which have not been 'individually negotiated', that is terms which were drafted before the contract and which the consumer has not been able to influence. Even where some of the terms have been individually negotiated, the Regulations will still apply if the contract as a whole appears pre-formulated. But they do not affect terms which merely identify the goods – as long as they do so clearly – or state the price. Other things being equal, in other words, someone who pays a high price for shoddy goods cannot complain of unfairness. For the purposes of the Regulations, 'services' may include contracts relating to land, for example those made with estate agents. 'Consumers' are individuals acting for purposes outside their businesses: Regulations 2 and 3. Schedule 1 of the Regulations excludes also contracts

51

of employment, succession rights under family law, company incorporation or partnership contracts, and any terms required in contracts by law. The Regulations do, however, cover a major area which is outside the 1977 Act, namely insurance contracts.

2.22 **Unfairness** The key question, of course, is what is meant by 'unfair'. Regulation 4 answers the question in typical continental-style language. A term is unfair if 'contrary to the requirement of good faith [it] causes a significant imbalance in the parties' rights and obligations ... to the detriment of the consumer'. Fairness must depend to some extent on the nature of the goods or services, and on the more detailed guidance given as follows by Schedules 2 and 3 of the Regulations.

Schedule 2 says that a decision as to good faith turns on the bargaining power of the parties, whether the goods or services were supplied to the consumer's special order, and on any inducements given to the consumer. It will be seen that these criteria are much the same as under Schedule 2 of the Unfair Contract Terms Act, above. But the fact remains that the requirement of good faith is still a novelty as a general principle of English contract law.

Schedule 3 offers a long list, which it says is only indicative and not exhaustive, of the kinds of term which may be held unfair. If found unfair, the term is not binding on the consumer – though the rest of the contract may remain enforceable: Regulation 5. The examples given in the list show very clearly that the scope of the Regulations is much wider than that of the Act. They include terms entitling sellers or suppliers to keep consumers' pre-payments in certain circumstances; sellers' or suppliers' rights unilaterally to interpret the terms or end the contract; rights to end contracts of indefinite duration without reasonable notice; terms binding consumers although they have had no real opportunity to understand them; limits on consumers' rights to take legal action or terms obliging them to go instead to arbitration, and the like. The rights of suppliers of financial services to end or vary certain contracts on due notice are not affected.

A new obligation is imposed by Regulation 6, which requires written contracts with consumers to be in plain and intelligible language. Use of trade or legal jargon might of itself, therefore, invalidate a contract if it leads to obscurity or ambiguity. Any attempts by traders to evade the Regulations by making their contracts subject to the laws of non-EU states are nullified by Regulation 7, if the contract in question has a close connection with a Member State.

Regulation 8 concerns enforcement, and makes a significant step forward in terms of consumer protection. The Regulation obliges the UK Director General of Fair Trading to consider any complaint that a consumer contract term in general use is unfair. If he agrees that it is, he can then seek an undertaking from the trader to change or withdraw it, or, failing that, he may ask the High Court for an injunction to prevent further use. He cannot, however, take action without first receiving a complaint, and he cannot help individual consumers who seek redress.

The new powers have led to the establishment of a special Unfair Contract Terms Unit within the Office of Fair Trading. More than 1200 complaints were received in the first 18 months. It has been found that unfair terms are widely used and that most business sectors are affected. The Director General has taken effective action against a wide range of traders. He has, for example, warned several individual mobile phone airtime suppliers about the terms of their contracts. The contracts were said to be unduly burdensome for consumers and unduly favourable for suppliers. The Director criticised the small print, obscurely worded terms, and 'hidden' or 'surprise' terms. He objected specifically to price variation clauses, unreasonably long periods of notice which consumers had to give to end their contract, compensation requirements in the event of early termination, excessive disconnection charges and 'entire agreement' clauses excluding all pre-contract statements and promises. Many such terms have now been changed or abandoned. We note current proposals to give the Consumers' Association the same powers as the Director General to take action under Regulation 8 on behalf of the public.

We see, then, that the Regulations are in various respects both wider and narrower than the Unfair Contract Terms Act, and that the differences in approach raise several interesting – and unanswered – questions. The Act works, so to speak, by means of a black list and a grey list; some exclusion clauses are void wherever used, while others may be valid if reasonable in the circumstances. The Regulations have no black list; only a grey one. No particular kind of term is forbidden, but any term may be held invalid if contrary to good faith. What does good faith mean? How might the Regulations affect terms declared void by the Act? Presumably the specific prohibition in the Act would still be upheld. But what might be the effect of the test of good faith on clauses which the Act says are subject to the test of reasonableness? The tests are not identical, since good faith evidently involves a wider inquiry as to honesty and openness. We might hope, however, that the courts would be prepared to apply them in the same way. Despite the problems, one could hardly doubt that this particular EU contribution to UK law will bring about fundamental changes to our trading practices, at least in the consumer market.

2.23 Other statutory provisions

Apart from the Unfair Contract Terms Act and the Unfair Terms in Consumer Contracts Regulations, there are several other statutes controlling or forbidding the use of exclusion clauses in certain more specific contexts. So, for example, the Consumer Protection Act 1987 says that producers cannot opt out of the strict liability imposed upon them by the Act (para. 6.12). The Consumer Credit Act makes void any term in a consumer credit or hire agreement or a related agreement which is inconsistent with any provision in the Act or regulations made under it for the protection of the debtor or hirer. The Defective Premises Act 1972 imposes duties of good workmanship upon builders which by s. 6 cannot be excluded. A group of Acts concerned with domestic and international transportation should be noted. These are the Public Passenger Vehicles Act 1981, which makes void any provisions in a contract to carry a passenger in a public service vehicle which purport to restrict liability for his death or injury. The Carriage by Railways Act 1972 and the Carriage of Passengers by Road Act 1965 have similar effect regarding the international carriage of goods. The Carriage of Goods by Sea Act 1992, which gives effect to the Hague Rules, invalidates any clauses relieving the carrier of liability for loss of or damage to goods caused by his negligence. Similarly a carrier by air cannot escape his liabilities under the Carriage by Air Act 1961 (enforcing the Warsaw Convention), but such liabilities are subject to financial limits. Section 91 of the Arbitration Act 1996 prevents arbitration clauses in consumer contracts from taking away consumers' rights to go to court.

2.24 FORCE MAJEURE AND HARDSHIP CLAUSES

Many commercial contracts try to provide for extraneous events or changes in the parties' circumstances occurring after the contract has been made, which may make performance of the contract exceptionally difficult or effectively impossible for one side or the other. The events need not be unforeseeable, for example strikes or storms, but must be beyond the control of either party. The clauses dealing with these difficulties are called force majeure ('overwhelming events') or hardship clauses. They might perhaps be regarded as a species of exclusion clause, above, but are actually separate and distinct. Usually they list the kinds of problem the parties fear might upset their arrangements, such as Acts of God (natural calamities), acts of war, riots, strikes, storms, etc., and say that if and when they occur the contract will be suspended for as long as they last, or, as the case may be, will bring the contract to an end.

These clauses are generally enforceable if they meet three main require-ments: (i) the circumstances in which they apply must be adequately specified or exemplified; (ii) the problem which arises must be of the kind envisaged by the clause; and (iii) it must not be the fault of either party, and beyond the control of the party relying on the clause. These points are illustrated by cases such as the following. In *British Electrical Industries* v *Patley*, 1953, it was held insufficient just to refer to 'the usual force majeure clauses' because the meaning of the expression differs according to the context in which it is used. It was not enough, for example, to show that the clause allowed for delays because of strikes when the strike in question was a long lasting national strike. This was not at all the type of short-lived, local strike the parties had had in mind: *The Penelope*, 1928. In *B & S Contracts* v *Green*, 1984, the clause was invalidated because the employer could reasonably have avoided the strike which affected his business. Similarly in *Pyke* v *Cornelius*, 1955, the fact that the seller's supplier let him down did not amount to force majeure, because he could have obtained the goods from another supplier.

2.25   Frustration

The question then arises, what happens if a disaster occurs and there is no force majeure clause in the contract, or if there is a clause but it does not deal with a disaster of such magnitude? The answer lies in the legal doctrine of frustration of contract. This doctrine applies only when circum-stances change so completely, and without the fault of either party, that it is *impossible* or *impracticable* to perform the contract. Impossibility includes, for example, destruction of the specific subject matter of the contract, and subsequent illegality. We stress that a contract is not frus-trated merely because of greater difficulty in carrying it out, or the likelihood of loss instead of profit.

In the leading case of *Davies* v *Fareham UDC*, 1956, a builder contracted with the local authority to build certain houses for a fixed price. Because of delays beyond his control the costs of labour and materials rose so much that he would have made a substantial loss if held to the fixed price. He tried to escape from this provision and charge a higher price by arguing that the contract had been frustrated. The court held that he could not escape, because strictly speaking it was still possible or practicable for the houses to be built. The lesson of the case is that the courts will not help professionals who fail in their contracts to guard against the familiar risks of their own trade or industry, for example, here, by a price variation clause in the contract.

Tsakiroglou v *Noblee Thorl*, 1962, illustrates very clearly the courts' reluctance to release parties from their contractual obligations on grounds of frustration. The case concerned a ship on its way to Hamburg, caught south of the Suez Canal at the time of the Anglo-French invasion of Egypt in 1957. The cargo sellers claimed that the contract had been frustrated and refused to ship the goods further. The buyers sued for breach of contract. The House of Lords held that it was still possible and practicable to take the ship round the Cape – some 11 100 miles instead of the 4400 or so assumed by the contract – and so if the sellers refused they would be liable for breach. This answer depended, of course, on the goods not being perishables, and other such factors. Their Lordships also accepted that if an increase in costs were 'astronomical' they might have to give a different answer. (We note in passing that there is no UK case where inflation alone has been held to frustrate a contract.)

Interruption or ending of the supply of part of the goods contracted for does not of itself frustrate a contract. But if it is partly frustrated in this way, so that the seller cannot fulfil all his buyers' orders, it seems that he can do whatever is reasonable with the remainder of the goods. He might supply his customers *pro rata* if they agreed, or might supply the first to the exclusion of the others: *Intertradax* v *Lesieur*, 1978.

If the court accepts that a contract has been frustrated, the consequences are laid down by the Law Reform (Frustrated Contracts) Act 1943. Essentially all the contractual obligations are ended – not suspended, as usually happens under force majeure clauses. Money already paid under the contract is recoverable, while money due is no longer payable. Expenses on one side or the other are recoverable, but only out of any sums already paid or owing. 'Valuable benefits' obtained under the contract before the frustrating event must be paid for. These remedies are subject to the court's discretion and are not rights as such: *Gamerco* v *ICM*, 1995.

The 1943 Act can be excluded by express agreement between the parties, as where they contract on the basis of an appropriate force majeure clause. It does not in any case apply to contracts for the carriage of goods by sea, charter parties, insurance contracts, or contracts for the sale of specific goods which have perished without the fault of either party.

2.26 PENALTY CLAUSES

The purpose of a penalty clause – or, strictly, a liquidated damages clause – is to stipulate in advance the sums to be paid or forfeited in the event of a breach of contract. The party relying on the clause hopes thereby to avoid the difficulty of proving individual items of loss and the overall expense of litigation. We consider the effectiveness or otherwise of such clauses in the context of claims for damages in Chapter 4.

2.27   ARBITRATION

Business people are understandably reluctant to tangle with the law. Most prefer to settle their differences by means of arbitration. The advantages are generally thought to be speed, economy, informality and privacy; all of which should make the proceedings less antagonistic and disagreeable than they would probably be in court. These benefits cannot be guaranteed, however. Arbitrators (or, in Scotland, arbiters) can be very expensive. With the agreement of the parties or the permission of the court, their decision on questions of law may be subject to appeal – though the parties may agree beforehand to exclude this possibility. It should be borne in mind also that successful arbitration requires the full and continuing co-operation of both sides. We note that claims for less than £3000 (likely to be increased to £5000) may be dealt with equally or more efficiently and economically by the small claims procedure in the county court. Consumers' rights to use this procedure and not to be obliged to accept trade arbitration are safeguarded by s. 91 of the Arbitration Act 1996.

There is nonetheless a strong business preference for arbitration, as reflected in most standard form contract forms. The parties' rights are regulated partly by common law and, in England and Wales, by the Arbitration Act above. Usually the contract will nominate an arbitrator or panel of arbitrators, for example certain officers of the relevant trade association, or a person or persons appointed by a chamber of commerce. It is helpful also to specify the place of arbitration, the procedure – which may be as formal or informal as the parties wish – and time limits. The parties may if they wish agree to accept a decision based on fairness and convenience rather than the strict letter of the law. If not, the governing legal system should be specified. It may also be desirable to state the language of the proceedings. Arbitration awards under written agreements will be enforced by UK courts as if they were orders of the High Court.

2.28   CHOICE OF LAW

In any contract which, because of the nationality of the parties involved or the place where the contract was made or is to be performed, has any connection with another country, it is most important to state which country's laws govern the relationship. The system chosen will usually be that preferred by the stronger contracting party and will be accepted by the courts unless clearly intended to prevent or discourage litigation. Parties to UK contracts, however, are not allowed to choose another system simply in order to avoid the application of the Unfair Contract Terms Act, above. The contract should state which country's courts or arbitrators shall have jurisdiction, and, preferably, which language shall apply. A typical example of the kinds of problem which may otherwise arise is *The Assunzione*, 1954. After negotiations in France and Italy, French carriers chartered an Italian ship to carry goods from Belgium to Italy. The contract was made in France, but on an English standard form which said nothing as to the governing law. The Court of Appeal held that since the contract was to be performed in Italy it should be governed by Italian law.

The Contracts (Applicable Law) Act 1990 is intended to resolve 'forum' problems for European Union countries. The Act incorporates the 1980 Rome Convention on contractual obligations which are subject to conflicts of law. Questions of status, wills, matrimonial and family relationships, negotiable instruments, arbitration agreements, company law, agency duties, trusts and certain insurance contracts are outside the scope of the Convention. With these exceptions, the Convention says that contracts are governed by the system of law expressly or by clear implication chosen by the parties. If their choice is not clear, the law applicable is that of the country most closely connected with the contract. This is usually where the liable party lives or carries on business. If land is involved, the country most closely connected is that where the land is situated.

Article 5 of the Convention makes special provision for consumer contracts. It says that choice of law clauses cannot take away the protection of the consumer's own legal system if he made the contract in his own country after a specific invitation or advertising by the other party, or if the contract is for a package holiday. But contracts of carriage and contracts for services to be supplied in another country (such as car hire or time-share agreements) are not protected in this way. We note here also that the Brussels Convention on Jurisdiction and Enforcement of Judgments, 1968, given effect in the UK in 1982, makes judgments in EU states reciprocally enforceable.

2.29 SUMMARY

In this chapter we have examined certain aspects of the vocabulary of English contract law and a wide range of terms commonly used in commercial contracts. We have noted the distinctions between representations, conditions and warranties, and the resulting rights and remedies, and noted the classification and use of 'innominate terms' as a way of determining the appropriate remedy for breach of contract. Among the express terms examined, those of particular importance include provisions as to the quality and fitness of goods, ownership and risk (noting that under English law, risk passes with ownership unless otherwise agreed), sellers' rights to retain ownership of goods until paid, exclusion clauses and force majeure or hardship clauses.

The problems which might arise both for commercial parties and consumers through the use of exclusion clauses are now largely resolved by the Unfair Contract Terms Act of 1977 and the Unfair Terms in Consumer Contracts Regulations 1994 – although it is fair to say that no attempt has been made to co-ordinate the two provisions. The Act declares void clauses or notices which exclude liability for personal injury caused by negligence and other clauses affecting fitness of goods in consumer transactions. Various other types of exclusion clause or notice will be upheld only if the supplier can prove them reasonable in accordance with the standards laid down in the Act. While the Act may benefit small businesses as well as consumers, the new Regulations refer only to consumer contracts. On the other hand, the Regulations apply not only to exclusion clauses but to many other potentially unfair clauses. All such clauses are now subject to a test of good faith, failing which they will be declared void.

NOTE

Due to the changes in the law during the publication of this book, the following now applies:

1. The Late Payment of Commercial Debts (Interest) Act 1998 entitles unpaid business suppliers of goods or services to claim interest at base rate plus 8 per cent as from 30 days after payment is due. The right to interest cannot be excluded or varied unless the contract provides an alternative substantial remedy. Initially the statutory right is available only to enterprises with fewer than 50 employees.

3 Implied terms of quality and fitness in contracts of sale

3.1 COMMON LAW TERMS

A seller's primary obligations are those he or she expressly agrees with the buyer, in writing or by word of mouth, in the contract of sale. We examined some typical terms in the last chapter. More often than not, however, the terms expressly agreed between the parties do not cover every aspect of their agreement, nor answer in advance every question or grievance which might arise. When problems do arise to which there is no apparent answer in the contract, one side or the other may then look to the law to fill in the gaps by adding appropriate terms to the agreement.

These terms may be added or 'implied' either by common law or by statute. So far as the common law is concerned, the judges are generally reluctant to intervene and rewrite contracts to deal with problems which they think the parties should have dealt with themselves. They will not add terms simply to make a contract more fair and reasonable, or, unlike the rule in continental systems, solve problems by importing a general obligation of good faith in contracting. But they may be willing to help if the proposed terms are based on provable trade custom, or, more commonly, are *necessary*. The test of necessity is a strict one. In effect it must be shown that without the proposed term or terms the contract would not make commercial sense. So in *Liverpool City Council* v *Irwin*, 1977, the House of Lords held that a corporation tenancy agreement which stated only tenants' duties would be meaningless unless it was deemed to include Council obligations as to maintenance. By reference to the test of necessity, judges have decided, for example, that in the absence of any specific agreement on the point, work under a contract must be begun and completed within a reasonable time – *Aries Powerplant* v *Ece Systems*, 1997 – and a reasonable price paid. What is reasonable in any given case is decided by the judge on the facts of the case.

Other miscellaneous examples of judicial attitudes to this problem include the case of *Stag Line* v *Tyne Repair*, 1984, where a ship repairer was held impliedly under a duty to tell the shipowner of a serious fault in the repairs. Conversely, in *Ault* v *Sure Service*, 1983, the judge refused to imply a term which would have stopped a sales agent who had contracted to use his best endeavours for his principal from working also for his principal's competitors.

3.2 STATUTORY TERMS

Much more important for present purposes are the terms imposed by Act of Parliament. These are usually intended to provide some form of 'safety net' in all transactions of a particular kind. Sometimes the terms apply only in the absence of agreement between the parties, but may on occasion represent minimum standards of fitness or fairness, as the case may be, enforced regardless of the parties' wishes.

So far as sales law and sellers' liabilities are concerned, the most important terms are those implied by the Sale of Goods Act 1979. We take account also of the Supply of Goods (Implied Terms) Act 1973 – which deals with goods supplied on hire purchase and by redemption of trading stamps – and the Supply of Goods and Services Act 1982, which regulates hiring and rental agreements and goods provided under service or repair contracts. Premium offers and free gifts are not controlled by statute. Drugs supplied by doctors' dispensaries and by chemists on prescription are not regarded as goods sold but as services provided: *Appleby* v *Sleep*, 1968. Intellectual property rights as such are not covered by the 1979 or 1982 Acts. So, for example, while computer disks may be considered as goods, programs are not. But a disk with a defective program would be regarded as defective goods: *St Albans DC* v *ICL*, 1996.

Sellers' and suppliers' duties under these various Acts are essentially the same, and so far as they apply in England and Wales are nearly all classified as 'conditions' or 'warranties'. In Scotland they are all described as 'terms'. As mentioned in Chapter 2, the Acts define conditions to mean basic terms whose breach entitles the innocent party to repudiate the contract, unless he has accepted the goods (para. 3.16), and/or to claim damages. Warranties are defined here as less important terms, breach of which entitles the innocent party only to claim damages. This apparently simple distinction between major and minor terms and remedies may create difficulties. If what seems a minor breach of contract is classified by the Act as a breach of condition, the resulting all-or-nothing solution can be unjust. Judges are naturally reluctant to set aside contracts for no good reason, but the Act may leave them no alternative. As we see below, a distinction is now drawn between consumer contracts and business contracts as regards remedies, which may help to overcome this problem. The proposed EU Consumer Guarantee Directive makes the same distinction, again with regard to the type of remedy available: para. 3.10.

3.3 THE SALE OF GOODS ACT

The Act of 1979, reproduced in part in Appendix 1 as amended in 1994 and 1995, is still basically a restatement of the first Sale of Goods Act of 1893. The most important differences and developments are that sales are made subject to the Unfair Contract Terms Act 1977 (see Chapter 2) and sellers' powers to opt out of the liabilities we shall examine are thus much reduced. The rules on quality and risk are also updated.

It should be noted that the word 'seller' covers equally manufacturers, distributors, retailers and private individuals if and insofar as they enter into contracts of sale. Section 14 of the Sale of Goods Act – concerning quality and fitness of goods – applies only to business sales, but otherwise all are bound to their buyers by the same terms of the same Act. So far as retailers and distributors are concerned, we should observe that they are almost always in business on their own account and thus personally or corporately liable on their contracts. They may well be described in the sales literature as 'manufacturers' agents' or 'franchised dealers', but that alone does not make them agents in law. Only where one person genuinely contracts for and on behalf of someone else does he make that other liable for his own breach of contract.

Commercial agents as such – self-employed intermediaries authorised to buy or sell goods on behalf of another – are covered by the Commercial Agents Regulations 1993. The Regulations impose duties of good faith on both principal and agent, and give the agent a right to a written statement of the terms of the agency, reasonable remuneration, certain continuing commission rates, and notice.

3.4   Title

The first of the relevant rules in the Act is s. 12, but it requires only brief mention for present purposes. The section says there is an implied condition in all contracts of sale that the seller has a right to sell the goods, and implied warranties of freedom from prior rights over the goods and of quiet possession of them except in so far as any limitations are disclosed before sale. Thus a seller is liable for infringement of a third party's patent rights, whether deliberate or inadvertent: *Microbeads A G* v *Vinhurst*, 1975.

A seller who sells goods which, unknown to him, have been stolen, is liable under s. 12 to repay the full price to the innocent buyer as and when the true owner reclaims the goods: *Rowland* v *Divall*, 1923. The Office of Fair Trading reports that some 500 000 stolen cars are sold every year. A buyer in the used car market would be well advised to use a credit reference agency such as the AA to make sure he or she has a good title. The agency service may include insurance in the event of error.

We should mention here in passing another common problem of car ownership – that which arises when hire-purchasers sell their cars before they have paid all the instalments due. A helpful rule of law in s. 27 of the Hire Purchase Act 1964 resolves the problem at least in part, by saying that the first private purchaser (i.e. not a dealer) of a vehicle originally sold in breach of an h.p. agreement gets a good title to the vehicle if he or she purchases it in good faith, whether from the original hire-purchaser or from a dealer.

3.5   Description

Section 13 says that in sales by description there is an implied condition that goods will conform with their description; that is, that the buyer will get what the seller promised. In sales by both sample and description the bulk of the goods must also correspond with the description.

The key question is as to the meaning of the word 'description'. The word clearly does not encompass *everything* said or written by the seller about his goods, for instance, in the way of sales talk. Nor on the other hand does it necessarily presuppose a spoken or written statement. Many goods 'describe themselves' by the way they are packed or displayed. The judges have held that 'description' is confined to those express or implied statements which actually identify the goods or are otherwise part of their essential attributes; the sort of thing one might perhaps write on a sales or receipt note to define one's purchase. If the goods do not conform with these particulars then s. 13 enables the buyer to reject them and demand his money back, subject always to the question of acceptance noted in Chapter 2 and below.

Difficulties naturally arise in distinguishing between essential and inessential attributes. 'New', for example, is an essential element, while 'in good condition' probably would not be because it is merely a question of degree: *Cehave* v *Bremer* 1975. Even then the precise meaning of 'new' is open to argument. In *Phillips* v *Cycle Corp.*, 1977, a motorcycle sold as new was held to be so even though it was five years old, because it had not previously been sold by retail. This was surely a quite incorrect test in the circumstances. In *Rogers* v *Parish*, 1987, the fact that a car had been stored in the open for several months, and had deteriorated accordingly, was not thought to affect its newness. Conversely if the goods are indeed 'new', or otherwise as specified, the fact that they are defective in some other respect does not of itself prove breach of s. 13. So in *Grenfell* v *Meyrowitz*, 1936, the buyer ordered a particular kind of safety glass which then broke and injured him, but he had no claim under s. 13 because he got the type of glass he asked for. Presumably there is a point at which an article is so defective that it cannot properly be given the same description as if it were in working order, but such situations must be rare.

Normally therefore the scope of s. 13 is limited to situations where the buyer orders 'A', but is delivered 'B'. If 'A' is delivered but found defective the buyer's remedy if any is usually in the quality and fitness requirements of s. 14. We shall see that these requirements may sometimes be matters of degree, and so should bear in mind the possibility of using s. 13 to define quality and avoid the doubt which might otherwise arise. This can be done only by the use of very precise language which as we have said identifies or defines the goods. A good example is *Tradax* v *European Grain*, 1983, where the buyer ordered a consignment of animal feeding stuffs with 'maximum 7.5 per cent fibre content'. On delivery the consignment was found to have up to 9.25 per cent fibre content. It was held that the statement as to fibre content was part of the description of the goods, and the buyer was thus enabled to reject the goods under s. 13 without having to argue questions of suitability or fitness under s. 14.

As a rule then the judges attach much weight to precise specifications of this kind. In *Arcos* v *Ronnaassen*, 1933, for instance, $\frac{1}{2}''$ staves were ordered but staves of $\frac{9}{16}''$ supplied. The buyer was held entitled to reject them even though they could still be used for his intended purpose.

> A ton does not mean about a ton, nor a yard about a yard. Still less when you descend to minute measurements does $\frac{1}{2}$ inch mean about $\frac{1}{2}$ inch. If the seller wants a margin he must and in my experience does stipulate for it.

This very strict approach is, of course, open to abuse. It may give a buyer who has changed his mind about the wisdom of his purchase a gratuitous and quite unnecessary opportunity to renege on his contract. More recently the courts have preferred to ask simply whether the seller's deviation from contractual requirements is of any real significance: *Cehave* v *Bremer*, above; *Reardon Smith* v *Hansen Tangen*, 1976. So if there is only a very minor shortfall or excess in quality or quantity, the buyer's claim will probably be rejected. In contrast with the *Tradax* case above is *Tradax* v *Goldschmidt*, 1977, where a contract for the sale of barley allowed for up to 4 per cent impurity but the barley delivered contained 4.1 per cent of foreign matter. The buyer was not allowed to reject the goods on this pretext. The case is a good example of the 'de minimis' rule; that is, that the law will ignore very small and immaterial faults or breaches of contract.

One last point about s. 13 is that the more the buyer examines the goods and satisfies himself they are what he wants, the less he can claim to rely on the seller's description of them. There may be no 'sale by description' at all, or none at least in respect of those aspects of the description his examination was intended to confirm. So in *Harlingdon* v *Hull*, 1990, an expert buying on the basis of his own judgment a painting wrongly attributed by the seller to a certain artist had no claim under this section. In *Beale* v *Taylor*, 1967, two halves of cars had been welded together and sold as one. The buyer had tested the car before buying it, but the welding was not the kind of fault he was looking for, and so he was still protected by s. 13. It should follow that when goods are sold 'as seen' or 'as is', s. 13 should apply only to hidden faults: *Cavendish Woodhouse* v *Manley*, 1984.

3.6 Quality and fitness

For product liability purposes by far the most important duties imposed by the Sale of Goods Act are those in s. 14. Their main provisions are that where goods are sold in the course of business they must be of *satisfactory quality* and *reasonably fit for their purpose*. For the purposes of English, but not Scottish, law, these requirements of quality and fitness are both *conditions*. As noted above this means that if goods fail to meet these standards the buyer can reject them and recover his money, together with compensation for any personal injury or economic loss directly caused by the goods. The right to reject goods is lost once the buyer has accepted them – ss. 11 and 35 (see below) – and in that event he has only a claim for damages.

3.7 **Business or private sale?** It is of interest first of all that these rules as to quality and fitness apply only to business sales, whereas ss. 12, 13 and 15 apply to all sales including those between private individuals. It follows that if Mr A sells his own car to Mr B and it then breaks down completely, Mr B has no redress under s. 14 of the Sale of Goods Act, nor, unless there is fraud or negligence, under any other rule of law. As between private individuals the policy of the law is still summed up in the maxim *caveat emptor*: let the buyer beware. A person who buys goods from his neighbour must satisfy himself of their worth, or have only himself to blame. Since the law will not help him he must help himself, and the most useful way of doing that, apart from having an expert examine the goods, is to extract some appropriate and preferably written promise from the seller as to their quality or quantity before purchase. This promise, so long as it is factual and not mere sales talk, then becomes an express term of the contract and if broken can be sued upon according to the general principles of law discussed in Chapters 1 and 2. Failing any express contractual commitment, a private seller could only be liable on grounds of negligence; in other words that he knew or ought to have known that the goods were likely to cause injury or loss but failed to warn the buyer: *Hurley v Dyke*, 1979. In a private sale the buyer might well find it difficult if not impossible to prove the seller at fault in this way.

Because private sellers are not liable to the same extent as business sellers, the latter sometimes try to hide their identity. In the 'small ads' columns of newspapers, for example, it may be very tempting for the business seller to masquerade as a private individual and thus escape the burdens of s. 14. The purpose of the Business Advertisements (Disclosure) Order 1977 is accordingly to compel advertisers selling in the course of business to state that fact. Failure to do so is a criminal offence. Sales by auction or competitive tender are outside the Order, as are sales of agricultural produce gathered or produced by the seller.

There may occasionally be difficulties in deciding whether a particular sale is indeed in the course of a business. The Sale of Goods Act defines business to include a profession and the activities of public authorities, so it is not merely a question of seeking to make a profit. It is certainly not necessary to be a manufacturer of the goods in question, nor even to deal frequently in such goods, as where for example a coal merchant might sell his lorry. There is no single test, whether of intention or frequency or any other element. An overall objective view is necessary. In *Blackmore v Bellamy*, 1983, a postman had a hobby of buying, improving and then selling old cars. Since it was his hobby he neither sought nor made any significant profit. He was prosecuted for breach of the 1977 Order, above.

The magistrates accepted his evidence that his activities were no more than a hobby, and acquitted him. Another case of interest is *Davies* v *Sumner*, 1983. A self-employed courier used his car almost entirely for the purposes of his job. He likewise was prosecuted when he sold it as a private individual, and he also was acquitted because the sale was not in the course of his trade or business. But a person who sold his own used goods in his own shop was acting in the course of business: *Southwark BC* v *Charlesworth*, 1983.

If a private person sells through a business agent, for example an auctioneer, then under s. 14(5) the conditions of quality and fitness bind the business agent unless he makes it clear to the buyer that the seller is not acting in the course of business.

3.8 Satisfactory quality

We observe first that this basic requirement in s. 14(2), until recently expressed as a requirement of 'merchantability', does not apply as regards defects pointed out to the buyer before sale, nor to faults the buyer should have seen in any examination of the goods he may have carried out. He is not obliged to examine the goods beforehand, and indeed very often cannot do so, for example because they are sold when in transit.

The immediate question arising under this sub-section is in deciding what 'satisfactory quality' actually means. There is a very broad definition in sub-section 2A. The goods must 'meet the standard that a reasonable person would regard as satisfactory, taking account of any description of the goods, the price (if relevant) and all the other relevant circumstances'. Sub-section 2B adds that

> the quality of goods includes their state and condition and the following (among others) are in appropriate cases aspects of the quality: fitness for all the purposes for which goods of the kind in question are commonly supplied; appearance and finish; freedom from minor defects; safety; durability.

This definition is vague, but perhaps inevitably so. What is aimed at is the *norm* of performance or fitness or appearance, rather than perfection. Whether goods reach a norm, the generally acceptable standard, depends on the nature of such goods. It is usually easy enough to decide whether an article with only one or two functions, for example an electric kettle, is in acceptable condition and working properly, but very much more difficult where multi-functional and extremely complex products such as cars are involved. Buyers' reasonable expectations also depend, of course, on whether the goods are new and if so whether expensive and said to be of good quality, or cheap and therefore perhaps less reliable and durable, or secondhand, and if so on their age and appearance and the reduction in price.

Let us illustrate the problems a little further. Satisfactory quality, like merchantability, must include the 'saleability' of the goods. But saleable to whom and as what? In *Sumner Permain* v *Webb*, 1922, the buyer bought goods he intended to export to Argentina. Unknown to him the Argentine government had prohibited the import of such goods. But the fact that he could not sell them there, and the object of the contract thus defeated so far as he was concerned, did not mean they were not saleable. He was still able to sell them elsewhere, though at lower prices. Similarly, in *Buchanan-Jardine* v *Hamilink*, 1983, an unavoidable delay in the exercise of the buyer's right to resell goods was held not to affect their merchantability. In *M/S Aswan* v *Lupdine*, 1986, plastic containers were found merchantable even though they melted and ruined their contents when exposed to extreme heat.

If goods can only be resold at a lower price that does not of itself prove them unsatisfactory under their original description, but that depends, of course, on the extent of the reduction and the reason for it. There is always the possibility of the market dropping in the meantime, or the goods may be usable for some other more economical purpose than that originally intended: *Brown* v *Craiks*, 1970. Conversely a resale price only just below the price first agreed does not necessarily prove the goods satisfactory, for example as new goods, as we see immediately below.

3.9 **Minor defects** Another question is how much importance the law should attach to scratches or blemishes or other purely cosmetic defects. A person given a choice of, say, washing machines, all identical except for one with a scratch or dent, clearly would not buy that particular one, at least at the full price. It should follow that an article may not be satisfactory because of very minor and superficial faults and even though otherwise in good working order. But could that article likewise be rejected by the buyer after he has taken delivery of it?

The Canadian case of *IBM* v *Shcherban*, 1925, is instructive here. The buyer ordered a $300 computer scale. It was delivered with a broken dial glass which would have cost only 30 cents to repair and which did not affect the working of the machine in the slightest. The court held the machine unmerchantable and the buyer therefore entitled to reject it. Whether or not one agrees with the decision it is obviously very much on the borderline. Section 14 (2B) says that goods must be satisfactory in appearance and finish and freedom from minor defects – but we must remember that the test is still one of *satisfactory* quality, not perfection. No commodity can be perfect. There must come a point when a scratch or mark, particularly on industrial rather than consumer goods, is so trivial that no reasonable buyer would take account of it and a court would certainly refuse to acknowledge it.

Ultimately the problem is how to discourage shoddy workmanship while at the same time preventing buyers from seeking to reject their purchases without good reason. The Sale of Goods Act now recognises the need to distinguish for this purpose between consumer goods and commercial or industrial goods. Section 15A says in almost as many words that very minor or cosmetic faults could usually justify rejection – if at all – only in consumer sales, and that in business contracts the buyer's rights in these circumstances, if any, will probably be limited to a claim for damages. Such a claim might, of course, be for so small a sum as not to be worthwhile, and might preferably be met by negotiating a reduction in price. If a plaintiff does have a right to reject for cosmetic faults, such right would almost certainly be lost within a very short time after delivery.

From the seller's point of view it is helpful, as mentioned earlier, to try to avoid these difficulties by specifying tolerances or approximations within which his goods are sold, or by using 'anti-technicality' clauses giving him the right to repair the goods before the buyer can exercise any right to repudiate he might otherwise have. The seller must be careful to ensure that these provisions cannot be regarded as exclusion clauses, which are closely regulated by law: Chapter 2.

3.10 Durability Section 14(2)(B) also specifically recognises the durability of goods as an aspect of their quality and fitness. What that might mean in any particular case would depend on the normal life expectancy, wear and tear, price and quality of the product. The appropriate period should not be affected or reduced by the terms of any express warranty given with the goods: *Hunter* v *Syncrude*, 1989 (Can.).

A similar issue is whether goods should be regarded as unfit if no adequate repair service is provided, as when a new model is introduced and spare parts for the old one immediately become unobtainable. Many so-called consumer durables are made virtually worthless in this way. Certain Canadian statutes on agricultural machinery require manufacturers or suppliers to carry spare parts for up to 10 years after sale, and New Zealand's Consumer Guarantee Act 1993 obliges manufacturers to ensure facilities for repair and spare parts for a reasonable time – but there are not yet any comparable UK provisions. The Office of Fair Trading has, however, approved various codes of practice, such as the one on domestic electrical appliance servicing, which says manufacturers should stock spare parts for five to 15 years, depending on the item, which might suggest that goods could properly be regarded as defective if the absence of spare parts meant they could not be repaired within their normal life span. Commercial buyers might be well advised to make the continued availability of spare parts or servicing facilities an express term of their contracts. The question may soon be resolved at least in part by the proposed EU Consumer Guarantee Directive. In its draft form this gives buyers of consumer goods the right as against their sellers to demand where practicable the replacement or repair of defective parts – or eventually a full refund – for up to two years, depending on the type of goods in question. We should also note that manufacturers' or suppliers' arbitrary refusal to make or supply spares could be illegal under competition law as an abuse of a dominant market position.

3.11   **Motor vehicles**   We look now more specifically at a range of problems of quality and fitness associated particularly with cars, new and used – though the problems are, of course, typical of many mass-produced goods. The first issue is that of safety. A leading case is *Farnworth Finance* v *Attryde*, 1970. This was a contract of hire purchase rather than sale, but involved the same issues of fitness and quality. The machine was a new Enfield motorcycle. It developed a series of lethal defects: a pannier fell off and made the machine slide about the road; the headlight failed at night and at speed once because the dip switch was corroded and twice more because the terminals came off the wires; the chain broke and the lubricating system was faulty. The hire-purchaser was not impressed. In the Court of Appeal their Lordships agreed this was a 'most formidable list of defects', making the motorcycle 'thoroughly unsatisfactory' and 'not really a workable machine on the road'. It was accordingly held to be neither reasonably fit for its purpose nor of merchantable quality and the hire-purchaser was able to repudiate the contract and recover all he had paid. In view of the inconvenience he had suffered he was not obliged to make any allowance for the 4000 miles he had in fact driven on the machine.

One could scarcely doubt the rightness or obviousness of this decision, but the important point is that it clearly identifies *danger* as a breach of condition; not, of course, *any* danger however trivial or remote, but a real risk of a significant injury.

With this landmark before us we turn to the Scottish case of *Millar* v *Turpie*, 1976, which concerned a new Ford Granada. The day after taking delivery the buyer noticed a leak of oil from the power assisted steering box. He took it back to the dealer. In due course the dealer told him he had mended it and the buyer took the car home again. Next day he found another leak from the same source. At that point he evidently decided he could trust neither car nor dealer and told the dealer to take the car back and return his money.

The question was therefore whether two oil leaks made the car unfit and unsaleable, since that was the test in s. 14 of the Sale of Goods Act and the equivalent hire purchase rules. Our only guide so far is that of imminent danger. How dangerous is an oil leak from the steering box? On the basis of the expert evidence put before him, the judge thought there was no immediate likelihood of any serious risk, if only because so much oil would have to be lost before any risk at all could occur that the driver would have been bound to see it and have the car properly repaired. Although the dealer had failed to do the job on the first occasion, the fact remained that this was a minor fault, easily and cheaply remedied. That being so, said the judge, there was clearly no 'material breach' of s. 14. And that in turn meant that the buyer could not rescind the contract. Although this case was decided before the Act was amended to refer specifically to freedom from minor defects, one might guess that the answer would be the same today. The law still does not require perfection.

Millar's case raises in passing the interesting question whether a buyer of defective goods can reject them straightaway if the fault is serious enough, or whether he must first take them back to the seller and give him the chance to try to mend them; and, if so, how many times has the seller the right to try but fail? On the face of it goods must be reasonably fit and of satisfactory quality *at the time of sale* and for whatever period is appropriate thereafter. If the buyer had a legal duty to return goods for repair before he could think about rejecting them that would mean the goods were only required to be fit after that time, and that any kind of trial run was always at the buyer's risk. That would seem absurd, and the Canadian case of *Friskin* v *Holiday*, 1977, makes it clear that such is not the law.

On the other hand the judgment in *Millar* makes it equally clear that the buyer was wrong in not giving the dealer another chance to mend the leak. If the fault had been one the dealer and perhaps another independent expert had both tried but somehow failed to remedy, then and only then might the buyer have succeeded. In effect he would have proved that the defect was not as we said above easily and cheaply remediable. But that seems to be the same as saying that the buyer *does* have a duty to return goods for repair before he can reject them, so how can the arguments be reconciled?

The answer may be that – except as regards immediate dangers – some goods, such as cars, are sold 'subject to service', that is on the basis that work remains to be done on them. In that case the buyer has no alternative but to return the goods to the dealer to find out exactly what is wrong with them. Unless he does that it may be difficult if not impossible to say whether the fault is serious or trivial and repairable or not. In practice then, if not expressly in law, the buyer must behave reasonably and the seller will often get another chance to put things right. This conclusion is supported by *Leaves* v *Wadham Stringer*, 1980, where the buyer complained about the brakes on his new Leyland Princess. The dealers accepted that if a brake fault rendered the car unroadworthy the buyer was entitled to reject it. But an independent engineer found later complaints unjustified, and the judge held on the facts that there were no significant defects in the brakes *after their repair.*

The main points we have sought to establish so far, however, are the limits of the seller's liability. If his goods are so defective in normal use as to represent a real danger to life and limb the buyer can reject them and recover his money (subject to the problem of 'acceptance', below). But conversely if faults appearing after delivery are 'normal' or do not substantially affect the value of the goods or their safety then the buyer may have no remedy at all.

We come now to what is probably the commonest problem area, that of goods whose faults put them somewhere in the middle of this spectrum of liability, with little or no element of danger but frequent failures in operation or many minor faults or blemishes.

3.12   Teething troubles and poor workmanship   Until relatively recently, the standards of design, workmanship and overall reliability of new cars accepted by English judges were dismally low. In *Spencer* v *Rye*, 1972, for example, the judge would not allow the buyer to reject a car despite its many 'most irritating' faults because 'they were all capable of adjustment or being put right without too much trouble'. It seemed as if the test was simply whether the car would go more often than not. But within the past 10 or 15 years a much more realistic view of consumers' expectations has prevailed.

Two of the most interesting and important cases are *Bernstein* v *Pamson's Motors* and *Rogers* v *Parish*, both decided in 1987. *Bernstein* is notable also regarding the issue of acceptance, para. 3.16, and we note the facts of the case at that stage. Its importance here is in Mr Justice Rougier's general remarks about the kinds of problem likely to arise in buying a new car, and the proper responses to such problems.

No system of mass production can ever be perfect: mistakes and troubles of one sort or another, generally minor, are bound to occur from time to time, being often referred to as teething troubles. Nowadays the buyer, even the buyer of a new car, must put up with a certain amount of teething troubles and have them rectified, albeit generally under some sort of manufacturer's warranty.

In attempting to define teething troubles, aside from those involving basic safety obligations, his Lordship said:

> The time which is taken and the expense of rectification, evidencing as it does the seriousness of the defect, are relevant considerations. The work of a moment such as would be comprised in attaching a battery lead... would hardly, if ever, justify rescission. Many days spent off the road in the repair shop might have a different effect... Clearly there could come a stage when an army of minor unconnected defects would be evidence of such bad workmanship as to amount *in toto* to a breach of condition of merchantability... It may well be that in appropriate cases cosmetic factors will also apply, depending on the description and price applied to any individual car. No buyer of a brand new Rolls-Royce Corniche would tolerate the slightest blemish on its exterior or paintwork; the purchaser of a motor car very much at the humbler end of the range might be less fastidious.

The second of these leading cases, *Rogers* v *Parish*, concerned a new Range Rover. Six months after delivery and despite several attempts at repair the engine was still misfiring at all speeds and there was excessive noise from the gearbox and transfer box. The vehicle had substantial bodywork defects. Its condition was said to reflect 'great discredit' on factory inspection procedures. After driving it for some 5500 miles, 'albeit', said the judge, 'in a manner which gave him no satisfaction', the plaintiff attempted to rescind the contract. The trial judge held that although the car was substantially defective at the time of sale most of the faults could be or had been cured, and so it was of merchantable quality and fit for the purpose of being driven.

This bizarre but at that time typical conclusion was rejected by the Court of Appeal. The purpose for which the car was required, said the Court, was not merely that of driving from one place to another, but of doing so

> with the appropriate degree of comfort, ease of handling and reliability, and... of pride in the vehicle's outward and interior appearance... Deficiencies which might be accepted in a second hand vehicle are not to be expected in one purchased as new... The factor of price is also significant... The buyer is entitled to value for his money... These defects lie well outside the range of expectation.

The buyer's claim was upheld accordingly. This decision was clearly right, and is confirmed by the more consumer-oriented terms of the 1994 amendments to s. 14 of the Sale of Goods Act, with their references to [...] finish and (substantial) freedom from minor defects.

3.13 **Used cars** We turn now to the still more controversial area of the secon[...] hand car market. In *Selling Second Hand Cars*, published in 1997, the Office of Fair Trading said this was the sector which attracted more consumer complaints than any other. Some 8 million used cars are sold every year. One purchase in every six is found to lead to problems within six months.

Section 14 of the Sale of Goods Act applies as much to used goods as to new ones, but its effects necessarily differ. Contrasting cases include *Bartlett* v *Marcus*, 1965, and *Crowther* v *Shannon*, 1975. In *Bartlett*, the dealer sold a used Jaguar car for £950, warning the buyer that minor clutch repairs might be needed. They became necessary almost immediately and cost the buyer £45. His claim for damages was rejected because the car was 'in usable condition even though not perfect . . . It was fit to be driven along the road in safety'. 'Driveability' and safety were all the buyer could expect. Secondhand cars are likely to need repairs, and expensive cars need expensive repairs.

Similarly, in *Thain v Anniesland Trade Centre*, 1997 (Scot.), the plaintiff bought a 5- or 6-year-old car, mileage reading 80 000 miles, for £2995. Two weeks later the differential bearing in the automatic gear box began to fail. The dealer would not replace the gear box, as the plaintiff demanded, but offered other cars. The court refused the plaintiff's claim to reject the car and recover the price, on the ground that the failure could have occurred at any time and was an accepted risk of buying a car of that age and mileage.

But it is all a question of degree, as illustrated in *Crowther* v *Shannon*, 1975, another case concerning a Jaguar. The car was sold for £390 with 80 000 miles on the clock. After the buyer had driven it 2000 miles in the following few weeks the engine failed completely and had to be renewed for another £400 or so. The Court of Appeal distinguished this case from *Bartlett*. In *Crowther* the defect was such that the car was not fit for the road, and on the basis of expert evidence that Jaguar engines were supposed to last for some 100 000 miles the buyer had got very much less than he was reasonably entitled to expect. His claim succeeded accordingly.

Feast v *Vincent*, 1974, finally, is an instructive New Zealand decision. A company specialising in heavy road building equipment needed another engine for one of its road rollers. The right type of engine could not be found but eventually the company came across another one in the hands of a small dealer which it was thought might be suitable. The engine was bought without a test and for about one-third of its price when new. It ran

:d up and became completely unusable. It was
edress, partly because of his greater expertise
⹁ce of reliance on the seller's skill and judgment,
Ѕ⹁ause this was very much a speculative purchase, leaving
⹁ın no ground for complaint if things went wrong.

ⱀeasonable fitness

In disputes over commercial contracts, for instance for the sale of machinery, questions of the quality, fitness and suitability of goods are probably more likely to turn on issues of fact and technical detail than on the meaning or effect of the law. The basic question will be whether the product meets the specifications originally agreed – which may be a very complex matter. Each side may call its own expert witnesses – typically engineers or scientists – to give evidence on performance characteristics and capabilities, and the extent of compliance or non-compliance. Expert witnesses are notoriously expensive, but – contrary to continental practice – it is very unusual for English courts to appoint their own experts and save time and money accordingly. Experts are presumed to speak independently and objectively, and must try to guard against being influenced by the point of view of the party who called them. Given their often flatly contradictory advice, the judge must then decide as best he can which evidence he prefers and where the truth lies.

So far as points of law are concerned, however, we should note first that while disputes over satisfactory quality (s. 14(2)) often involve also questions of reasonable fitness for purpose (s. 14(3)), they are not bound to do so. The two requirements are separate and distinct. Goods may be unsatisfactory, for example, for a variety of reasons which do not affect their fitness for a particular purpose. Cosmetic defects are unlikely to affect a machine's efficiency. And conversely, goods which are perfectly satisfactory for the open market may not be fit for a buyer's more specific purpose. An aggrieved buyer need not prove that the goods fail both requirements; only that they fail one or the other.

As with satisfactory quality, so the requirement of reasonable fitness depends on certain qualifying factors. We have mentioned one of the most important already, that the sale must be in the course of business. The buyer must also have informed the seller expressly or by implication of the purpose for which the goods are required. As a rule this presents no difficulty because the purpose of most goods is self-evident: clothes for wearing, cars for driving, and so on. It is only necessary for the buyer to state his needs expressly when they are in some way more specialised or demanding than the normal purposes or uses of the goods. But the mere fact that the buyer tells the seller what he wants to do with the goods does not of itself oblige the seller to ensure the goods are fit for that purpose. In *Teheran Europe* v *Belton*, 1968, for instance, the seller knew that the buyer intended to export the goods to Iran, but was not liable when they proved unsaleable there. Circumstances alter cases, however, and it may be that such information becomes part of the buyer's contract requirements: *Carpet Call* v *Chan*, 1987 (Aust.).

Another prerequisite of sub-s. 3 is that the buyer has relied upon the seller's skill and judgment in selecting his goods. Reliance is normally presumed and does not have to be proved. 'A buyer goes to the shops in the confidence that the tradesman has selected his stock with skill and judgment': *Grant* v *AKM*, 1936. But this presumption may be displaced by evidence, for example, of the buyer's own expert examination of the goods, or that they were made to the buyer's design, in which case, depending on the extent of reliance upon his expertise, the seller may be answerable only for the quality of the materials he uses and not the overall success of the design: *Cammell Laird* v *Manganese Bronze*, 1934; *Dixon Kerby* v *Robinson*, 1965. The mere fact that the buyer specifies his requirements in detail, for example by reference to BSI standards, does not of itself prove he is not relying on the seller's skill, nor, therefore, exclude s. 14: *Central Regional Council* v *Uponor*, 1996. In the very unsatisfactory case of *McDonald* v *Empire Garage*, 1975, the seller escaped liability because of the buyer's expert examination of the goods, even though the fault could not have been found on any reasonable examination.

Subject to these provisions, sellers must ensure that their goods are reasonably fit for their purpose, or, if not, take them back and return the price. Fitness for purpose may be determined not only by the goods themselves, but, for example, by the adequacy and/or accuracy of their advertising, packaging, labelling, or instructions. Allegedly vague or misleading instructions on the use of herbicides have led to several cases, including *Wormell* v *RHM Agriculture*, 1987, and *Caners* v *Eli Lilly*, 1996 (Can.). *Caners* observed that any uncertainty or ambiguity in the instructions should be interpreted against the supplier. In *Amstrad* v *Seagate*, 1998, the seller was liable for the failure of a consignment of computers to function reliably within the ranges stipulated in his product manual.

We emphasise once more that reasonable fitness is not a standard of perfection. What it means in any given case depends entirely on normal usage and expectation, and on the complexity of the goods and their age and price, as illustrated in the many cases noted above on the requirement of satisfactory quality.

3.15 Sale by sample

Section 15 of the Sale of Goods Act should be briefly noted. It provides that in contracts of sale by sample there are implied conditions that the bulk of the goods shall correspond with the sample in quality, that the buyer shall have a reasonable opportunity of comparing the bulk with the sample, and that the goods shall be free of any defect making them unmerchantable which would not be seen on reasonable examination of the sample. The only significant point is that for a sale to be by sample an express or implied term of the contract to that effect is necessary (s. 15(1)), and accordingly the fact that a product is used for purposes of demonstration or illustration by the seller does not of itself bring the sale within s. 15. The section will help the consumer only in cases where off-cuts of cloth, carpet, etc. are produced to 'speak for themselves': *Drummond* v *Van Ingen*, 1887; *Thorne* v *Borthwick*, 1956 (Aust.).

3.16 Acceptance

A plaintiff loses his right to reject goods for breach of express condition or one implied by ss. 12, 13, 14 or 15 of the Sale of Goods Act if he 'accepts' the goods. His only claim then is for damages. This rule, which does not apply in Scotland, is laid down by s. 11 of the Act, and acceptance is defined by s. 35. It takes place if (i) the buyer tells the seller he will keep the goods, or (ii) after taking delivery and having a reasonable opportunity of inspecting the goods, the buyer acts in a way inconsistent with the seller's continued ownership of them. Reselling the goods or repairing them does not prove acceptance. A buyer may accept one part and reject another. (iii) Most important for present purposes, the buyer accepts goods if he keeps them for more than a reasonable length of time without notifying the seller of his rejection. To put that another way, the longer the buyer holds on to goods the more difficult it must be for him to say they are not what he wanted. The trouble is that defects in consumer durables in particular may not appear for some considerable time after they have been bought and used. The question then arises whether the idea of 'acceptance' is meaningful unless it involves both knowledge of the defects and the intention to keep the goods despite them. Lord Denning said in *Guarantee Trust of Jersey* v *Gardner*, 1973, that that was indeed the position: 'A person cannot be said to affirm a contract unless he has full knowledge of the breach and deliberately elects to go on with it.'

Rightly or wrongly, however, that is not the position under the Sale of Goods Act, except as it applies to Scotland, below. We refer again to the leading English case of *Bernstein* v *Pamson's Motors*: para. 3.12. The plaintiff here bought a new Nissan car. In the next three weeks he drove it for some 150 miles. It then broke down on the motorway and could not be restarted. The fault proved to be that a piece of sealant had entered the lubrication system and cut off the oil supply to the camshaft, which then seized up. The plaintiff, having lost all confidence in the car, sought to return it and recover the price. The judge agreed that although this was a freak occurrence, and although the car was subsequently restored under warranty to be as good as new, the fact remained that the car had been dangerous at the time of delivery and as such in breach of the conditions of quality and fitness. He nonetheless refused to allow the plaintiff to rescind the contract, and awarded damages only – a token sum for inconvenience, waste of petrol, etc. – on the ground that three weeks' use of the car constituted acceptance. The judge said that the purpose of the 'reasonable time' which buyers have before being deemed to have accepted goods was only to 'examine and try out the goods in general terms' – to ensure, in other words, that the goods were what they had ordered. This period would, of course, vary considerably with the complexity of the goods. But at all events, the nature of any defect or the speed with which it might be discovered were in his Lordship's opinion irrelevant.

This ruling is undoubtedly strict – and if three weeks, why not three days? – and contrary to what one might have thought were the vital issues in the case. It is also contrary to several other cases which have applied the acceptance rule more leniently. In *Spencer* v *Rye* (para. 3.12), for example, the buyer's right to reject was upheld despite three months' possession and intermittent use. In *Burnley Engineering* v *Cambridge Engineering*, 1997, a High Court judge said it might not be too late to reject defective machinery after allowing about a year for installation and commissioning. We note that there is no acceptance rule as such in hire purchase law, and in some cases hire-purchasers have been allowed to return defective vehicles after several thousand miles' driving: *Farnworth Finance* v *Attryde*, para. 3.11; *Laurelgates* v *Lombard*, 1983.

In Scotland, the problem is treated differently. Section 15B of the Sale of Goods Act allows repudiation of a contract because of any 'material breach'. The only obligation on the buyer then is that he or she should exercise this right within a reasonable time of discovering the breach – which is very much the continental view. Scottish judgments which might be thought preferable to *Bernstein* include *Knight Machinery* v *Rennie*, 1994 (see also para. 2.20), where rejection of defective machinery was allowed several months after delivery. In *Burrell* v *Harding's Executors*, 1931, the defect was discovered only when goods were taken out of store two years after delivery. The court held that it was not necessarily too late to reject even at that stage.

Continental legal systems, and the proposed EU Directive on consumer guarantees (para. 1.17), have no acceptance rule like that in the Sale of Goods Act. They require only that the buyer notifies the seller within a specified or otherwise reasonable time of discovering the defect that he wishes to reject.

3.17 Strict liability

In the rules examined above we find one of the most important principles of English sales law. It will be recalled that under s. 14 of the Sale of Goods Act goods sold in the course of business *must be of satisfactory quality and reasonably fit*. How or why they fall short of these standards is immaterial. The seller may be no more than a conduit for goods made and packed by others over whom he has no control, but he must still guarantee to the buyer their reasonable suitability and safety. He remains liable, in other words, whether the defect is known or unknown, or even unknowable, and whether or not he tries or is able to remedy it. So in *Frost* v *Aylesbury Dairy*, 1905, the defendants were liable for selling milk with typhus germs though at the time quite unable to detect the presence of the germs.

The primary liability for the quality and fitness of goods is thus upon the seller and not the manufacturer, a basic rule of English law remarkably little known even in commercial circles. The rule may be modified by the use of exclusion clauses and proposed EU imposition of new liabilities on manufacturers, but certainly as it stands it is very much in the buyer's interest since the seller is probably close to hand and the more responsive to threats of legal proceedings and attendant bad publicity. And in any case it seems right that a person who makes his livelihood out of selling should take some responsibility for what he sells. The seller might, of course, argue that it is unfair to blame him for defects which are the manufacturer's fault, but the immediate answer is that he can sue the distributor or manufacturer under the same section of the same Act for an indemnity. His claim may then depend on the validity of any exclusion clause there may be in the contract between them, as explained in the previous chapter.

This form of liability without personal fault is called strict liability. But strict liability is by no means the same as absolute liability, under which a seller would be responsible for any and every injury caused by his goods. The effect of strict liability is to require redress only for injuries or loss which are the reasonably likely consequences of the defects proved, but which the buyer could not be expected to guard against for himself. So where detergents or dyes or clothes safe for everyone else cause dermatitis in one or two individuals because of their own wholly abnormal and undisclosed susceptibilities, the seller is not to blame: *Board* v *Hedley*, 1951; *Griffiths* v *Conway*, 1939. Nor would he be liable for supplying goods which proved unusable only because of undisclosed problems on the buyer's premises; *Slater* v *Finning*, 1996. There is, of course, no precise answer as to the number of people who have to be injured before goods will be regarded as unsafe, nor as to the requisite seriousness of injury. The more serious the harm, the fewer the number who need suffer it before a product is condemned. So in *Kendall* v *Lillico*, 1969, the judge said: 'I should certainly not expect food to be held reasonably fit if even on very rare occasions it killed the consumer.' But conversely a seller is not necessarily liable even when his buyer suffers a most serious injury. In *Heil* v *Hedges*, 1951, for example, the plaintiff suffered trichinosis after buying raw pork chops infected with worms. She sued the butcher for selling her these injurious goods, and lost. The court said that as raw meat the chops were in a normal condition and it was for her to cook the meat properly to eliminate this normal risk.

There are many such cases in which the buyer might be injured through failing to carry out his own responsibilities under the sale, for example where he buys a car but does not bring it back to be serviced, or where he sees or ought to see the goods are not fit for use and so should stop using them: *Lambert* v *Lewis*, 1981. The seller is then most unlikely to be liable for any resulting injury.

3.18 HIRE PURCHASE

The same conditions laid down by sales law as to title, description and quality of goods are applied also to hire purchase transactions by ss. 8–10 of the Supply of Goods (Implied Terms) Act 1973, with the same consequences in terms of strict liability. Depending on the form of credit, however, the responsibilities may fall on different parties. If the dealer himself provides credit facilities then he remains liable as if he were the seller. But if as more commonly happens credit is provided by a finance company, it is the company as owner of the goods which is responsible for passing good title to them and ensuring their quality and fitness. The dealer's function then is essentially that of independent intermediary. He displays the goods and acts as credit broker, that is he enables the consumer to make a hire purchase contract with the finance company, and having done that his responsibility is usually at an end: *Drury* v *Buckland*, 1941 – dealer in h.p. transaction not liable under Sale of Goods Act.

As we saw in Chapter 1, there may be exceptions to this general rule. It may be recalled that in the case of *Andrews* v *Hopkinson* a dealer expressly promised a customer that the car in question was 'a good little bus' and that he would have no trouble with it. In response, the customer took the car on hire purchase from a finance company. The court held that he thereby gave consideration for the dealer's promise and so could enforce the promise against him. It is not yet clear whether the dealer might alternatively be liable for breach of an *implied* promise as to quality and fitness. The judge in *Andrews* suggested that he should be, because the transaction was so like a sale that the common law should imply obligations akin to those in the Sale of Goods Act. This argument was adopted in *Robotics* v *First Co-operative Finance*, 1983, but seems not yet generally accepted.

In the absence of any express undertaking by the dealer, therefore, the position may still be as decided in *Drury*, above. For the consumer this is less agreeable than the sale situation. He may well think he has contracted with the dealer who supplied the goods, who is as we said responsive to threats of legal action and bad local publicity, only to find that he must make his complaints to a finance company probably at the other end of the country and correspondingly less interested in his problem. One might then have expected the Consumer Credit Act 1974 to impose additional liability on dealers, but instead it went in the opposite direction and strengthened consumers' rights against finance houses.

Manufacturers involved in giving credit to individuals to finance the purchase or hire purchase of their goods should take very careful note of ss. 56 and 75 of the Consumer Credit Act. Both apply only to regulated agreements, that is where credit up to £25 000 is given. Section 56 makes the creditor liable to the consumer for anything said or done by the dealer in the course of negotiations leading up to the making of a hire purchase, conditional sale or credit sale agreement. 'Negotiations' include advertisements and 'any other dealings'. Even though a dealer is usually an independent party he is regarded for the purposes of this section as the creditor's agent (and may also be so for the purpose of receiving deposits: *Branwhite* v *Worcester Finance*, 1969). So in *Andrews*, above, the consumer could now sue either dealer or finance house or both, and leave them to sort out their liability between themselves.

Section 75 affects what are usually called 'connected lending' transactions, where a creditor lends money to a debtor to enable him to *buy* goods from a third party supplier under pre-existing arrangements between creditor and supplier. Purchases with credit cards are within this section, unless as with American Express and Diners' Club cards prompt repayment in full is required. The object of the section is to give the debtor the same protection against the creditor as if he had obtained the goods on hire purchase, and the rationale is that the creditor here has much the same kind of continuing interest as in a hire purchase transaction. The section provides accordingly that whatever rights the debtor might have as buyer against seller he can exercise equally against the creditor. The creditor thus becomes responsible for any misrepresentation by the seller or for the seller's breach of an express promise or implied condition as to title or description or fitness under the Sale of Goods Act. In the Scottish case of *UDT* v *Taylor*, 1980, a debtor/buyer returned a defective car to the seller and under s. 75 was also held able to rescind the finance agreement with the creditor. The section gives the buyer a useful alternative remedy where the seller denies liability or is insolvent or goes out of business. As with s. 56 the present rule does not apply to leasing agreements. Unlike s. 56 the scope of s. 75 is limited according to the cash price of the goods. It applies only where the cash price is between £50 and £30 000.

3.19   SERVICE AND HIRE CONTRACTS

Until 1982 there was no equivalent of the Sale of Goods Act or hire purchase legislation to define consumers' rights in relation to goods supplied not by way of sale or hire purchase but under contracts for services or on lease or hire. These various different types of contract were regulated only by the somewhat uncertain standards of the common law. The object of the Supply of Goods and Services Act 1982 was accordingly to clarify the law in this area and bring it more clearly into line with existing legislation. The Act does not apply in Scotland, where the situation is still governed by common law.

As a result of the Act it is not often as important as it once was to decide whether a particular contract is primarily for the supply of goods or primarily for the supply of work and materials; a contract for services. But the liabilities still differ, as described below, and so the distinction may still have to be made. Very broadly the question is whether the contract is essentially for the exercise of skill and care, or for the transfer of ownership of goods. The problem is, of course, that each kind of contract may include an element of the other. Each case turns on its own merits and no definite rule or guide can be given. A contract to paint and then sell a portrait is a contract for services – *Robinson* v *Graves*, 1935 – but the issue is not often so clear. When a hairdresser applies a hair dye, that could be said to be half supplying a service and half supplying goods: *Watson* v *Buckley*, 1940. Building and installation contracts are generally seen as contracts for work and materials: *Aristoc Industries* v *Wenham*, 1965 (Aust.).

Sections 1 to 5 of the 1982 Act concern goods supplied under contracts for services, for example installation or repair contracts, and ss. 6 to 10 goods supplied on hire or loan. The obligations imposed on the supplier are essentially the same as those under ss. 12 to 15 of the Sale of Goods Act and ss. 8 to 10 of the Supply of Goods (Implied Terms) Act. Standards of quality and fitness for purpose are therefore strict, as illustrated in *Myers* v *Brent Cross Service*, 1934, where a garage was liable for an accident caused by fitting a component with a hidden defect in the course of a car repair. But as we have said before, strict liability is no guarantee of perfection. A burglar alarm, for example, might still be reasonably fit for its purpose even though it can be wrenched off the wall and silenced: *Davis* v *Afa Minerva*, 1974. In any case, liability is strict only in relation to the other contracting party and not, as in a car case, for example, to his or her passengers or other road users. Their only claim could be for negligence, which in a case like *Myers* they would be unable to prove against the garage: *Sigurdson* v *Hillcrest Service*, 1977 (Can.).

Liability can be avoided or reduced if the consumer does not – or in the circumstances should not – rely on the supplier's skill or judgment. This might happen where for example the consumer specifies exactly the type of material or product to be used, in which case the supplier does not warrant fitness for purpose but only the quality of the goods: *Young* v *McManus Childs*, 1968.

The 1982 Act also covers contracts for services which do not necessarily involve transfer of ownership or possession of goods. The most important provision is s. 13, which says that in contracts for the supply of services in the course of business there is an implied term that the services will be carried out with reasonable care and skill. The duty thus imposed in relation to services is different from that affecting goods. A supplier of goods must ensure they are reasonably fit, whereas a supplier of services undertakes only to act in accordance with the normal standards of his trade or profession, for better or worse. He may nonetheless find the duty quite far reaching, as in *Taylor* v *Kiddey*, 1968, where a garage was held liable for failing to check a wheel under the terms of a service contract specifying attention only to steering. An architectural design must be reasonably fit for its purpose: *Greaves* v *Baynham Meikle*, 1975.

Another rule worth noting is in s. 14, requiring that if no time is fixed for the performance of a contract it must be performed within a reasonable time, depending of course on the type and scale of the work to be done. Cases include *Aries Powerplant* v *Ece Systems*, 1996; *Charnock* v *Liverpool Corporation*, 1968, where a garage was held liable for taking eight weeks over repairs which should have taken five, and thus had to pay for three weeks' car hire; and *Stanners* v *High Wycombe Borough Council*, 1968, where the local authority was held responsible for a delay in completing building work which enabled thieves to break into a warehouse next door.

3.20 SUMMARY

Terms may be added into contracts at common law and by Act of Parliament. Generally the judges will only add terms into particular contracts to express a trade usage taken for granted by the parties, or if it is necessary to do so because otherwise the contract would be wholly one-sided or lack business efficacy. Terms added by Parliament on the other hand are intended to lay down minimum standards of performance or fitness for all contracts of a particular type. Such statutory terms are most important in contracts of sale and hire purchase of goods if the parties themselves fail to specify their requirements in detail. So far as sellers' liabilities are concerned the key provision is in s. 14 of the Sale of Goods Act and its equivalent in legislation for h.p. and service contracts. In effect the section requires business sellers to guarantee the reasonable quality and fitness of their goods. If this implied condition is broken the buyer can reject the goods – unless he has already accepted them – and recover his money. The seller's liability in this respect is strict, which means that he is liable for breach of the condition even though he may be in no way personally to blame for it. But unless barred by an exclusion clause the seller can then sue his own supplier to recoup his losses, and so on back up the line until the manufacturer carries the responsibility.

4 Liability and remedies for breach of contract

4.1 REPUDIATION

We saw in Chapter 2 that a sufficiently serious breach of contract would justify the innocent party in repudiating the contract and/or claiming damages. We discussed there – and pursue the question a little further in para. 4.6 below – the difficulty of deciding whether any particular breach would in fact justify repudiation, and noted also that in contracts for the sale of goods the right to repudiate is lost if the innocent party accepts the goods. At this point it may be helpful just to remind ourselves that such serious breaches of contract are usually described as breaches of condition, as distinct from breaches of warranty which entitle the innocent party only to claim damages, and to say a little more about their effects.

Repudiation for breach of condition brings the contract to an end. As a general rule, obligations under it are thereupon cancelled, and each party should so far as practicable be returned to his or her original position. Goods delivered are returned; money paid is repaid, possibly subject to deductions for use of the goods. If it is not possible to restore the original position, as where the wrongdoer has done faulty work under a contract for services, the innocent party cannot recover all advance payments unless he can show he has received nothing of value in return: para. 2.5.

Ending a contract for breach of condition does not, however, mean that the contract is then or always has been void. A broken contract is not the same thing as a void contract. So, for example, the wrongdoer could not by his own breach of condition free himself from confidentiality obligations entered into as part of the contract. If third parties acting in good faith have acquired rights in the property which is the subject of the contract, those rights cannot be disturbed. But when a contract is void from the outset, as with fundamental mistake, no such rights arise.

4.2 DAMAGES

By far the most usual remedy under English law for breach of contract is an award of damages. The standard continental remedies of reduction in price, or replacement or repair of defective goods, are not currently available as of right (apart from the buyer's right under s. 30 of the Sale of Goods Act to withhold part of the price for short delivery), though widely used in practice in settlement of claims. The proposed EU Directive on consumer guarantees makes these latter remedies generally enforceable at law. We note also the right of an unpaid seller to hold back goods promised or belonging to the buyer. This right of lien, given by s. 41 of the Sale of Goods Act and the common law, does not affect the seller's claim for damages.

The purpose of an award of damages for breach for contract is to compensate the victim, not to punish the wrongdoer. The court's inquiry, therefore, is as to the extent of the victim's loss, not as to the reasons for the wrongdoer's failure. To put the point another way: a contract usually requires certain things to be done. If they are not done, there must (as a general rule) be a breach of contract. *Why* they are not done – whether the wrongdoer is personally blameworthy, or was unable to fulfil the contract because he was himself let down by someone else – is usually immaterial. Liability which arises regardless of fault or absence of fault is called strict liability. Strict liability is the basis of English contract law.

As always, there are exceptions. If the contract requires the defendant to take reasonable care, or use his best endeavours, or imposes some other such qualified or conditional obligation, then his liability will depend on whether the breach was due to his personal failure to act or to circumstances beyond his control – including perhaps the contributory negligence of the plaintiff: *Barclays Bank* v *Fairclough*, 1995. We have seen also that liability may sometimes be limited or excluded by express exclusion or force majeure clauses or, very occasionally, by the doctrine of frustration (para. 2.25).

Our main inquiry, however, is how the courts establish the extent of the victim's loss. The object of an award is to put him where he would have been if the contract had been carried out, so far as money can do that. But that is much easier said than done. The appropriate figure – the *quantum* – cannot be established just by proving that the breach caused certain specific losses, that is, merely by proving cause and effect. Effects of causes may go on indefinitely in all kinds of completely unlooked for and extraordinary ways. In the interests of fairness to both parties and of justice and certainty in the law, it is necessary at some point to draw the line and end the wrongdoer's liability. The problem for every legal system is to say when and how the line should be drawn.

4.3   THE TEST OF REMOTENESS

English law's answer is to require a certain degree of foreseeability or probability of loss, and to hold that losses which do not meet this requirement are too 'remote' and therefore irrecoverable – even though directly caused by the breach. Any attempt to define the requisite degree of foreseeability must begin with a reference to the leading case of *Hadley* v *Baxendale*, 1854. Very briefly, the case concerned a delay in the delivery of a mill shaft. Since this was the only available shaft, the delay meant that the mill had to stay closed for a longer period. The mill owners sued the carriers for damages for the delay, claiming the cost of closure for that period. The carriers admitted liability for the delay, but contested the amount of damages.

In a ruling which eventually became the basis of English, Commonwealth and American law on the subject, the judge said that recoverable losses

> should be such as may fairly and reasonably be considered either arising naturally, i.e., according to the usual course of things, from such breach of contract itself, or such as may reasonably be supposed to have been in contemplation of both parties at the time they made the contract as the probable result of the breach.

Liability is thus imposed for (i) the kind of losses which *usually* arise in a particular situation, and/or (ii) for those *exceptional* consequences of which the defendant had special knowledge and for which expressly or by implication he had agreed to take responsibility. The first rule or test is objective; the second more subjective. A simple example of the first rule would be an award of the difference in price between goods ordered but not delivered and the cost of obtaining other such goods. For the purposes of the second rule, it is not enough just to show that the defendant was told of the consequences of breach. It would be a question whether in all the circumstances, including in particular the price charged for the goods or services in question, the defendant could reasonably be regarded as undertaking such additional liability. If possible, the difficulty should be dealt with expressly in the contract, for example by saying 'for the avoidance of doubt the sellers hereby acknowledge that it is within their contemplation that [late delivery etc.] is likely to cause the buyers exceptional expense arising out of [loss of profits, future trading losses, loss of good will, interest charges, etc.]' – preferably with some precise indication of the nature of such expense. Where the seller is the stronger party he may, of course, try expressly to reject any such extended liability.

If we apply these two rules to the facts of *Hadley*, we see that the mill owners were bound to fail in their claim for all the losses arising from the closure of the mill. They had not told the carriers that this was the only shaft they had, or that delay would lead to closure. The carriers had in fact every reason to believe that such a large enterprise would have a spare shaft. In the end, therefore, the mill owners recovered only a token sum to compensate for the relatively minor inconvenience which might normally be expected from late delivery of goods.

4.4 Some leading cases

Countless cases have been decided since *Hadley*, seeking to apply and explain the two rules – not all equally successfully. Important examples include *Victoria Laundry* v *Newman*, 1949. The defendants' failure here to supply the laundry with a new boiler in the time agreed resulted in the laundry suffering general loss of profits, and also led to the loss of a particularly lucrative government contract. This wholly unexpected contract was offered after the laundry had ordered the boiler, but the laundry was unable to take it up because of the lack of extra capacity which the boiler represented. The Court of Appeal held the defendants liable for the laundry's loss of normal profits, but not for the exceptional or 'windfall' loss which neither side had contemplated at the time the contract was made.

Victoria Laundry is noteworthy also because of the Court of Appeal's attempt to restate and simplify the *Hadley* rules. The Court said that losses caused by breach of contract were recoverable if they were 'reasonably foreseeable'. In *Czarnikow* v *Koufos*, 1969, the House of Lords rejected this formulation. Their Lordships argued that many kinds of losses were reasonably foreseeable, but not at all *likely*. In their Lordships' opinion, *Hadley* required that damages could be claimed only for *likely* losses. Several Commonwealth countries have nonetheless adopted the test of reasonable foreseeability: *Asamera Corp.* v *Sea Oil Corp.*, 1979 (Can.).

The *Czarnikow* case concerned a consignment of sugar which in breach of contract arrived late at Basrah, where there was a sugar market. Having missed the market, the shippers lost a resale profit they would otherwise have made. The House of Lords held that they were entitled to recover this loss under rule (i) of *Hadley*. The case is thus an important recognition of the kinds of loss likely to be caused by delays in fulfilling commercial contracts. But no claim can normally be made for loss of a wholly exceptional resale profit: *Coastal Trading* v *Maroil*, 1988. Where, as in these cases, a seller of defective goods knows or should know that the buyer intends to resell the goods, damages may alternatively be assessed by reference to the buyer's liability to compensate sub-purchasers for the expenses they in turn incur: *Bence* v *Fasson*, 1996.

Ruxley v *Forsyth*, 1995, is an interesting case concerning a contract to build a swimming pool. The pool was to be 7 ft deep at its deepest point, but when built it was only 6 ft deep there, though still safe for diving. Should the damages represent the difference in value between a 6ft pool and a 7ft pool – a negligible sum – or the cost of rebuilding the pool in accordance with the contract? The House of Lords accepted that the cost of rebuilding the pool would be out of all proportion to the 'loss' suffered by the buyer, and so awarded damages representing the difference in value, and a token sum for loss of amenity and enjoyment. Their Lordships thought it most important that the overall sum awarded should be reasonable – perhaps a new element in the application of the *Hadley* rules. The decision may be acceptable on its own facts, but it does not give a very satisfactory answer to the familiar problem of suppliers winning contracts by undercutting their competitors and then failing to do the job properly. Is it right that they should be able to buy their way out of liability by paying only a token sum?

Another illuminating example is *Parsons* v *Uttley Ingham*, 1978. The contract here was for the supply of a pig food hopper. The hopper was installed defectively so that the food went mouldy. Many pigs died through a rare disease resulting from eating the mouldy food. It was held that the natural and foreseeable consequence of the defective installation was that the food would go mouldy and that the pigs would suffer accordingly. Since some form of harm was likely it made no difference that the actual damage was both more serious and more extraordinary than might have been expected. The owner of the pigs therefore recovered their value, but not the additional profit he might have made on resale, this latter loss being regarded as too remote.

It can be seen from *Parsons* in particular that apparently minor breaches of contract, or breaches which seem minor because the price of the goods or services is so small, may have quite disproportionately expensive results. The seller of a fire extinguisher, for example, could theoretically be liable for the destruction of a complete building and for the injuries of people escaping from the fire if the extinguisher failed to work at the vital moment, if and insofar as these were the reasonably foreseeable consequences of the defect – which would in turn depend on the type of building, need for other extinguishers or fire escapes, etc. Still more clearly might a car or aircraft component seller be liable to his buyer for the total cost of an accident caused by a hidden fault in the component. Such extensive and possibly ruinous liability might be avoided or reduced by insurance and/or by clauses to that effect in the contract of sale, subject once again to the Unfair Contract Terms Act (see Chapter 2).

We might observe that many contracts purport to deal with these problems by dividing the losses which might arise from the breach into 'direct' and 'consequential'. Liability might then be accepted for direct loss but rejected for that which is deemed consequential. A warranty on machinery, for example, might undertake to supply new parts to replace those found defective but refuse liability for injuries caused thereby. It will be seen that this division is not in accordance with the 'foreseeability' rules of common law. Any attempt to override the rules in this way would probably be negated by the court interpreting 'direct' losses to mean those which come within the terms of rules (i) and (ii) of *Hadley* v *Baxendale,* and interpreting 'consequential' losses as these which are in any case too remote because they fall outside these rules: *Ogilvie* v *Glasgow DC,* 1994 (Scot.); *British Sugar* v *NEI Power,* 1997. Alternatively, any such purported limitation or exclusion of liability would probably be held to be void under the Unfair Contract Terms Act or Unfair Terms in Consumer Contracts Regulations.

Damages for breach of contract are usually only to compensate for economic loss, but may be awarded also for physical injuries caused by defective goods or services. They will not usually be awarded for anxiety and stress, unless the contract is intended to provide peace of mind – such as a holiday contract. The fact that a loss may be very difficult to quantify does not of itself preclude a claim: *Chaplin* v *Hicks,* 1911 – damages awarded for loss of opportunity to attend a selection interview (presupposing at least a reasonable prospect of success). Damages may be awarded for pre-contract expenditure brought about by and known to the party in breach: *Anglia TV* v *Reed,* 1971. They may also be given to cover interest on a debt, for example where the wrongdoer knows the innocent party has had to borrow to meet his contractual commitments. A statutory right to interest on late payments is now available: para. 2.13.

Where the contract gives one party a choice as to how to fulfil it, he or she may still have to exercise that choice in a responsible way. In *Lee* v *Zehil,* 1983, for instance, the defendant had broken his contract to buy a large quantity of clothing from a range of five different grades. The contract did not specify how many items of each grade should be bought. The court rejected the defendant's argument that he might have bought the whole consignment in the cheapest range. He had to make his choice in a reasonable way, consistent with the commercial purpose of the contract.

4.5 MITIGATION

Another basic rule on the assessment of damages, but one we need not pursue in detail, is that the law usually expects the victim of a breach of contract to do his best to reduce or 'mitigate' his own losses. If a seller fails to deliver goods, his buyer who wishes to use them for profit should try immediately to obtain similar goods elsewhere, and if a buyer refuses to accept delivery the seller should try to find another buyer – though not on a 'give away' basis. Inaction will reduce any damages which might otherwise be awarded. But if reasonable attempts to mitigate loss only make matters worse the further expense is recoverable. The duty to mitigate does not apply where the plaintiff's claim is not for damages at large but for payment of a specific debt. Thus an unpaid seller can claim the full price of goods delivered after ownership has passed to the buyer, or after the due date of payment: ss. 49, 50, Sale of Goods Act.

4.6 ANTICIPATORY BREACH

Finally we should mention the problem of 'anticipatory breach'. This occurs where one party to the contract makes clear before the due day that he has no intention of carrying out his promise. The innocent party then has a choice. He may either 'accept' the repudiation, refuse to carry out his own obligations and claim damages for the loss he has suffered *at the date of repudiation*, subject to his duty to mitigate his loss, or treat the contract as still in being and claim (probably more substantial) damages for the loss he sustains *at the time it should have been carried out*.

Both courses of action present difficulties. Before he can give up his own obligations, the innocent party must be sure the other's conduct entitles him to do so. If the innocent party is not justified in ending the contract, he may find himself liable for breach of contract. It is far from clear what kind of conduct constitutes repudiation, but a few examples may be helpful. When the seller re-sells the contract goods to a third party, for instance, he clearly repudiates the contract: *Graham* v *United Turkey Red Co.*, 1922 (Scot.). Late payment was regarded as repudiation in *Carter* v *Dalton*, 1996. But when the seller demands a higher price than previously agreed, or claims legal justification for withdrawing from the contract, such conduct has been held not necessarily to constitute repudiation, nor, therefore, to entitle the other party to end the contract: *Vaswani* v *Italian Motors*, 1966; *Woodar* v *Wimpey*, 1980.

If the innocent party treats the contract as still in being, despite the other's repudiation, the curious result is that he can act in a way which flatly contradicts the duty to mitigate. According to *White & Carter* v *McGregor*, 1962, a buyer who has second thoughts and cancels an order immediately after making it may still be liable to the seller for the seller's total loss of profit on the transaction, a surprising and indeed alarming conclusion! In *Hounslow LBC* v *Twickenham Garden Developments*, 1970, however, the rule was said not to apply where the innocent party needed the other side's 'co-operation', for example where the object of the contract was that the innocent party should do some work on the land of the 'wrongdoer' but the wrongdoer changed his mind and refused entry. Clearly the innocent party could not then force his way in and do the work regardless.

The argument was taken a stage further in *Clea* v *Bulk Oil*, 1984, where the question was said to be simply whether continued performance of the contract by one side against the wishes of the other was reasonable in the circumstances. In this case a ship chartered for two years needed major repairs after the first year. The charterers rejected the ship but the owners insisted on repairing it, which took six months. The owners' conduct was held to be unreasonable and they were unable to claim hire-charges for this period.

4.7 PENALTY CLAUSES

In construction contracts in particular, but also in many other types of contracts, it is common practice to include clauses quantifying in advance the damages payable if the contract is broken (not to be confused with terms requiring deposits or bonds to be forfeited on breach). The purpose of such clauses is to avoid the problems of proving and valuing every item of loss and having to satisfy the court that each and every item was foreseeable or probable within the terms of *Hadley* v *Baxendale*, above. They might, for example, state a sum payable for each week's overrun beyond completion date, or simply subtract a certain percentage of the purchase price.

These clauses are widely called penalty clauses, but should properly be called 'liquidated (i.e. fixed) damages' clauses. They are enforceable as long as the court considers they are genuine pre-estimates of the losses likely to be suffered on breach. In that event, all the plaintiff has to do is to prove the breach, and he is then entitled to the specified sum. He is not required to prove in detail how much he has lost. On the other hand, he cannot claim more than the specific sum, even though his losses may in fact be much greater, unless, it seems, the contract expressly enables him to do so: *Cellulose Acetate* v *Widnes Foundry*, 1933; *Raymer* v *Stratten Woods*, 1988 (Can.).

If the clause is not a genuine pre-estimate, however, and is indeed 'penal' or 'punitive' in its effect, that is by threatening to make the other party liable for a wholly disproportionate sum if he is in breach, then it is void and unenforceable. Unlike the practice of almost every other legal system, English judges will not reduce excessive penalties to more reasonable amounts. The curious result of declaring a clause penal is that the party relying on it – usually the buyer – is then free to prove his losses in detail, and may thereby claim more than the liquidated sum.

It is very difficult to predict whether a court will find a liquidated damages clause acceptable or declare it void. The usefulness of such clauses is correspondingly doubtful. In the leading case of *Dunlop* v *New Garage*, 1915, the House of Lords said that the question was not simply whether the contract described the clause as being for liquidated damages or a penalty, but whether at the time the contract was made 'the sum stipulated for is extravagant and unconscionable in amount in comparison with the greatest loss which could conceivably be proved to have followed from the breach'. Requiring a larger sum to be paid on failure to pay a small sum is likely to be penal – but it is, of course, still legal to require a debtor to repay the whole sum if he does not comply with the terms of the loan: *The Angelic Star*, 1988. A clause which requires the same sum to be paid for various kinds of breach, some important and others less so, will probably be unenforceable, as illustrated in *Duffen* v *FRA BO*, 1998, a Court of Appeal decision. Against that, however, may be the difficulty of settling a suitable figure for each and every different kind of loss.

The penalty rules have defied rationalisation, as Lord Justice Diplock remarked in *Robophone* v *Blank*, 1966, and have indeed been strongly criticised. In his *Remedies for Breach of Contract*, Professor Treitel observed:

> The common law rules for distinguishing between penalties and liquidated damages manage to get the worst of both worlds. They achieve neither the certainty of the principle of literal enforcement, since there is always some doubt as to the category into which the clause will fall, nor the flexibility of the [continental law] principle of enforcement subject to reduction, since there is

no judicial power of reduction. On the other hand, they place an undue premium on draughtsmanship . . . The chief danger is to 'home-made' clauses which may be invalidated even though they are not intrinsically unfair.

4.8 SPECIFIC PERFORMANCE

A decree or order for specific performance is a court order to the defendant to fulfil his or her contract, additional to or instead of an award of damages. In practice such orders are relatively rare, because English courts do not see themselves as competent to compel contracting parties to carry out contracts they have repudiated. In the commercial context damages are usually an adequate substitute for performance of the contract. A disappointed buyer can probably find other similar goods on the market and charge the seller for the difference in price and consequential inconvenience, while conversely a disappointed seller can usually sell to someone else.

In effect it is only when the subject matter of the contract is unique or irreplaceable, or damages impossible to calculate, that specific performance is likely to be ordered. These conditions apply almost exclusively to contracts for the sale or lease of land. Under s. 52 of the Sale of Goods Act the court can order specific performance of contracts for the sale of specific goods, but it will do so only in very exceptional circumstances. An example is in *Behnke* v *Bede*, 1927, where the buyer was compelled to take goods which the seller had made to the buyer's personal requirements and which therefore had no general market value. Ships will probably be treated as unique goods. Exceptional hardship to the innocent party is another possible ground for such an order. So in *Sky Petroleum* v *VIP Petroleum*, 1974, the court ordered specific performance of a contract for the supply of petrol as being the only way to avoid the particularly serious consequences the buyer would otherwise have suffered during an acute petrol shortage.

In theory at least, continental legal systems are more favourably inclined towards issuing orders equivalent to specific performance. An example is the 'astreinte' order available under French law, enforceable by a penalty sum payable initially to the court and ultimately to the plaintiff for every day of default. In America, ss. 2–809 and 2–716 of the Uniform Commercial Code enable the courts to order specific performance whenever justified by commercial needs.

4.9 TIME LIMITS

The Limitation Act 1980 lays down time limits within which claims for breach of contract or tort (the non-contractual wrongs which are the subject of Chapters 5 and 6 of this book) must be brought. In contract, the basic rule is that a claim must be begun within six years of the breach, that is, as the Act says, 'the date on which the cause of action accrued'. The danger here is that a contracting party may not know immediately whether or when the contract has been broken, and so may risk losing his right to sue before he knows he has that right. But if the breach has been concealed from him by the defendant's fraud he has six years from the time when he discovered or should have discovered the fraud.

Claims in tort must also be begun within six years of the cause of action accruing. In tort, however, that is not necessarily when the tort is committed, but only when actual loss or damage is suffered, which may well be at a much later date. A plaintiff who has a claim both in contract and in tort may take advantage of whichever cause of action gives the longer limitation period. In claims for damages for physical injury, whether in contract or tort, the time limit is three years from the date of injury or the time when the plaintiff knew or should have known he or she had a cause of action. Claims arising from breach of a promise in a deed must be brought within 12 years of breach. A Law Commission report in 1998 proposed reform and rationalisation of these various limitation periods.

4.10 SUMMARY

It is a general rule of English law that liability for breach of contract is strict. Liability is imposed, in other words, on proof of breach, and does not depend on the personal blameworthiness or otherwise of the wrong-doer. The usual remedy is an award of damages. The purpose of an award is to put the innocent party in the position where he or she would have been if the contract had been duly performed. Difficulties often arise in calculating the sum of money necessary to achieve this purpose. The innocent party has to show not only that the breach caused his loss, but that the loss was not too remote. Losses are too remote – or indirect or consequential – if they fall outside the rules of predictability laid down in the leading case of *Hadley* v *Baxendale*. Damages are recoverable under these rules for losses which are the 'natural' – or usual or likely – consequences of the kind of breach in question, and/or for losses which are not normal or likely but which both parties had in mind as likely in the event of breach of that particular contract.

Awards may be reduced to the extent that the innocent party fails to mitigate his or her loss, for example as buyer, by trying to obtain other goods from elsewhere following the seller's failure to deliver. But no reduction will be made for losses resulting from the innocent party's contributory negligence, unless the basis of his claim is that the wrongdoer has broken a duty to take reasonable care.

Sums specified in the contract as payable in the event of breach – liquidated damages – are enforceable only insofar as they are genuine pre-estimates of the innocent party's likely losses, and not penalties or punishments for non-performance. If the sum is held to be a penalty it is void and unenforceable, but the innocent party is still free to prove a claim for his or her actual losses.

5 Product liability (1) negligence

5.1 THE COMMON LAW

In this and following chapters we move away from the contractual rights and duties we have discussed so far, and consider the often more difficult and controversial issue of non-contractual ('tortious') liabilities. In particular we are concerned with the responsibilities of manufacturers to the ultimate users of their goods who suffer injury or damage to property because the goods are in some way defective. Manufacturers' non-contractual liabilities are usually classed as questions of 'product liability', originally an American expression, to distinguish them from sellers' liabilities for breach of contract. Product liability disputes may arise where, for example, the buyer is the injured party but cannot sue his or her seller because the seller has gone out of business, or where the injured party is, say, the buyer's employee or a member of the buyer's family, and so again has no contract with the seller.

Most legal systems have found it difficult to say exactly what, if any, obligations should arise outside contractual relationships. The UK answer was until quite recently to be found only in case law, beginning with the famous case of *Donoghue* v *Stevenson* in 1932. In 1987 the common law rules were overlaid – though not by any means entirely superseded – by statute; the Consumer Protection Act. In this chapter we discuss the common law rules, and in the next, the Consumer Protection Act. Many of the issues arising here are equally relevant under the Act.

5.2 REASONABLE CARE

We begin with a brief account of *Donoghue* v *Stevenson*. The facts were very simple. The plaintiff was bought a bottle of ginger beer by her friend. The bottle was opaque and sealed. After opening the bottle and drinking some of the contents the plaintiff poured out the remainder into her glass, and found a decomposed snail floating there. She suffered severe gastroenteritis. Who should she sue? There was at that time no statutory provision to help her, so she had to rely on common law. The basic problem was that she had no contract with the seller, or anyone else. She had to fight the case all the way up to the House of Lords which, after the greatest difficulty and by a majority of only 3 to 2, reached the painfully obvious conclusion that it was the manufacturer who should be liable for the contents of this bottle. Their Lordships laid down a general rule of liability in all such non-contractual cases, namely that suppliers of goods must take *reasonable care* to ensure the safety of the goods for those likely to use them – their 'neighbours', as Lord Atkin put it. Failure to take such care is the wrong or tort of negligence.

This is in fact just one instance of the duty we are all under, individually and corporately, legally and morally, to try to avoid harming each other. We could equally well say, for example, that employers owe a duty of reasonable care to their employees, vehicle drivers to other road users, doctors to patients and so on. It is a duty which cannot directly be delegated to others to fulfil. Sometimes, as under the Health and Safety at Work Act, this same duty is reinforced by the criminal law (see Chapter 8), but normally in cases of unintentional injury it is enforceable only by claims for damages.

Our next task therefore is to see what is meant by 'reasonable care'. It will be understood that this expression falls well short of a guarantee of safety. The law does not demand the impossible, nor say that one person must *always* be liable whenever he harms another, however indirectly and inadvertently, otherwise business would be impossible and trade unions illegal. When someone is injured by a product the question the judge asks himself is so far as possible an objective one: did the producer (or distributor, or installer, etc.) do what a reasonable man in his position should have done to try to avoid the injury? His answer will depend entirely on the facts put before him and on what seems to have been the proper course of action in the circumstances according to the accepted standards of expertise in the particular trade or industry. Judges naturally do not wish to appear only as wise after the event, or to condemn manufacturers when they have undoubtedly done their best, even though what they did might subsequently seem mistaken. But the possibility remains that the manufacturer's best may not be good enough in the light of advancing standards in society at large and within that industry in particular.

A quotation from a case on employers' liability indicates the general approach, bearing in mind as we said above that we could substitute 'producer' or 'distributor' for 'employer'.

> It is the duty of an employer in considering whether some precaution should be taken against a foreseeable risk to weigh on the one hand the magnitude of the risk, the likelihood of an accident happening and the possible seriousness of the consequences ... and on the other hand the difficulty and expense and any other disadvantages of taking the precaution.

There are then a number of clearly identifiable factors which will determine whether a consumer's claim should be successful. In effect these are the 'ingredients' of reasonable care, or, put another way, they are the main elements of the 'safety checklist' against which every product must be tested.

5.3 The burden of proof

Many of the difficulties faced by an injured party in proving a producer at fault have been overcome or at least reduced by the Consumer Protection Act, as we shall see in the next chapter. In circumstances not covered by the Act, an injured party may occasionally be helped by a rule of evidence. If the circumstances of an accident seem incapable of explanation on any ground other than that of the defendant's negligence, the judge may invoke the maxim *res ipsa loquitur* ('the thing speaks for itself' – though if so why does it not speak in English?) to reverse the burden of proof and require the defendant to *disprove* negligence. In theory he should then be able to show he took all due care by supervision of workers and tests of products to avoid the risk, but in practice the fact of the accident might be taken as conclusive proof that he had failed in his duty.

The point is illustrated in *Grant* v *Australian Knitting Mills*, 1936. The plaintiff bought a pair of underpants. They contained excess sulphites, which caused severe dermatitis. He sued both seller and manufacturers. In seeking to disprove negligence the manufacturers established that they had a very modern factory and had sold more than a million pairs of underpants without complaint. The court held:

> If excess sulphites were left in the garment, that could only be because someone was at fault. The (plaintiff) is not required to lay his finger on the exact person in all the chain who was responsible, or to specify what he did wrong.

Negligence is found as a matter of inference from the existence of the defects taken in conjunction with all the known circumstances.

In *Daniels* v *White*, 1938, on the other hand, lemonade manufacturers escaped liability for carbolic acid in their bottles by proving they had a 'foolproof' method of cleaning and filling bottles. This conflict may perhaps have been resolved by *Hill* v *Crowe*, 1978, where it was emphasised that proof of a 'perfect' system, that is discharge of the manufacturer's personal duty of care, did not rule out liability for employees' negligence. This issue of *vicarious liability* is discussed in para. 5.15.

It follows that if the judge cares to say that the *res ipsa* rule applies, the injured plaintiff is in a very strong position. The rule was invoked, for example, in *Steer* v *Durable Rubber Co.*, 1958, where a hot water bottle burst after only three months' use and scalded the plaintiff. It was invoked also in *Carroll* v *Fearon*, 1998, a Court of Appeal ruling on a road accident caused by the tread suddenly stripping off a tyre. The tyre was made in 1981, well before the Consumer Protection Act came into effect. The evidence suggested that the tread could only have come off because of a fault in manufacture, and the existence of that fault was prima facie proof of negligence. 'If the manufacturing process had worked as intended, this defect should not have been present.' The onus was then on the manufacturers to prove the accident happened for reasons beyond their control, for example subsequent misuse of the tyre, but they were unable to do so. We observe in passing that this particular exercise in compensating victims of negligence took 10 years from accident to judgment, including a 22-day trial on the way. The delay was said to be due in part to the technical nature of the inquiry, and the 'lamentable approach' of the manufacturers, Dunlops, but in many ways is inherent in the process of trial for negligence.

The fact remains that the *res ipsa* rule is used only relatively rarely, and not in many circumstances where one might think it could be. The burden of proof was not reversed in *Donoghue* v *Stevenson*, for example, nor was it suggested that it might be in the disputes over Thalidomide. As a rule, the whole burden of proving fault at common law lies on the injured party.

Happily, the Consumer Protection Act has resolved many of the problems of claiming damages for negligence. But as we shall see in the next chapter, it has by no means solved them all. There are still many circumstances in which the Act does not apply, and an understanding of the law of negligence thus remains vital both for the injured party and for all professional suppliers of goods and services. We now seek to explain and illustrate how the rules may work in a wide variety of factual situations. For the sake of convenience we shall divide the cases under the four general headings of Safety of materials, Safe design, Advice and warning, and Workmanship. But these headings are not mutually exclusive, and we may often find that issues arising under one heading may be resolved by reference to another.

5.4 SAFETY OF MATERIALS

The producer of raw materials faces immediately the problem that many of them are inherently dangerous, and most if not all involve further hazards in extraction and processing. If we really wished to avoid these dangers we could simply forbid the use of the materials, but will more probably find that society regards the materials as necessary for its comfort or convenience and so decides that someone must be employed to run the risks. Precautions will be imposed but they will be essentially second best, requiring, for example, safe storage or handling, use of respirators or safety clothing or barrier cream. In his capacity as employer the producer will then have to do his best to ensure that his employees observe these precautions, and if not will be liable to them in damages. If he sells the materials for others to use, he must ensure they are packed as safely as reasonably practicable and that the user has adequate information as to their proper use. Only very occasionally do we accept that the risks are so great that the product must be taken off the market. An early example was the Factories Act prohibition of white phosphorus in match making, to avoid the disease of 'phossy-jaw' commonly found among matchmakers in the nineteenth century. More recently blue asbestos has been banned and restrictions imposed on other forms of asbestos which make its continued use almost impossible and provide the strongest incentive to find alternatives. Certain other carcinogenic products and various drugs with exceptionally severe side effects have also had to be withdrawn. The lead content of petrol is gradually being reduced.

These various points, apart from the question of warnings and advice to users discussed separately below, are illustrated in a number of leading cases. First *Pearson* v *NW Gas Board*, 1968, and *Hawes* v *Railway Executive*, 1952, discuss problems of inherent danger and social utility in relation to gas and electricity supply. In *Pearson*, a gas main, buried at the standard depth and so far as was known in good condition, was fractured by an exceptionally severe frost. The result was an explosion in which a house was destroyed, the husband killed and his wife severely injured. She claimed compensation for these losses from the Board, on grounds of negligence. On that evidence the court held that the Board had taken all the normally effective precautions and could not be liable for failing to predict or prevent this tragic accident. The cost element was crucial here. If the Board were to be held liable in this quite exceptional case it would then have to spend limitless sums of money reburying all its pipes all over the country to try to avoid such accidents recurring, though of course no one could say for sure how much deeper they would have to be to *guarantee* safety. Further precautions were therefore impracticable.

The facts of the *Railway Executive* case were that Mr Hawes, a railway ganger doing minor maintenance work on a stretch of electrified railway line, slipped or tripped and was electrocuted on the live rail. Clearly his widow could prove the elements of likelihood and seriousness of accident listed above as the main ingredients of liability. She could also establish an easy and effective way of eliminating what might otherwise appear as an inherent risk, that is, by turning the current off. The Executive defended the case simply by denying it was under any duty to turn the current off. The court argued that her claim, pursued to its conclusion, meant that every time anyone did minor maintenance work the current would have to be off, and since such repairs took place all over the system all the time the railways would be in a state of complete and permanent dislocation. This result would be quite unacceptable to society as a whole. The widow therefore lost her claim because the cost of taking effective precautions was far more than society would be willing to pay. That in turn involves recognition of the fact that electricity is extremely dangerous and that there are limits to what we can do to make it safe. Some countries such as Germany deal with this problem by imposing strict liability on public utility suppliers. It is interesting to see that in America, where the position is governed by common law rules of product liability, their answer to problems like that in *Pearson* seems to be the same as ours: *Harris* v *Northwest Natural Gas*, 1979.

Again we might ask in passing whether these apparently neat and logical common law conclusions, which would not be affected by the Consumer Protection Act, represent acceptable ways of dealing with families which have lost their breadwinners. Society wants gas and electricity supplies; in a sense therefore it sentences to death or injury some of those who work on or use these products. Should it not then be society's responsibility to make sure that victims and dependants are adequately provided for, rather than left virtually destitute as may be the case at present?

Sometimes, of course, it is feasible and necessary simply to ban or withdraw an exceptionally dangerous product from the market. This may be achieved by statute or by a court ruling. In *Wright* v *Dunlop*, for instance, ICI made a product called Nonox S which they supplied to Dunlop for use in tyremaking. ICI discovered that the product carried a risk of cancer and took various steps including ultimately withdrawal of the product to safeguard their employees. The question then arose as to ICI's liabilities if any to Dunlop's employees as users of their product. The court held that ICI's duty was the same as that towards their own employees, at least if they knew how the product was being used and on the assumption that it was used as ICI intended, which was so here. ICI were then bound to

> take all reasonable steps to satisfy themselves that Nonox S was safe: 'safe' in the sense that there was no substantial risk of any substantial injury to health on the part of persons who were likely to use it or to be brought into contact with its use, the method of the use being such as was intended or contemplated or was at least reasonably to be expected as a normal and proper use.

The judge explained the possible courses of action as follows:

> It is obvious that the answer to the question: 'What are reasonable steps?' must depend upon the particular facts. It is obvious, also, that the duty is not necessarily confined to the period before the product is first produced or put on the market. Thus, if, when a product is first marketed, there is no reason to suppose that it is carcinogenic, but thereafter information shows, or gives reason to suspect, that it may be carcinogenic, the manufacturer has failed in his duty if he has failed to do whatever may have been reasonable in the circumstances in keeping up to date with knowledge of such developments and acting with whatever promptness fairly reflects the nature of the information and the seriousness of the possible consequences. If the manufacturer discovers that the product is unsafe, or has reason to believe that it may be unsafe, his duty may be to cease forthwith to manufacture or supply the product in its unsafe form.
>
> It may be that in some circumstances the duty would be fulfilled by less drastic action: by, for example, giving proper warning to persons to whom the product is supplied of the relevant facts, as known or suspected, giving rise to the actual or potential risk. Factors which would be relevant would be the gravity of the consequences if the risk should become a reality, and the gravity of the consequences which would arise from the withdrawal of the product.

In the event ICI were held liable for not telling Dunlop of the danger sooner and Dunlop were also to blame for not acting on the advice quickly enough.

5.5 SAFE DESIGN

From dangers created by the extraction or processing of materials we turn to those resulting from defective design or construction. The designer's objective is not to provide products incapable of causing injury, which as we stressed in Chapter 3 is impossible, but only to ensure they are reasonably safe in the circumstances of their likely use. They must not, in other words, give rise to unnecessary risk of injury; specifically, those which the user cannot foresee and guard against for himself. The law asks therefore whether the designer or producer knew or ought to have known of the likelihood of the product being used in a particular way. If so, was injury a reasonably foreseeable consequence? And if so again, what if anything could he and should he have done to avoid or reduce that risk?

The practical limits of product liability are well illustrated in the context of such obviously dangerous products as aeroplanes or cars, or, if it comes to that, cigarettes or whisky. The law does not ban the product, nor require it to be totally safe. Car manufacturers are not expected to build crashproof vehicles nor those 'incorporating only features representing the ultimate in safety', as was said in an American case. But while it is not commercially viable to build cars which will withstand high speed impacts there is increasingly the view that cars can realistically be expected to be safe in 5 or 10 or possibly 20 mph crashes, and injuries caused by splintering glass or steering shafts can and should be prevented even at higher speeds.

This problem area was instructively examined in the Canadian case of *Gallant* v *Beitz*, 1983. There was a collision between a car and a Datsun lorry. The lorry driver's injuries were caused in part by his being forced up against an iron bar which the manufacturers installed behind the driver's seat for use in tyre changing. The question then was whether Datsun were responsible for these particular injuries. On appeal it was held that on principle there could be liability

> for negligently designing a vehicle that is not reasonably crashworthy. Since motor vehicle manufacturers know or should know that many of their vehicles will be involved in collision and that many people will be injured in those crashes, they must turn their minds to this matter during the process of planning the designs of their vehicles and they must employ reasonable efforts to reduce any risk to life and limb that may be inherent in the design of their products.

That being so, it was for the trial court to decide whether the manufacturers should have foreseen the danger to occupants from the position of the bar.

Broadly, then, a manufacturer's duty is to provide goods which are reasonably safe *for what they are*. A cheap, light car or motorcycle is less safe than an expensive and well-constructed vehicle, but that does not mean that light cars or motorcycles must not be built. Taking the cheaper product as it stands, the court asks whether it has unnecessary dangers and if so whether it is practicable to reduce them. Feasibility can only be measured by reference to other comparable products and practices and to the cost of the proposed improvements.

Nicholson v *Deere*, 1987, is an instructive Canadian example of these design issues. The case concerned a motor mower designed with its petrol tank fitted close to the battery, thus creating a risk of fire by sparks igniting petrol vapour. The fire duly occurred, and burned down the user's house. The manufacturer was held to blame for not using other, safer designs, possibly more costly, when he knew or should have known of the danger. The Ontario High Court said:

> A manufacturer does not have the right to manufacture an inherently dangerous article when a method exists of manufacturing the same article without risk of harm. No amount of or degree of specificity of warning will exonerate it from liability if it does.

Some very helpful remarks on cost were made in *Turner* v *General Motors*, 1974, an American case. Speaking of an alleged defect in the design of a car, the judge said:

> If a change in design would add little to safety, render the vehicle ugly or inappropriate for its particular purpose and add a small fortune to the purchase price then the court should rule that the manufacturer had not created an unreasonable risk of harm.

The designer's or manufacturer's overriding concern in the light of these technical and economic considerations is as we have said to take whatever precautions are practicable against reasonably foreseeable hazards. Such hazards are not confined to those involving intended users or arising from proper or normal use. It is foreseeable, for example, that a defective car part might cause an accident and that the accident might involve passers-by or other car drivers or passengers. Brought thus involuntarily into contact with the product they are still 'users' and as such within the producer's duty of care. In *Lambert* v *Lewis*, 1981, a manufacturer of a dangerous caravan towing hitch was found 75 per cent to blame for an accident to an oncoming vehicle, even though the immediate cause was the owner's continued use of it despite knowledge of the defect (for which the owner paid the remaining 25 per cent). Similarly in *Stennett* v *Hancock*, 1939, a car repairer was held liable to a passer-by injured when a part he had fitted came off the car.

Again, the 'normal' – if not the 'proper' – use of goods includes certain predictable misuse or abuse of them. The designer's or manufacturer's responsibility does not of course extend to any and every conceivable form of misuse. He cannot, for example, stop people speeding or driving dangerously in the cars he designs or builds. He cannot stop a child burning itself on ordinary domestic heating pipes: *Ryan* v *Camden LBC*, 1982. See also paras. 5.10, 5.13. And although not concerned with product liability, the case of *Jolley* v *Sutton LBC*, 1998, is instructive here. The council admitted negligence in leaving a boat to rot near council flats, but still escaped liability when the boat fell on a child who had jacked it up in order to repair it. The accident was said to be 'of a different type and kind from anything which the council could reasonably have foreseen'.

Designers' and suppliers' civil liabilities are illustrated in cases such as *Williams* v *Trimm Rock Quarries*, 1965, and *Hindustan SS Co.* v *Siemens*, 1955. In *Williams* manufacturers of a new type of drill were liable for injury caused when it moved and fell. The judge said:

> Before sending a machine like this out for demonstration and putting it on the market, the toolmakers should have guarded against the possibility of its rising up and toppling over, and should have investigated those possible sources of danger. Since this accident they have taken steps to that end and all is now well; but reasonable foresight would have discovered it before the machine was issued.

The *Hindustan* case concerned a ship's telegraph system so designed that 'full astern' could easily be misinterpreted as 'full ahead'. It was held that the manufacturers would have been liable for the resulting collision, but for the fact that the ship's officers were now familiar with the problem and should have guarded against it themselves.

Certain employment law cases are also very helpful, even though neither designers nor suppliers were directly involved in them. The employee in *Tearle* v *Cheverton & Laidler*, 1970, worked on a machine with a sloping control panel from which the starting button projected at waist height. Behind the control panel were the moving parts. The employee was instructed to adjust these parts. He stopped the machinery and intended to turn it off also at the mains, but unfortunately was distracted and forgot this further precaution. He then removed the guard on the machine and got on with the job of adjustment. While doing this he inadvertently pressed on the starting button with his body and injured his hands in the machinery. He sued his employers, not because of any failure to fence or isolate the machine itself, because that was not how the accident happened, but because of the position of the starting button. The judge held the employer liable for negligent failure to hood the button so as to prevent this foreseeable occurrence of someone pressing it on by accident and being injured as a result. It will be seen that the same charge of negligence could have been made against the designer or supplier of the machine, with the same outcome. In passing, however, we should note that the plaintiff here lost two-thirds of his compensation because of his own forgetfulness. Similarly in *Farr* v *Butters*, 1932, the plaintiff lost his claim altogether because he could see the machinery he was assembling was defective but nonetheless continued to use it.

5.6   Research

We have stressed the manufacturer's duty to keep up to date. In effect he is obliged to conduct continuous research into safety aspects of his products; in particular to seek and respond to information from users as to operating hazards. In appropriate cases that will mean establishing feedback systems such as those agreed between doctors and drug manufacturers and between car dealers and manufacturers. It is most important that he should keep records of research findings, either to show he then took the necessary precautions or to avoid charges of destruction of evidence which if proved would be virtually conclusive of liability.

Reasonable care does not, of course, require a manufacturer to begin at the beginning and find out for himself all over again that which is already well established, as is recognised, for example, by s. 6 of the Health and Safety at Work Act (see para. 8.6). He is entitled to rely on common knowledge within the industry. But how can we say what level of knowledge is or ought to be common within an industry at any given time? *Vacwell* v *BDH Chemicals*, 1970, is an illustration of the problem. Pharmaceutical manufacturers were held to blame here for marketing a new and possibly dangerous combination of chemicals, with disastrous results, without consulting all reasonably accessible literature on the subject. Conversely a Health Authority's treatment of a patient's minor hand and ankle disabilities with Butazolidin, which resulted in near blindness, was held after much conflicting evidence not to be negligent in the light of medical knowledge at that time: *Sheridan* v *Boots & Kensington AHA*, 1981. A similar issue arose in *Girdler* v *SE Kent HA*, 1997, and was similarly resolved.

The manufacturer's duty is particularly stringent in relation to new drugs, perhaps the most vexed of all product liability issues. The trials necessary to meet the requirements of the Committee on Safety of Medicines are rigorous, but even followed to the letter still cannot eliminate the possibility of some totally unlooked-for or delayed reaction causing serious injury. The plaintiff's position in these cases is still a very difficult one, despite the help given by the Consumer Protection Act. In a negligence case, though not under the Act, there is as we have said usually no presumption in his favour, however disastrous his injury, as illustrated by *Sheridan*'s case above. From outside the industry he might have to prove that the manufacturer failed to follow normal test procedures, and that these procedures would have revealed the risk in question. The manufacturer for his

109

part will have his own battery of experts to say that all the right precautions were taken and no indications of danger appeared.

It is impossible to predict the outcome of such conflicts of evidence. All one can say with any degree of certainty is that the claim will be very hard fought, may take many years to reach final appeal, and may then result in defeat for the plaintiff who will have achieved nothing to compensate him for his loss but will probably be irretrievably ruined by legal costs. These were no doubt among the considerations facing the parents of children harmed by Thalidomide. Although the cause of the harm was clear the last thing the parents wanted to do was to go to court. In effect they fought for compensation with both hands tied behind their backs, and suffered accordingly delays of 12 or more years before public sympathy induced the manufacturers to offer reasonable sums in settlement. This tragedy became a mainspring for the reform proposals which eventually led to the enactment of the Consumer Protection Act.

Even if his product is approved by some independent authority the manufacturer's responsibilities are not necessarily at an end. The Canadian case of *Willis* v *FMC*, 1976, is an instructive example. The plaintiff was a farmer and turnip grower. He bought an insecticide and a new herbicide. The sellers made the insecticide themselves but were merely distributors of the herbicide. The herbicide had undergone limited trial use for one year, and then the manufacturers applied for and were granted Canadian government approval of their product for general field use. It was intended that both products should be used together. When the plaintiff did use them together, however, they interacted and damaged his crop. He sued the seller for breach of the Canadian Sale of Goods Act and the herbicide manufacturers for negligence. The seller was liable for the damage done by the herbicide. Although effective for its purpose it was still not reasonably fit since it could not be used with certain insecticides and carried no warning to that effect. The court also found the manufacturers liable in negligence. They were at fault in not allowing a longer period for the testing of the herbicide, because otherwise it might clearly cause a great deal of damage, and they could not escape liability by relying on government approval. On the one hand the duty to carry out proper tests was on them alone, and on the other there was always the possibility that the government's approval might itself have been given negligently.

The significance of the *Willis* case may be put another way. It shows that even when one acts in accordance with a government directive or licence or other guideline, for example, one set by the Health and Safety Commission or BSI, that of itself does not rule out the possibility of negligence. Compliance with specific statutory duties does not necessarily absolve a producer or anyone else from his general common law duty of care.

A relevant English case is *Perrett* v *Collins*, 1998, where the Court of Appeal held an aircraft safety certifier liable for negligent certification resulting in injury to a passenger. Where professional negligence of this kind contributes only to an economic loss, liability is less likely to be imposed: *Marc Rich* v *Bishop Rock*, 1996.

5.7   New safety devices

In the course of research a manufacturer will sooner or later find a way of making his product safer than it has been in the past. He might, for example, invent a new safety device for it. What, if any, liability does this discovery or invention create in relation to his existing products already out on the market? Common sense suggests that if the product was reasonably safe when first put on the market there can be no continuing duty to recall and update it. Inevitably the older the product the greater the danger attached to its use. But the fact that the discovery is new does not of itself mean it could never have retrospective effect. Exceptional cases might arise where, depending on the extent of the danger which might now be averted, a recall or renovation programme might conceivably be both feasible and necessary. For an American example, see *Kozlowski* v *Smith*, para. 7.5.

Before further consideration of recall and renovation programmes we should note the case of *Birnie* v *Ford*, 1960. This was an unusual decision where employers were held liable to an injured employee despite the fact that it was not until several months after the accident that they devised precautions which would have prevented it. On the face of it this may seem to penalise the employer or manufacturer for the successful outcome of his research. But the problem, that of injury from razor-sharp car body panels, was a relatively simple one and it was clear that if the employer had applied his mind sooner and put a fully trained safety engineer on the job he would almost certainly have made the invention in time to prevent the accident. Essentially therefore it was a matter of holding the employer liable for failing to exert himself sufficiently to resolve a familiar but serious danger – a lesson equally applicable to manufacturers and distributors.

5.8   New hazards

Research or other subsequent events may reveal or confirm previously unsuspected or insufficiently appreciated dangers. The proper response must vary with the circumstances, but may include at least a publicity campaign, perhaps warnings to individuals – *Hobbs* v *Baxenden Chemical Co.*, 1992 – quite possibly a recall programme, and conceivably even a complete standstill if the danger is sufficiently great; for example the grounding of aircraft when a structural defect is discovered.

By way of illustration we refer first to *O'Connor* v *British Transport Commission*, 1958. The BTC, predecessor of British Rail, discovered through various accidents and incidents with which we are not here concerned that their carriage door handles were not as safe as they had thought, and in particular that they could be opened all too easily by children. What should they do then? Warning notices would be defaced or ignored. The only solution was to embark upon a long-term programme of modifying the door handles. While this programme was under way a child opened the door of an unmodified carriage and was injured. BTC was held not liable for his injuries because they had taken the only course of action open to them. There were thousands of carriages and the doors could not all be altered overnight. In the meantime there was a continuing risk, but since it was unavoidable no one could be blamed.

This answer is only valid if the necessary precautions, repairs or alterations are undertaken as soon as reasonably practicable. The consequences of delay are shown in the Canadian cases of *Swanson Estate* v *Canada*, 1991, where a government agency was blamed for not taking sufficiently prompt action against an airline after complaints about safety, and *Malat* v *Bjornson*, 1981. In *Malat*, a highway authority was held liable for failure to install a particular type of barrier, which had been available for 10 years, to meet a serious danger recognised for 13 years. An English example to the same effect is *Rimmer* v *Liverpool City Council*, 1983. The plaintiff injured himself falling against a 3 mm glass panel, a standard fitment on certain types of corporation housing built in 1959. He had complained at the beginning of his tenancy that the panel was dangerous for children but had been told it was standard and nothing could be done about it. The judge found that although in 1959 the corporation architect had no code of practice to guide him on the safety of glass 'an intelligent reading of the 1966 and 1972 codes of practice would have called to the minds of the architects' department the risk of danger to anyone stumbling against that glass'. He held that the department was not relieved from reconsidering the position in the light of after-acquired information since they then knew that the flat contained this foreseeably dangerous and easily substituted panel. It is worth noting that the plaintiff's own knowledge of the danger did not affect his claim, because in the circumstances there was nothing he could do about it. *J* v *Staffordshire CC*, 1997, is a similar case on an education authority's failure to comply with BSI recommendations on school windows.

5.9 Recalls

So far as recalls are concerned, there is a helpful statement of the position in *Walton* v *British Leyland*, 1978. The plaintiffs here were involved in a disastrous accident in 1975 after a wheel came off the Austin Allegro in which they were passengers. By the beginning of 1967 BL had received over a hundred reports of 'wheel adrift' problems on this model. They knew the risk was a real and serious one. A recall would have cost some £300 000 and, of course, damaged their image. Instead they instructed their dealers to fit larger washers, though without fully explaining the risk. Non-franchised dealers were told nothing at all about the problem. This particular car had been serviced by both franchised and non-franchised dealers. The plaintiffs claimed against the dealers, who all escaped liability since they were unaware of the dangers, and against BL. The judge held BL wholly to blame, not for use of the component which caused the accident, which was manufactured by a reputable third party and not in itself faulty, but for failure to recall the cars and give adequate public warning. The crucial passage in his judgment was as follows:

> The duty of care owed by Leyland to the public was to make a clean breast of the problem and recall all cars which they could, in order that the safety washers could be fitted. I accept, of course, that manufacturers have to steer a course between alarming the public unnecessarily and so damaging the reputation of their products, and observing the duty of care towards those whom they are in a position to protect from dangers of which they and they alone are aware. The duty seems to me to be the higher when they can palliate the worst effects of a failure which, if Leyland's view is right, they could never decisively guard against. They seriously considered recall and made an estimate of the cost at a figure which seems to me to be in no way out of proportion to the risks involved. It was decided not to follow this course for commercial reasons. I think this involved a failure to observe their duty of care for the safety of the many who were bound to remain at risk, irrespective of the recommendations made to Leyland dealers and to them alone.

In 1979 a Code of Practice for the Motor Industry was agreed between the Department of Transport and the Society of Motor Manufacturers. The Code, revised in 1992, applies to cars up to 10 years old. It does not and cannot specify exactly the nature or number of defects requiring action but obliges manufacturers, importers and dealers concerned about the number of faulty vehicles to tell the Department of the faults and resulting dangers and their proposed precautions. They must then take all suitable steps to inform vehicle owners, sending at least two letters if necessary, recall the vehicles if that seems desirable and notify the Department of action taken. Some one million cars are recalled annually in the UK. The Department may put forward its own proposals as to the appropriate precautions and publish such warning information as it thinks necessary.

From time to time the Committee on Safety of Medicines withdraws its approval for the marketing of a drug when serious side effects are reported. Under the Code of Practice (Rules and Guidance for Pharmaceutical Manufacturers and Distributors, 1997) for the recall of such products a manufacturer who can prove he has taken all feasible steps to withdraw or recall his products when necessary will escape liability for negligence if in any particular case his efforts fail, for example because the distributor or user cannot be contacted or ignores the warning. If injury results from the continued prescribing of a disapproved drug liability seems almost inevitable, but there is always the possibility that as between immediate pain and suffering and continued use of the drug the latter might be upheld as the lesser of two evils. The doctor would of course have to advise the patient of the risks involved. We discuss this problem area below and in the next chapter.

A manufacturer who recalls his goods or modifies or even withdraws them does not *thereby* admit liability for them. He might for example have been prompted to take remedial action by some unforeseeable accident for which he would not be liable, and his action might serve only to demonstrate his anxiety to ensure that no such accident should happen again.

5.10 Obvious dangers

We turn now to another aspect of design; the question of liability for injury caused by dangers which are or ought to be obvious to the user. There must, of course, be a point at which a risk is so obvious that there can be no ground for complaint, as when one hits one's thumb with a hammer or cuts oneself when shaving. American cases have observed that there is no need to warn against the unwisdom of landing on one's head on a trampoline, or of prematurely releasing one end of a rubber exerciser: *Garrett* v *Nissen*, 1972; *Jamieson* v *Woodward*, 1957. But that is not the issue here. These products were, we presume, fit for their normal purposes and without any risk other than those plainly inherent in their use. What should the law's response be when the danger is obvious but not inherent?

An excellent illustration of the problem is provided by the English case of *Crow* v *Barford*, 1963. In this case a person using a motor mower with a large grass ejection aperture inadvertently put his foot in the hole and was injured by the rotating blades. He sued the manufacturer on grounds of negligent design. The judge rejected his claim, simply because the danger was so clear. One might very well doubt, however, whether this was the right answer. Surely the question ought not to be 'Was the danger obvious?' but 'Was it *necessary*?' Otherwise manufacturers could put on the market whatever shoddy designs they pleased and escape liability simply by pointing to their glaring imperfections.

American courts have had to deal with disputes of this kind, as discussed at more length in Chapter 7, and have examined the issues perhaps rather more realistically. In *Wright* v *Massey Harris*, 1969, for instance, the judge in a similar sort of case cited this passage from an article on power lawn mower injuries in *The American Surgeon*:

> [A]pproximately 30 per cent of all power lawn mowers are made by companies whose primary objective is to turn out a lower priced, sometimes poorly constructed machine for a profit. These companies have given little or no consideration to safety features of their products and some do not bother to caution the buyer of the machine about its inherent dangers. The low cost of these mowers makes them attractive to the unsuspecting customer. On the other hand, some of the more reputable manufacturers have attempted to construct mowers which meet rigid safety standards. These also usually attach a card or booklet for instructions regarding proper operation of the machine and emboss special warnings at the danger points on the machine housing.

In the light of these considerations the judge directed the jury that the machine in question was one whose design disregarded the basic safety principles. The issues of contributory negligence and consent referred to at the end of this chapter must not be overlooked, but it may still be thought that such cases reflect safety needs more accurately than *Crow* v *Barford*.

5.11   Durability

When we discussed the standard of reasonable fitness required by the Sale of Goods Act we asked how long goods were expected to last. The same question arises in the present context. 'A reasonable time' is not a satisfactory answer, but it is the best we can manage. Nobody expects manufacturers to produce goods which will never wear out, nor suffer from the consequences of wear and tear. What matters is whether the goods were reasonably safe when first sold and used. Passage of time and the possibility or proof of intermediate handling may suggest that the fault could not be the manufacturer's. In *Evans* v *Triplex Safety Glass*, 1936, the plaintiff lost his claim against the manufacturers for injuries received when his windscreen shattered for no apparent reason a year after he bought the car. The court rejected his claim because of the length of time between purchase and the accident, the possibility that the glass might have been strained when installed in the frame by the intermediate seller, and lastly because the breakage might have been for some reason other than a defect in manufacture. Again it appears that American courts might take a rather more rigorous view and assume fault upon the manufacturer in the absence of compelling evidence to the contrary: *Henningsen* v *Bloomfield Motors*, 1960. And even after several years it might still sometimes be possible to prove that the goods were defective in the first place.

5.12 Packaging

Design liabilities extend to the safety of packaging, for example, provision of containers which do not break or leak or open too easily, particularly when they may be harmful to children or others ignorant of their contents. Common law duties are reinforced by stringent obligations of the criminal law, notably the Chemicals (Hazard Information and Packaging for Supply) Regulations 1994 and the Carriage of Dangerous Goods by Road and Rail (Classification, Packaging and Labelling) Regulations 1994.

Examples of the scope of packaging liabilities are *Hill* v *Crowe*, 1978, and *Samways* v *Westgate*, 1962. In *Hill* the manufacturer of a packing case was sued by a lorry driver injured when he stood on the case while loading it. It collapsed because it was badly made, without sufficient nails in the boards, and liability was imposed because the manufacturer should have known it might be used for standing on. *Samways* did not concern manufacturers' duties as such but nonetheless illustrates the need to pack goods with due forethought of those likely to use them. In this case a refuse collector was injured as he picked up a box without noticing a sliver of glass left sticking out through the side. His claim against the company which left the box out for collection was successful.

If packaging is undertaken by a third party such as a distributor and not by the manufacturer, the latter may still be liable for negligence if he fails to take care in selecting a reputable contractor and giving him the information and specifications necessary to enable him to do the job safely. Other aspects of packaging and labelling are considered further under the next heading.

5.13 ADVICE AND WARNING

We have emphasised that even the most safety conscious of manufacturers cannot build complete safety into their products. Inherent dangers and possibilities of misuse create irreducible risks. In such cases, where a manufacturer has done all he can realistically be expected to do in terms of design and construction, the only precaution left open to him may be to give advice and warning as to use.

The kind of information he must give varies infinitely with the product. It may be a simple matter of marking 'on' and 'off' in the language of the country to which goods are exported: *Goodchild* v *Vaclight*, 1965, below. Another salutory reminder of language problems was in *French* v *Olau Lines*, 1983, where a cleaner suffered chlorine gas injuries because he had mixed two cleaning agents contrary to warning labels printed only in foreign languages. Or it may be necessary to specify in detail the various hazards and precautions, as with warnings against heat and light on aerosol tins. In *Lambert* v *Lastoplex Chemicals*, 1971 (Can.), for example, a general warning of the danger of inflammability was held insufficient to meet the danger of a lacquer sealant which could be ignited even by the spark of an electric light switch. The same conclusion was reached in the hair-raising American case of *Martin* v *Bengue*, 1957, where the plaintiff's chest ointment caught fire while he was smoking in bed. These cases contrast with the decision of the Australian court in *Norton* v *Streets*, 1968, where it was held that a general warning of the inflammability of an industrial adhesive should have been sufficient to stop the buyer using a burner only 20 feet away from a tray of adhesive in a badly ventilated room.

Different levels of information may be necessary for different purposes and different classes of users. Where the safety or suitability of a product is likely to be decided by a third party before it reaches the end-user, the information given by the manufacturer must be appropriate to the needs of the third party rather than the user. So, for example, doctors must be given very detailed information about possible adverse reactions to drugs before they can prescribe them.

Notable Canadian examples of this 'learned intermediary' rule are *Buchan* v *Ortho Pharmaceutical*, 1986, and *Dow* v *Hollis*, 1996. In *Buchan* the plaintiff suffered a stroke after taking oral contraceptives on prescription. The manufacturer was liable both for failure adequately to warn the doctor of this possible reaction and for promotional sales materials suggesting the product was quite safe. It was held also that even if the doctor had negligently failed to pass on a warning, that would not have relieved the manufacturer of his duty. Nor, in the court's opinion, could the manufacturer require the plaintiff to prove she would not have taken the drug if properly warned. In *Dow*, a case concerning post-operational ruptures of breast implants, the Supreme Court confirmed that the manufacturer's duty to warn extended to dangers coming to his notice after manufacture and distribution of the product. By a majority, the court also accepted the plaintiff's evidence that if she had been properly warned she would not have had the operation. It was not necessary to try to establish what a 'reasonable person' would have done in the circumstances. A repairman was held liable in *Nicholson* v *Deere*, above, for not telling his customer that a safety device was missing from the machine he had repaired. In the English case of *Holmes* v *Ashford*, 1950, the manufacturer knew his hair dye could be dangerous to certain skins. Hairdressers were told of the dangers by notices on the containers. The injured customer's claim that she also should have been warned was rejected.

The issue of a plaintiff's likely response to any warning or advice which he or she should have been given, but was not in fact given, seems more significant under English law than in the Canadian cases above. In *McWilliams* v *Arrol*, 1962, the House of Lords held that an employer should escape liability for failing either to provide or advise on safety equipment when he proved that the employee would almost certainly have ignored such precautions. This highly questionable line of argument is known as the 'doctrine of hypothetical causation'

Another instance of the need to warn intermediaries is in connection with contracts of carriage. It would very clearly be negligence, as well as breach of contract, to fail to inform a carrier of the potential dangers of the goods in question. As noted above, the consignor would very probably also be guilty of a criminal offence under the Carriage of Dangerous Goods by Road and Rail (Classification, Packaging and Labelling) Regulations 1994.

Where products are intended to reach end-users directly, without intermediate inspection, the manufacturer must be particularly careful to ensure that any necessary advice or warning is clear, obvious and unambiguous. If at all possible it should be inscribed on or attached to the product. There is always the possibility that information accompanying but separate from the product – safety manuals and the like – will not reach the user or will quickly be forgotten or lost. In some circumstances it might even be possible and desirable to overcome risks of indifference or ignorance by sending out periodic reminders to known users.

Instructions as to use must also warn adequately of the dangers of foreseeable misuse. The American case of *Spruill* v *Boyle-Midway*, 1962, is an instructive example. The product in question was floor polish, known by the manufacturer to contain poison. A householder left a tin where a child found it and ate some of the polish. This might seem an extraordinary use for polish, but since the polish was to go on the floor where children might play it was nothing if not predictable. The manufacturer was therefore held to blame for not marking the contents as poison, not so much to deter children as to encourage their parents to keep the tins out of harm's way.

If suitable instructions are duly given then, of course, the user has only himself to blame if he fails to observe them. The point was clearly made in *Allard* v *Manahan*, 1974, a Canadian case about an experienced worker killed by the ricochet of a nail he had fired from a nail gun. In the worker's dependants' claim against the manufacturers of the gun the judge observed:

> It is true that a person in the position of the defendant, who deals in firearms, must exercise a high standard of care in the conduct of his business, but that does not mean to say that he is obliged to supply or recommend every safety device which is on the market or can be made available. The manual which is supplied with the tool described these devices and a person renting the tool can avail himself of this additional protection if he so desires.

As indicated in *Allard* and other cases previously mentioned, contributory negligence by a user, or conduct which seems to amount to consent to run a risk, may well defeat his claim against a manufacturer. This would still be so today under the Consumer Protection Act. But this result of disregarding advice or warning notices must not be confused with the effect of manufacturers' notices expressly excluding liability if anything goes wrong. Exclusion clauses are rigorously controlled by the Unfair Contract Terms Act, as we saw in Chapter 2, and by the Consumer Protection Act itself: para. 6.12.

5.14 WORKMANSHIP

This last category of the causes of accidents includes negligent handling, processing, packaging or distribution of safely designed products, thereby creating new and unnecessary hazards. The relevant principle of law here is the common law doctrine of vicarious liability; that is, liability for someone else's wrongdoing.

5.15 Vicarious liability

Employers are held liable under this rule to persons injured by their employees' wrongful acts if committed in the course of their employment.

The employee's act or omission is in the course of his or her employment if it is a wrongful way, for example a disobedient or careless way, of doing what the employee was supposed to do. The injured party's task therefore is to prove negligence against an employee, not the employer. Conversely the fact that the employer might have been quite unable to prevent the accident does not in any way reduce his liability. Two main arguments are advanced to justify the rule. First, the employer is in control of the operation and so should take responsibility for the outcome. Second, if the careless employee alone were liable he or she would not usually have the resources to compensate the injured party, who would thus go without redress. We have noted the effect of the rule already in decisions such as *Hill* v *Crowe* where the manufacturer had to pay for an accident caused by an employee's faulty construction of a packing case.

It might, of course, be very difficult to prove which particular employee was at fault at any given point on the assembly line. The judges accept therefore that if a plaintiff can show that he was injured by the product and that the nature of the injury is such that there must have been negligence somewhere within the employer's enterprise, he need not 'lay his finger on the exact person in all the chain who was responsible': *Grant* v *Australian Knitting Mills*, 1936; *Carroll* v *Fearon*, 1998. It follows that vicarious liability claims are almost impossible for an employer to refute and represent a form of strict liability. On the other hand such liability is usually only civil and unlike the employer's personal duty of care it is not reinforced by the criminal sanctions of the Health and Safety at Work Act (see Chapter 8). Criminal acts of sabotage of the employer's goods by disaffected employees would seem unlikely to result in employer's liability to injured consumers.

5.16 Sub-contractors

As a general rule the doctrine of vicarious liability is confined to the relationship of employer and employee. In other less tightly regulated relationships the law sees less reason for imposing liability on anyone other than the party actually at fault. That in turn means that when an accident is caused by a defective part supplied by a sub-contractor, as distinct from the manufacturer's own employee, the manufacturer who incorporated that part in his own product will not be held vicariously to blame. The manufacturer might still be liable for breach of his own personal duty of care if he failed to select a reputable sub-contractor, provide him with all necessary specifications and test or sample the parts supplied: *Rogers* v *Night Riders*, 1983; *Winward* v *TVR Engineering*, 1986. Even when all these things are done, however, a defective part might still slip through, and in that event he could not be liable in tort (though he could, of course, be liable for breach of contract, if there were in fact a contract between himself and the injured plaintiff). So in *Taylor* v *Rover*, 1966, an employee's claim in negligence against the manufacturer of chisels was rejected when it was proved that the faulty part was supplied by a reputable sub-contractor and that it could not have been found by the manufacturer's sample testing system. The law here was simplified by the Employers' Liability (Defective Equipment) Act 1959, holding employers primarily liable for such hidden defects. Another exception to the general rule is in the Package Travel Regulation 1992, which make tour operators liable for independent agents' negligence.

While the liability of the sub-contractor himself might not be in doubt, the problem from the plaintiff's point of view if suing in tort is first that of finding whether a sub-contractor was involved in the production process – and perhaps being time-barred by the time he discovers this – and second the danger of incurring liability for costs for suing the wrong party. These difficulties have been overcome where the Consumer Protection Act applies.

5.17 DISTRIBUTORS' LIABILITIES

In most of the cases considered so far we have seen that if anyone is to blame for a dangerous product it is the manufacturer. This is not necessarily so, however. It is always possible that someone else in the chain of distribution might be guilty of negligence. If the manufacturer also has been negligent then the burden will be shared between them in whatever proportion the court thinks just, or each may be held wholly liable and left to recover what he can from the other. Alternatively the manufacturer may for one reason or another be relieved of all liability and the whole burden imposed upon the retailer, installer, repairer, inspector, certifier, distributor or importer, as the case may be, who has failed to take reasonable care.

The possibilities are illustrated in the following cases. In *Fisher* v *Harrods*, 1966, a person bought a bottle of jewellery cleaner from Harrods which he sent to Mrs Fisher. When she came to use it the bottle 'exploded' and the liquid went into her eyes, causing pain and temporary blindness. The explosion occurred because of the build-up of pressure of the contents and the way the bottle was sealed. There was no warning of danger on the bottle. From what we have said above it might be thought that liability for the contents and sealing of the bottle, and for the absence of any warning, must be upon the manufacturer. But in this particular case the manufacturer was a 'man of straw'; someone not worth suing because he had no money. Mrs Fisher therefore had no choice but to sue Harrods if she was to sue anyone at all. But while Harrods were the sellers Mrs Fisher was not the buyer, and so because there was no contract between them she had to prove that Harrods were negligent and not merely that the bottle or contents were not reasonably fit for their purpose.

Harrods had tested the product originally to see whether it did what it was supposed to do, that is clean jewellery, and on being satisfied of this they sold it. Evidence was given by Harrods and a buyer from another leading store that it was not their practice to do anything more than test the efficiency of goods they sold, which the judge accepted as normally quite sufficient. To prove negligence Mrs Fisher therefore had to show there was something abnormal about this particular article which demanded exceptional precautions by the retailer, such as inquiries about the safety of the goods or their containers, or the qualifications of the manufacturer. She succeeded because Harrods knew or ought to have known that a solvent strong enough to clean jewellery was inherently dangerous. This should have put them on their guard to inquire about the manufacturer's qualifications, which were in fact virtually non-existent, and the safe packaging of his goods.

The same conclusion would no doubt be reached with regard to electrical or other scientific or mechanical equipment with a range of hazards known to experts but hidden from consumers: *Nicholson* v *Deere*, above. In *Goldsworthy* v *Cataline Agencies*, 1983, a Canadian court held both a cycle manufacturer and a retailer liable for an accident, the one for making cycles without lock washers to hold the front wheel axle to the fork and the other for assembling the machine without washers and/or failing to warn of their absence. This case and *Burfitt* v *Kille*, 1939, illustrate in passing the particularly heavy duty of care of retailers supplying potentially dangerous goods – in the latter case, petrol – to children. Conversely if there were no reason to expect any danger there would be no reason for the retailer to make tests or inquiries and so no liability for accidents which might otherwise have been avoided.

Goodchild v *Vaclight*, 1965, is an interesting case on the duties of distributors – here, importers. The facts were that the plaintiff's husband bought an electric cleaner from a door-to-door salesman. The fan was not properly guarded or isolated and the on/off signs were in German. A couple of weeks later Mrs Goodchild suffered a severe electric shock while using the machine. She could not sue the seller because she could not trace him. Suing the German manufacturer would have been extremely expensive and speculative. The only remaining possibility was the importer. The difficulty here is that a person who is merely a conduit for another's goods is on the face of it unlikely to be responsible for their safety. But in this case, as the judge said,

> [T]he defendants were more than mere distributors. They bought about 40 000 machines over five years from the German manufacturers, having at the start stripped and tested one, and they serviced them. The defendants' name was prominently displayed on the machine and they gave a guarantee card and an instruction booklet with their address.

In effect then the importers passed the goods off as their own and were certainly in a position to appreciate the strengths and weaknesses of the product. The judge held them liable as if they were the manufacturers because they should have warned against the inherent dangers of the machine, clearly marked the switch positions and insulated the fan. But the judge also said that Mrs Goodchild as a prudent housewife, uncertain whether the machine was on or off, should have unplugged it or switched it off at the mains before trying to make it work. Her failure to take this precaution cost her half her damages.

Lastly we should note the case of *Devillez* v *Boots*, 1962. The plaintiff bought a bottle of corn solvent from the defendants. After a bath he put some solvent on his corn. As he was putting the bottle away it tipped over, the cork came out and the contents spilled over his private parts. He wiped himself and looked at the label on the bottle to see what else he should do, but no warning or advice was given. Later he suffered extreme pain and had to undergo plastic surgery. He sued Boots in all their capacities – as sellers, distributors and manufacturers of the product. We have no information about his claim in contract, but he might well have lost under that heading because the corn solvent was undoubtedly reasonably fit for its purpose, whatever harm it might do elsewhere. In alleging negligence Mr Devillez was also in difficulty because Boots established that over the previous 30 years they had sold some 20 million bottles of this preparation under the same label and in the same type of bottle. During that time they had had only a dozen minor complaints. The judge accepted that such a successful and safe commercial record was very much in Boots' favour. He nonetheless held them liable for essentially the same reason we saw in *Fisher*, that they knew the preparation had quite a strong concentration of acid in it and should have anticipated danger to other more tender parts of the body by providing a safer bottle and clearer warning.

5.18 DAMAGES

So far as possible the object of an award of damages is to compensate the plaintiff for the extent of his loss; to put him back at least in financial terms where he was before the accident. In practice this objective is rarely if ever achieved. In the first place the law cannot compensate for all losses but only for those which are the most direct and reasonably foreseeable consequences of injury, such as loss of earnings. Those more 'remote' will be disregarded. Even more clearly no amount of money can make up for the loss of an eye or an arm or a leg or other pain or suffering. Sums awarded for personal injuries can never be more than tokens. There will in any case be no agreement on the amount of the token, which depends entirely on the circumstances of the individual plaintiff. Only the judge can decide what is appropriate, reaching his conclusion by reference to awards in comparable cases. Current maximum awards for total permanent disablement are of the order of £500 000–1 million.

Awards may be reduced in accordance with the Law Reform (Contributory Negligence) Act 1945 if the judge considers that the plaintiff was partly responsible for his or her own injury. Careless or reckless or improper use of goods, disregard of safety instructions, etc., may lead to very substantial deductions, perhaps amounting to as much as 100 per cent of the award. Examples of judges' (wholly unpredictable) assessments of contributory fault appear in cases noted above such as *Tearle* and *Goodchild*. If the plaintiff's conduct suggests his or her entirely voluntary agreement or consent to run a known risk, then no award at all will be made – as in *Farr* and *Crow*, above.

Most negligence cases involve physical injury and/or damage to property. As a general rule, *no claim can be made for negligence causing pure economic loss*, that is financial loss which does not arise from physical injury or damage to property: *Murphy* v *Brentwood DC*, 1990. So, for example, loss of profit suffered by a business because of defective machinery cannot be recovered from the manufacturer unless bought directly from him, even though it is his fault the machinery does not work. Such claims are seen as matters for contract law alone, to be resolved by the buyer's claim against the seller. If the seller is insolvent, the buyer is left without redress. There is one exception to the general rule. It arises where financial loss is caused by *negligent advice or information* given in circumstances where the adviser knows the recipient depends on the advice being given carefully and will suffer loss if it is not: *Hedley Byrne* v *Heller*, 1964.

5.19 SUMMARY

As compared with relatively more straightforward claims for breach of contract (Chapters 1–4), it will be seen that common law claims for damages for negligence are often overwhelmingly difficult for the injured party – not only in terms of the basic legal issue of proof of fault but for all the familiar consequential reasons such as inordinate delay and astronomical cost. From the point of view of the manufacturer or distributor, it may be no less difficult to establish what 'reasonable care' requires as regards safety of design, ensuring appropriate instructions and warnings are given to consumers, and controlling component suppliers. International concern over injuries caused by pharmaceutical drugs and the patent failures of the law led eventually to the enactment of the Consumer Protection Act, the subject of the next chapter. But we shall see that the Act does not replace the common law altogether, and that distributors in particular are still at risk of liability for negligence.

Product liability (2) the Consumer Protection Act 1987

6

6.1 THE NEED FOR REFORM

In the previous chapters we examined what were until a few years ago the only remedies available under UK law to people injured by defective goods. We have noted the strengths and weaknesses of these remedies, which are still available and often used. We saw that a buyer from a business seller could hold the seller liable under the Sale of Goods Act simply by showing that the goods he or she had bought were not reasonably safe, and without needing to prove that it was the seller's fault the goods were dangerous. From the buyer's point of view the benefits are clear. Sellers are usually both accessible and responsive to such claims. But this strict liability regime has obvious limitations. If the seller goes out of business, or has not the resources to meet a large claim, or – most importantly – if the injured party is not the buyer, then the legal position changes completely.

In the past, an injured person not suing under a contract of sale has had no redress unless he or she could prove that someone had been negligent, and that that negligence was the cause of his or her injury. Most claims for negligence arising from use of goods have in the nature of things been made against manufacturers, although action has sometimes been taken against others closer to hand in the chain of supply. The greatest difficulty in all such claims is that of establishing the level of precautions which should have been taken, and then proving that the defendant failed to take them. The mere fact of injury does not prove that someone has been negligent. The injured person typically has no means of knowing what precautions are normal or desirable in a particular trade or industry, nor whether the designer, manufacturer or distributor, as the case may be, observed these precautions. If the precautions were taken, the defendant escapes all liability, however serious the accident might be.

The burden of proof in negligence cases in particular is a substantial one at the best of times, and if goods are manufactured or bought abroad the practical obstacles are (and remain so despite reform) all but insuperable. Many people might therefore suffer pain and poverty through no fault of their own, and yet have no redress against the manufacturer or supplier whose product caused their injury.

This state of affairs was accepted almost without question as part of the natural order of life for a great many years, both in Britain and abroad, perhaps because the injured had no sufficient voice or vote. In the 1960s and 1970s, however, it became a matter of general public concern. The mainspring of this concern was the international Thalidomide drug tragedy, with all that was suddenly seen to be involved in terms of human suffering on the one hand and legal and commercial obstructivism on the other. There were other causes also, notably the pressures of American product liability law and the inequality of trading conditions as between Member States in the Common Market which Britain had just joined.

In 1970 the Council of Europe, representing the UK and 17 other countries, appointed a committee of experts to consider how to harmonise the product liability laws of member states. At about the same time the Commission of the European Communities, now the European Union, began work on a Directive which would have the same effect within the Community. In due course the Council produced what became known as the Strasbourg Convention, while the Commission published a draft Directive.

The British government in the meantime had invited the English and Scottish Law Commissions to investigate the effects of our own rules on product liability. The Commissions' inquiries were overtaken by the work of the Royal Commission on Civil Liability and Compensation for Personal Injury under the chairmanship of a senior judge, Lord Pearson, which reported in 1976, but eventually their conclusions were broadly the same. These in turn were generally in agreement with the proposals in the Strasbourg Convention and the draft Directive.

There were significant differences on points of detail, but the basic direction of the proposed reform was clear. It was fundamental and far-reaching, but can be briefly stated. It was that producers of goods which are not reasonably safe should be strictly liable for personal injury caused thereby. The need to prove negligence in non-contractual claims would be ended accordingly, or, to put the point another way, the liability of manufacturer to ultimate user should be much the same as that of seller to buyer.

These proposals fell initially on stony ground, in Britain as well as in certain other European countries. There was opposition both from industry and governments, and in particular from Mrs Thatcher and her government. In a debate in Parliament in 1981, for example, Sally Oppenheim, then Minister for Consumer Affairs, went so far as to say: 'In no way would I wish to see any reform which undermines the law of tort in this country. That law is part of the fabric of society, depending as it does on the philosophy of duty and personal responsibility.' This patently absurd remark ignored all the lessons of the previous hundred years as to the entirely fortuitous and grotesquely unfair operation of the law and the evasion of personal responsibility by insurance, but certainly reflected the attitude of the government.

6.2 THE CONSUMER PROTECTION ACT

The European Commission nonetheless continued with its work, reaching compromises where it could, and offering governments the right to opt out of one or two of the more controversial provisions. In 1985 it finally produced Directive no. 85/374/EEC, generally known as the Product Liability Directive. Member States of the European Union are bound as a condition of membership to give effect to Directives through their own laws. The long-awaited result in the UK was the passing of the Consumer Protection Act in 1987.

The new law of product liability is stated in Part I of the Act – the first 9 sections – reproduced in full in Appendix 3 of this book. In the rest of this chapter we offer a commentary on the meaning and effect of the rules, section by section. The sequence may be summarised as follows. Section 1 states the purpose of the Act and defines 'product' and 'producer'. Section 2 imposes on producers and certain other parties strict liability for damage caused by defective products. Section 3 explains the meaning of 'defect'. Section 4 provides defences to liability. Section 5 defines 'damage'. Section 6 relates the Act to other Acts on personal injuries. Section 7 forbids exclusion of liability. Sections 8 and 9 provide respectively for amendments and the Act's application to the Crown. Reference is also made to s. 45, another interpretation section.

6.3 PRODUCTS

Section 1 says first that the Act is intended to give effect to the Directive – a vital provision, as we shall see when we reach s. 4 – and then offers at least a partial definition of the two key words; 'product' and 'producer'. Products are very broadly defined as any goods or substances, including, for the purposes of the Act, gas and electricity. Products contained in other products, whether as components or raw materials, are also included, as are goods attached to land (e.g. building materials, scaffolding, etc.), but not buildings as such. Ships, aircraft and vehicles are specifically included by s. 45. No direct distinction is drawn between new and used goods, but the Act applies only to goods supplied after 1 March 1988. The Act takes no account of defective *services*, unless involving defective goods.

Two types of goods are excluded; 'derogations' which are allowed by the original Directive. They are game and agricultural products, including fish, unless they have undergone an 'industrial process' It is not immediately easy to explain or justify these exceptions. Under current EU proposals, they may soon be ended. Perhaps the normal understanding of 'product' in the present context is of something man-made, but one might equally well say that foodstuffs in their natural form are certainly capable of causing illness, for example salmonella from eggs, and so it is quite arbitrary to exclude liability for them. Again, it might be said that the 'defects' in question are inherent and cannot justly be blamed on the farmer, but against that are farming practices, such as the use of pesticides, which are well known to create health hazards. There are other practical arguments as to the difficulty of tracing the source of, say, a couple of pounds of potatoes. But some critics say that the exclusions merely prove the strength of the farming lobby in the European Union. However that may be, all the Member States except Greece, Luxembourg, Finland and Sweden have taken advantage of this opt-out clause.

Pending reform, the game and agricultural products exemption ends when these goods undergo an industrial process. This expression is not defined, although s. 1(2)(c) indicates that the process must be one which affects the 'essential characteristics' of the goods. Thus packing, canning, cutting, freezing and cooking would be industrial processes, but presumably spraying or washing would not be.

While the exemption applies, its effects might be as follows. Suppose, for example, a consumer bought a few loose apples from a greengrocer, and then became ill after eating them because the grower had treated them with a harmful pesticide. Because of the exemption the consumer would not have a strict liability claim against the grower. But the consumer might be able to sue the grower for negligence, if he or she could show that the grower knew or should have known the pesticide was harmful (which would seem very unlikely). Alternatively or additionally, the consumer might sue the manufacturers of the pesticide, either for negligence or, since the exemption would not apply here, on the basis of strict liability under the Act. A claim might also be made against the greengrocer. This would be for breach of the Sale of Goods Act requirement that the apples be reasonably fit and of satisfactory quality; a relatively straightforward claim in which the question of the greengrocer's negligence or otherwise would not arise. But if the consumer who ate the apples was not the person who bought them, he or she as a non-contracting party would have no claim under the Sale of Goods Act. Any claim against the greengrocer would therefore require proof of negligence, which again would seem unlikely in this situation. The consumer would, however, have the same rights as above to sue the grower or the manufacturers of the pesticide.

6.4 PRODUCERS AND SUPPLIERS

The next definition is that of 'producer'. Usually that person is the manufacturer of the product, but the definition goes further. The producer may also be the person who 'won or abstracted' products which are not manufactured, such as raw materials, or, for products neither manufactured, won or abstracted, the person who carried out the industrial or other process which gave them their 'essential characteristics' (as in the example above, the person who packaged the goods). We note that someone who merely supplies a product containing other component products is not for that reason alone the supplier of the components: s. 1(3). This rule is important in limiting liabilities which suppliers might otherwise incur under s. 2(3), below.

6.5 THE BASIC RULE

Section 2(1) states very briefly the rule which is the fundamental reform brought about by the Consumer Protection Act. We discuss the details below. The basic rule is that where any damage is wholly or partly caused by a defect in a product, which it is for the injured party to prove, any of the following parties may be liable: (i) the producer, as just defined; (ii) anyone holding himself out as producer by putting his name or trade mark on the goods (the 'own-brander'); or (iii) anyone who has imported the product into the European Union from a country outside the Union in order to supply it in the course of his business to another person: s. 2(2).

If the injured person finds it difficult to trace any of these three parties, as may often happen, he or she may benefit by the alternative provided by s. 2(3). This holds anyone further down the chain of supply of the product – perhaps even a street-corner shopkeeper – liable for the injury if the injured party asks him for the name of his supplier and he fails to give it. Such request must be made within a reasonable time after the injury and in circumstances where it is not reasonably practicable for the injured party to identify the producer or importer. The rule is clearly one of last resort for the injured person, but makes it important for all suppliers, particularly of goods supplied in bulk from several sources, to record batch numbers and the like. In hire purchase transactions the supplier in question is the dealer, not the finance house.

These various rules give injured parties a choice of defendants. They may sue, for example, the maker of the defective car, or the maker of the component which made it defective, or, to be on the safe side, both. If both are liable, each is liable to the full extent of the claim: s. 2(5). They will then sort out between themselves what share of the losses each will bear, usually in accordance with their contract. This rule of 'joint and several' liability overcomes the problem illustrated by *Taylor* v *Rover Co.*, para. 5.16.

Section 2(6) notes that the new rule of strict liability does not affect existing legal rights. As we have seen, an injured buyer might still for reasons of convenience prefer to pursue a claim in contract against his seller, while non-contractual claims requiring proof of negligence might still be useful in the many situations not covered by the Act, as, for example, in cases like *Goodchild* v *Vaclight*, para. 5.17.

We return to the basic rule in s. 2(1) and its consequences. The essence of the rule is that it makes the producer, or the other possible defendants, liable for injury *without proof of fault* against him or them. The result is that the plaintiff need prove only cause and effect; that his or her injury was wholly or partly caused by a defective product. He or she is no longer obliged to show that the producer was negligent in failing to foresee or reasonably to guard against the injury. As it stands, the new rule represents a great step forward in both the development of plaintiffs' rights and the simplification of the law. Many problems remain, of course; problems as to interpretation and application. In practice it is always doubtful whether rights can be converted into remedies. There may be other and preferable ways of solving personal injury disputes. But in terms of legal principle, the Consumer Protection Act must be recognised as a major reform.

6.6 DEFECT AND DAMAGE

The next step is to say more precisely what s. 2(1) means by the key words 'defect' and 'damage'. These words are defined in ss. 3 and 5 respectively. Section 3 holds a product defective 'if the safety of the product is not such as persons generally are entitled to expect'. This safety require- ment extends to component parts of the product and to risks of damage to property as well as personal injury, but not to pure economic loss. The section says that what persons generally are entitled to expect depends on all the circumstances of the case, including the way the product has been marketed, its uses, 'get-up', instructions or warnings, and what might reasonably be expected to be done with or to the product. The time when the producer supplied it is important. If a safer version subsequently comes onto the market, that of itself does not prove the original product defective.

Producers and consumers alike may find the standard of 'general expec- tation' somewhat vague and unhelpful. The difficulties of interpretation are undeniable, but it is obviously impossible to lay down safety standards which would be equally clear to everybody and equally applicable to every product from aeroplanes to aspirins. The best the law can do is usually to put forward a very general rule, which can then be backed up by other more detailed regulations for specific kinds of dangerous products. Some of these may be rules of civil law – to help those already injured; others may be criminal – to seek to prevent further injuries. Our concern with this part of the Consumer Protection Act is with the civil law, while the relevant rules of the criminal law are noted in Chapter 8.

General rules of law can be understood and explained only in the light of particular cases. We see in Chapter 7, for example, that many American judges have sought to resolve the issues raised by their own product liability rules by applying 'cost–benefit' or 'risk–utility' tests. They try to decide liability by asking whether the social benefit of a product outweighs the risk of injury it creates. But how can the convenience of cars be measured against the casualties they cause, or the benefits of life-saving drugs be set against their sometimes disastrous side-effects? In reality, 'social benefit' is not a test or yardstick, but merely a line of argument or matter of opinion – one among many.

6.7 THE STANDARD OF SAFETY

The same kind of questions, of course, arise under the 'expectation' test in the Consumer Protection Act. We cannot reasonably expect drugs not to have any harmful side effects, whether or not we are warned of them, but what sort or extent of adverse reaction must we be prepared to accept? Patients and doctors and manufacturers may well disagree over the acceptability of what might be called 'relatively minor' reactions. Again, we cannot and do not expect mechanical products never to fail or wear out, but it is extremely difficult to say what 'tolerance' we should afford them. If a car component fails within a year or two of purchase and so causes an accident, does the consumer have to accept that perfection is not required and that failure is inevitable at some point, or will it be said that the product must have been defective? Sadly, there is no means of knowing. The parties can be reasonably confident that each case will be decided on its own merits, but that is no great consolation to an injured plaintiff who is finally left without redress.

In the end, only a judge can say what the safety standard in s. 2 (1) means and how it applies in any given case. It is his responsibility to weigh the evidence and balance the arguments put before him. He is no longer concerned with the producer's negligence as such, but will be guided, as the Act tells us, by the way the product is presented, and by its packaging and any accompanying instructions and warnings. He may have to decide very technical questions, such as whether the danger was inherent and inevitable, or could have been 'designed out'. He will not be concerned with what the consumer in the case knew about the product, so much as with what he or she should have known, nor with whether he or she read or understood the instructions but more probably with whether he or she should have done so (see para. 5.13). Ultimately, much will depend on the judge's own understanding of the common knowledge of the use, abuse, and dangers of the product in question.

Putting it briefly, the judge's task is essentially to decide what is reasonable in the circumstances – and that is in fact the crux of the matter. Contrary to the fears of many producers, and perhaps the hopes of some consumers, ending the test of negligence does not mean imposition of a guarantee of safety. Goods need not be and cannot be incapable of causing injury. For better or worse, all that the Act requires is that *goods must be reasonably safe in normal use*. They must meet the normal or typical or average standard of safety. In the absence so far of any major UK cases under the Act, readers may find most helpful the American examples discussed in Chapter 7.

6.8 DEFENCES: THE STATE OF THE ART

We have now established that if goods cause injury because they are not reasonably safe, the producer – or own-brander or importer – is liable without proof of fault. But that general principle is subject to a number of escape clauses, most of which, we might say, are necessary and obvious exceptions to the rule and do not seem to require any further comment.

Thus, section 4(1) says producers are not liable if they can prove any of the following. The first defence, in s. 4(1)(a), arises on proof that the defect in the product was brought about by compliance with other requirements of British or EU law. Under s. 4(1)(b) it is a defence that the defendant himself did not supply the goods, or (c) that he did not supply in the course of his business and was not a 'producer', or (d) that the defect did not exist at the time of supply. It is therefore a good defence to show the defect was caused by subsequent wear and tear in the user's hands, or by someone else's repairs.

Much more controversial, however, is the defence offered by s. 4(1)(e) – that at the time the producer supplied the goods the state of scientific or technical knowledge was not such that he or another producer of such goods might be expected to have discovered the defect if it was in fact present in goods under his control. This provision is variously known as the 'state of the art' or 'development risk' defence. If there is a difference, the state of the art signifies that the product was made in accordance with the latest safety data, while development risk recognises that the danger was unknown at the time.

Whichever way one might put it, this defence is a major inroad into the principle of strict liability (and one which is not available to professional sellers sued under the Sale of Goods Act). Those who framed the Product Liability Directive in its original form – and many supporters such as the UK Consumers' Association – were very much opposed to its inclusion. As the Royal Commission Report on Civil Liability and Personal Injury (the Pearson Report) said in 1973: 'to exclude developmental risks from a regime of strict liability would be to leave a gap in the compensation cover through which, for example, the victims of another Thalidomide disaster might easily slip'. Against this was the view of most of British industry, strongly supported by Mrs Thatcher's government, that if a new product unexpectedly caused injury it was unjust to hold a manufacturer liable when he had observed the highest known safety standards, and more generally that imposing liability in these circumstances penalised and inhibited research and innovation. This view perhaps indicated a basic ignorance of the law, since as we have seen, para. 3.17, it has always been possible to pass the strict contractual liability of business sellers on to manufacturers, albeit only after prolonged and expensive and unnecessary litigation. The objections to strict liability without a state of the art defence were not, of course, confined to British industry and the British government, but certainly Britain was a main opponent of the proposed reform. In the event the opposition was successful (leaving British consumers somewhat worse off than their counterparts in Germany, where drug manufacturers have been under a form of strict liability since 1978). The state of the art defence was included in the final form of the Product Liability Directive as an option – which all EU countries except Luxembourg and Finland have taken up.

Even after the Consumer Protection Act was passed, doubts remained as to the precise effect of the state of the art defence in the UK, because the wording of the section was not the same as that of the Directive. The producer escapes liability under the Act when he *might not* be expected to have known of the danger, whereas the Directive says he can escape liability only if he *could not* have known. There is surely a fundamental difference between these two propositions. The Act also asks what other producers of such goods knew or might have known at the time – inevitably a very difficult line of inquiry for the injured plaintiff, and one which does not appear at all in the Directive.

These doubts eventually led the EU Commission to take Britain to the European Court of Justice, on the ground that Britain had failed properly to transpose the Directive into its own legal system. Somewhat surprisingly, the Court held in *Commission of the European Communities* v *UK*, 1997, that the Act did comply with the Directive. Its main reason was that any difficulties in interpretation or application were resolved by s. 1(1), which, as we noted, states that the Act must be interpreted so as to fulfil the terms of the Directive. The contradictions between the two might still make this rather easier said than done.

The remaining defence is in s. 4(1)(f). This says that producers of component parts are not liable if their products fail *only* because of the nature or purpose or design or construction of the 'subject product' of which they become part. Component producers are not to be blamed, in other words, for parts which are in themselves safe, but become unsafe because of the requirements of subsequent producers.

With the possible exception, then, of the state of the art defence, these various defences in s. 4 appear reasonably clear and non-controversial. But all of them represent an important principle, which is that if a producer hopes to escape liability for injury caused by his product, the onus is on him to *disprove* responsibility. Section 2, it may be recalled, presumes that he is to blame. Even if it achieves nothing else, therefore, the Act greatly reduces the plaintif's burden.

6.9   DAMAGE TO PROPERTY

Section 5 tells us what kind of 'damage' producers may have to pay for under the general rule in s. 2. The main concern of the Act is to ensure compensation for death or personal injury, but within certain limits producers may also be liable for loss of or damage to property, including land. By s. 5(2) they are not liable for defects which damage or destroy either the products themselves (e.g. faulty wiring which destroys electrical equipment), or products supplied with and incorporating their products. So, for example, if a person bought a car fitted with a defective tyre, which later burst and caused an accident in which the car was damaged, the tyre manufacturer would not be liable under the Act either for the damage to the tyre or to the car. Strangely enough, however, liability could be imposed if the tyre had been bought as a new replacement. This distinction illustrates the great difficulty faced by the Commission in drafting the Directive and deciding whether producers should be liable at all for damage to property, and, if so, how far.

If the defective product does in fact damage or destroy property other than itself or its containers, as in the new tyre example above, the producer's liability depends on whether that property is for domestic or commercial use. He is not obliged to pay for damage to commercial property, but may have to compensate for loss of or damage to property normally intended for private use or consumption, and intended for that purpose by the person suffering the loss (who need not be the owner). Some difficult border-line cases may arise here, particularly with regard to computer and other home-office equipment. Liability for damage to domestic property only arises, however, when the cost of replacement or repair is more than £275: s. 5(4). This apparently arbitrary figure is the equivalent of the figure of 500 ecus (or euros) laid down by the Directive. It can be increased by government order to keep pace with inflation. We note in passing here a minor problem of translation from the Directive: certain EU countries have understood the rule to mean that consumers must always bear the first 500 ecus' loss themselves. Claims for compensation for damage to property must be made within three years of the earliest time at which the plaintiff knew or should have known of his or her right to claim.

6.10   CONTRIBUTORY NEGLIGENCE

Section 6 of the Consumer Protection Act explains how the Act relates to various other statutes concerned with personal injury litigation. From the point of view of both production managers and consumers, probably the most important provisions are those in ss. 6(4) and 6(6). The first of these says that claims are subject to the rules of contributory negligence (para. 5.18). These rules may seem inappropriate in the context of liability without fault, but nonetheless their effect is that a plaintiff may lose part or all of his or her claim because of his or her careless or reckless use of the product. The fact that the producer's liability may be reduced or ended in this way reinforces the point made earlier, that strict liability is by no means the same as absolute liability.

As we saw in s. 3, however, one of the tests of the defectiveness or otherwise of a product is 'what might reasonably be expected to be done' to or with it. As in negligence cases, therefore (para. 5.5), the judge has to consider whether the producer took adequate precautions not only against the risks of normal use but also against foreseeable *misuse* of the product. It should follow that the producer's liability will not be greatly affected where injury is caused by predictable error or folly, but will be very much reduced or ended altogether where consumers injure themselves by more extreme or bizarre uses of the product. It is all a question of degree.

6.11   TIME LIMITS

Section 6(6), taken together with Schedule 1 of the Act, imposes time limits on plaintiffs' claims for breach of the Act. Claims must be begun within three years of the time the plaintiff first knew or should have known he or she had a right to claim, and in any case within 10 years from the time the producer first commercially supplied the actual product which caused the injury. If the producer (as defined in s. 2(2) above) cannot be identified, so that a middleman becomes liable as provided by s. 2(3), then the 10 years run for him from the last time he was supplied by the producer.

The 10 year cut-off does not, of course, imply that any or every product should last for at least 10 years. The rule represents a compromise between the interests of producers and consumers – which may not wholly satisfy either side. On the one hand it could be said to be unfair to producers to have the fear of liability hanging over them indefinitely, while on the other they must accept that their products may remain, and perhaps be intended to remain, in circulation for many years. A product's full potential for harm may not appear until very much later still, as is all too clear from the many products subsequently found to be carcinogenic. If a claim under the Act becomes barred by the 10 year rule, a plaintiff may still have the right to sue for negligence under the limitation rules noted in para. 4.9.

The Directive allows Member States to limit liability for any one product to 70 million ecus. Greece, Germany and Portugal have adopted this limit.

6.12 EXCLUSION CLAUSES

The few remaining rules of Part I of the Consumer Protection Act can be dealt with very briefly. Section 7 forbids any attempt by a producer or supplier to avoid liability under the Act by the terms of his contract, or by a notice, or in any other way. This specific prohibition is in addition to the more general rules on exclusion clauses described in Chapter 2. A possible problem with regard to s. 7 is that of distinguishing between exclusion clauses as such and instructions as to use, including warnings. A clear instruction or warning such as 'Danger: do not use for . . .' could have the same effect as an exclusion clause, but it would seem wrong to invalidate it for that reason.

Section 8 permits modifications of the Act if required by any amendment to the original Directive. Section 9 ensures that the Crown, in its various capacities as producer or supplier, is bound by the Act.

6.13 CONCLUSIONS

Having now examined the crucial principles of the new law of product liability, what conclusions might we draw?

We should perhaps note first the effect of the line drawn by the Act between goods and services. Injuries caused in defective goods are regulated by a regime of strict liability. Remedies for injuries caused by defective services depend on proof of negligence. Is there any rational justification for such different treatment? Undeniably there are differences in terms of the tangibility of the end product, and in the nature and feasibility of precautions, for example in medical services. From the injured consumer's point of view, however, the law's entirely different approaches to the two issues might well appear quite arbitrary and indefensible. Suggestions of strict liability for services were in fact made in EU circles some years ago, but were not well received. In 1991 a draft Directive on liability for defective services went no further than to reverse the burden of proof of fault. This in turn was abandoned in the face of considerable opposition, and there the matter rests.

As regards goods, the Directive did not quite achieve its object of harmonising the law of the Member States of the European Union. It allowed variations in responsibility for agricultural products (s. 2) and a ceiling on damages (s. 5). Different countries have different rules as to the assessment of damages. The rights of buyers against sellers under contracts of sale are not affected by the Directive, and so may still differ to some extent between one EU country and the next, for example as regards proof of fault in claims for damages, and ancillary matters such as time limits. Overall, however, there is no doubt that within its limits the Directive has brought the law of EU countries and neighbouring countries, including Norway, Switzerland and Hungary, very much into line. Several others, much more distant, have followed closely, as we see in the next chapter.

In retrospect it may seem quite difficult to understand why product liability reform was thought so controversial, and why it was resisted for so long. Probably the explanation lay in fears of the unknown, of a tidal wave of litigation, or, more specifically, of some of the more extreme and well publicised consequences of American product liability law. We note in the next chapter some of the characteristics of American law which (fortunately) do not appear in the English system. Their absence may help to explain why producers' fears have proved unfounded. Fears of prohibitive insurance premiums have also proved unfounded. To the best of the writer's knowledge, supported by research, there is no evidence of any significant increase either in claims or in insurance costs arising under the Consumer Protection Act. We might in any case suppose that if a company found itself unable to obtain or to afford insurance cover, it would probably hesitate to market an untried high-risk product, even though there is no obligation to insure. If that were so, it would seem that the law had achieved a substantial public benefit.

One final reflection, perhaps a little surprising at this stage, is that the reform we have described is not necessarily the best or only answer to the problem in hand. Many injuries will still go without redress. Claims against producers are easier than they were, but still useless if the producers are 'men of straw', without the resources to meet such claims. Compensation may still be reduced or denied because of contributory negligence, although the plaintiff's needs are no less. The dividing line between strict and absolute liability remains, as consumers may find to their cost. Litigation will not stop, but for many people legal proceedings are an expensive and protracted ordeal. Can we not then find a way of helping the injured, not only consumers injured by defective goods but the countless thousands of others injured in the normal course of modern life on the roads, at work and elsewhere, without subjecting them to this distressing and often quite futile experience? Can we not devise a system which is fair also to the manufacturers upon whom much of our prosperity depends? Readers might consider, for example, the merits of the New Zealand system, described at the end of the next chapter.

6.14 SUMMARY

A person injured by a defective product may now be able to claim damages under one or more of three overlapping but separate and distinct sets of legal rights. Each set of rules has its own requirements as to the standard of proof, and its own limited application. The first rights arise where the injured person has bought the goods from a business seller. He or she may then have a claim for damages for breach of contract against the seller. As explained in Chapter 3, the seller's liability under the Sale of Goods Act is not to ensure the complete safety of the goods in all circumstances, but in effect to guarantee that they are *reasonably* safe. If he fails, he is liable without proof of personal fault. Such liability extends only to the buyer, not to any other person injured by the use of the goods.

The second possibility of redress arises where there is no contract of sale between the parties. An injured person may have a claim against anyone in the chain of supply – whether designer, producer, distributor or seller – if he or she can prove that that party's negligence caused the injury. We discuss what is meant by negligence in Chapter 5. Claims under contract or for negligence proved equally inadequate to meet the needs of injured consumers in the light of the drug tragedies of the 1960s. Following the European Commission's Product Liability Directive in 1985, the Consumer Protection Act of 1987 provides a third line of recourse, applicable to injuries caused by defective goods, but not by services, nor to injuries caused in any other circumstances. This chapter examines the details of that Act. A claim under the Act lies against the 'producer', as defined in the Act, if the injured person can show that his or her injury was caused because the goods were not reasonably safe. The producer's liability in that event does not depend on proof of personal fault. But pending the proposed reform no liability arises in relation to untreated agricultural produce; nor in any case where the danger could not have been anticipated, and liability may be reduced or ended by the user's own contributory negligence.

An injured person is not bound to succeed under any of these headings, however serious his or her injuries. Even if the claim is successful it may be only after years of expensive and traumatic litigation. Some form of insurance system might be thought more efficient and economical and less arbitrary in operation.

7 Product liability in America, the EU and other countries

7.1 AMERICAN LEGAL PROCEDURES

It is hoped that this chapter may help manufacturers and their agents exporting goods to North America to understand the basic principles of law they have to contend with there. The American experience is also of more general interest and importance. It offers guidance on a wide range of problems likely to arise under the broadly similar product liability regime which is now part of UK law.

We should note at the outset that there is not one system of law in America, but one for each State. While this survey sets out as 'American law' various generally accepted statements of principle, the possibility of significant variations from one State to another should therefore be borne in mind. But the Model Uniform Product Liability Act 1979, a Federal measure, has led to various statutory developments in individual states which have increased uniformity of practice, and helped to some extent to restrain some of the excesses of the system.

We should also remember there are many fundamental differences in legal procedure as between Britain and America; differences which may in part explain aspects of the American system probably quite unacceptable in Britain. These differences remain crucial in the operation of the law in the two countries, even though the rules of law themselves are now more directly comparable.

Perhaps the most important distinction between American and British civil trial procedures is that in America the major cases are still tried by juries. Juries are naturally very sympathetically inclined towards sick or injured plaintiffs appearing before them in claims against 'big business'. They are anxious to ensure that accident victims are compensated, and so may hold manufacturers – or, it seems, almost anyone else with a 'deep pocket' – liable without any great regard for the judge's detailed directions as to the law. They have no experience of determining the appropriate sum of damages and make awards which may be both excessively generous and wildly variable. Juries' awards may be appealed against, if they appear grossly disproportionate, but it is far from clear what that might mean in the American context. Awards may in any case be enormously increased by punitive damages if the manufacturer appears to the jury to have behaved particularly irresponsibly or discreditably. The practical problem then arises that insurance companies may refuse to cover punitive damages. The many millions of dollars awarded by way of compensation and punishment have resulted in prohibitive legal and insurance costs, inevitably reflected in the prices paid by end-users, and sometimes in bankruptcy and failure to compensate at all.

Another major factor is that the American jury is aware of the contingent fee system, under which the plaintiff's lawyer agrees to act without payment if the claim is lost, but to take perhaps a quarter or a third of the damages if successful. The jury increases its award accordingly to ensure that the plaintiff receives at least some of the benefit.

These factors play little or no part in the administration of justice in the UK. Juries are hardly ever used in civil proceedings. British judges adhere rigorously to the rules of law, and if they find in a plaintiff's favour will award damages within fairly well-defined limits. Their awards are incomparably more modest than those apparently normal in America, and exclude any punitive element. Finally, we have no contingent fee system, although plaintiffs may now have to accept the controversial conditional fee system. This method of funding claims allows the lawyer to increase his or her fee by up to double the usual amount if the case succeeds – but he or she receives nothing if it fails. It follows that the British response to product liability law reform should not be dictated by fear of the consequences we see in America.

7.2 THE BASIC PRINCIPLES OF MANUFACTURERS' LIABILITY

With these reservations and qualifications in mind, we look now at the basic principles of American product liability law. They are currently to be found in para. 402A and B of the second Restatement of Torts, an authoritative review of the findings of the courts published by the American Law

Institute in 1965. Headed 'Special Liability of Seller of Product for Physical Harm to User or Consumer', para. 402A declares:

> One who sells any product in a defective condition unreasonably dangerous to the user or consumer or to his property is subject to liability for physical harm thereby caused to the ultimate user or consumer, if (a) the seller is engaged in the business of selling such a product, and (b) it is expected to and does reach the user or consumer without substantial change in the condition in which it is sold. The rule ... applies although (a) the seller has exercised all possible care in the preparation and sale of his product and (b) the user or consumer has not bought the product from or entered into any contractual relations with the seller.

The principles stated in 1965 in para. 402A were little short of revolutionary in the common law world, applying as they did the familiar concept of strict liability in contract in situations which previously required proof of negligence. These rules have been the subject of countless cases in the American courts. Not all of the courts' conclusions have been equally satisfactory or desirable, whether in legal, economic or social terms. There has been much criticism of the law and many calls for reform at both State and Federal level; largely blocked so far because of the complexity of the issues and powerful vested interests. The American Law Institute is currently engaged in drafting a third Restatement of Tort, which may solve some of the problems considered below[1].

The practical effect of para. 402A as it stands at the moment is to make negligence almost – but not completely – irrelevant. It seems that negligence issues may still be involved as regards issues of defective design, inadequate warnings and dangerous drugs, but otherwise the plaintiff in America need prove only that the goods which injured him or her were not reasonably safe, that is that they fell below the normal expectation of their performance.

The Restatement's commentary on para. 402A explains the rule as follows: 'The article sold must be dangerous to an extent beyond that which would be contemplated by the ordinary consumer who purchases, with the ordinary knowledge common to the community as to its characteristics.' Many cases have sought to rephrase or adapt this test to resolve the questions it raises. An example is *Bacceleri* v *Hipter*, 1979: 'The test for determining when a product has an unreasonably dangerous defect is whether a reasonable person would be negligent if he sold the product knowing of the risk involved.' Other cases again emphasise the need to balance the possible benefits of the product against its possible harm – the cost/benefit or risk/utility analysis: *Barker* v *Lill*, 1978; *Feldman* v *Lederle Laboratories*, 1985. Such analysis is as we said earlier essentially a matter of opinion, but the court is perhaps as good a place as any for establishing the facts on which to reach an informed opinion.

7.3 UNNECESSARY DANGER

At all events, the position is broadly that if the plaintiff can show on the balance of probabilities that he or she has been injured by an unexpected or unnecessary danger in a product, the manufacturer is liable because and insofar as he has not taken the precautions necessary to avoid it. As a general proposition, what the manufacturer knew or ought to have known about the likelihood or remoteness of risk 'is of no moment': *Jackson* v *West Coast Paint*, 1974. Compliance or otherwise with 'state of the art' requirements has been said to be 'irrelevant' – *Gelsomino* v *Bliss*, 1973 – though as we shall see that is not so in every case.

Thus in *Elmore* v *American Motors*, 1969, a case involving a car crash thought to have been caused either by loose fastenings on the driving shaft or by metal fatigue, the court made no attempt to find which if either explanation was correct but stated simply that those 'engaged in the business of distributing automobiles to the public (are) strictly liable in tort for personal injuries caused by defects in cars sold by (them)', and so held both manufacturer and retailer liable. Where there are several possible causes of an accident, liability can be founded on any one of them which is sufficiently substantial: *Mavroudis* v *Pittsburgh Corning*, 1997. English courts in contrast seem firmly to have decided that it is no part of their duty to speculate as to the cause of an injury and that unless the *res ipsa loquitur* rule (para. 5.3) applies the plaintiff's claim must be rejected if he cannot prove how his accident happened: *Sumner* v *Henderson*, 1963. It is not clear how English judges might have decided *Elmore*, where one explanation for the crash, loose fastenings, was consistent with negligence, and the other, metal fatigue, probably not so.

Similarly in *Goodrich* v *Hammond*, 1959, manufacturers of 'blow-out proof' tyres were held liable without the plaintiff having to prove how or why the tyre burst. The manufacturer was also held responsible in *Henningsen* v *Bloomfield Motors*, 1960, where a new vehicle suddenly ran off the road and was so badly damaged that it was impossible to discover why it had done so. This kind of difficulty may often arise in serious accidents, but American courts are sometimes willing to say that the explanation must be that 'something was wrong', which in turn could only be the producer's fault: *Scanlon* v *General Motors*, 1974.

7.4 DESIGN PROBLEMS

The very strict standard of liability applicable to manufacturing faults seems not to apply in cases of design defects. The standard here is more clearly one of foreseeability of harm, much as in cases of negligence. In the draft third Restatement, liability is imposed where 'the foreseeable risk of harm posed by the product could have been reduced or avoided by the adoption of a reasonable alternative design . . . and the omission of the alternative design renders the product not reasonably safe.' The effects of these requirements in any given case depend upon the nature of the product, the possible nature and extent of the danger, costs and effects of modifications, etc. as we saw in *Turner* v *General Motors*, 1974 (para. 5.5). Opinions differ from one State to the next as to whether a plaintiff must prove the feasibility of an alternative design or the defendant must prove that the plaintiff's suggestions are not feasible[2].

7.5 WARNINGS

In the many cases where a product's dangers are inherent and irreducible, the manufacturer's liability may well turn on the presence or absence of warnings or instructions accompanying his product. One might think that manufacturers could not warn of dangers unless they knew of them, but that was not the view taken in *Beshada* v *Johns*, 1982. The defendants were held strictly liable here for failing to warn of the dangers of asbestos, even though no one knew of the dangers at the time the product was marketed. The reasoning in this case was subsequently confined to its own facts: *Feldman*, above. The result is again that disputes over warnings or their absence tend to be decided according to the standards used in negligence cases.

A manufacturer who becomes aware of a danger only after he has put his product on the market may have to try to notify users, if the risk of harm justifies such action: *Walton* v *Avco Corp.*, 1993. In *Kozlowski* v *Smith*, 1979, an exceptional case, the duty was found to subsist up to 30 years after marketing. This possible post-sale liability is bound up with the extent of a manufacturer's duty to test or monitor his products after selling them. The duty was explained in *Kociemba* v *Searle*, 1989:

> Limiting the continuing duty to test to cases where the manufacturer has knowledge of problems with a product alleviates defendant's concern that this duty will impose a crushing burden on manufacturers to retest products. If a manufacturer has no information concerning potential dangers associated with

147

a product, it will be under no duty to continually test the product. Conversely, if a manufacturer does obtain sufficient, credible information that a product already in use is potentially dangerous, the manufacturer should test that product to determine the extent of any danger, and then issue an appropriate warning or product recall.

Post-sale knowledge of a previously unknown danger is a different issue from that of the development of new safety equipment. There is usually no duty to recall products which were safe at the time of sale, by the standards of that time, in order to fit newly invented safety devices: *Gregory* v *Cincinnati Inc.*, 1995. Any other answer would penalise innovation. There may not necessarily be a duty to recall even where the product was defective at the time of sale, though that is clearly a more debateable point: *Eschenburg* v *Navistar*, 1993.

If warnings are in fact necessary, they must be obvious and unambiguous. A warning in very small print of the dangers of inhaling poisonous fumes was inadequate on a Safely-Kleen product: *Maize* v *Atlantic Refining*, 1945. Advice that such fumes were 'harmful' was likewise insufficient: *Tampa Drug Co.* v *Wait*, 1958. Manufacturers must ensure that their warnings are intelligible to those most likely to use or be affected by the product, for example unskilled or foreign workers: *Hubbard-Hall Chemical Co.* v *Silverman*, 1965. Where there is a considerable risk and only limited possibility of medical intervention, producers of medical products should ensure warnings reach users as well as doctors: *MacDonald* v *Ortho*, 1985. A user who ignores a clear warning will have no claim: *Town of Bridport* v *Sterling Clark*, 1997.

7.6 MISUSE

When deciding whether to give a warning, account must be taken also of predictable misuse of the product, particularly where children may be involved: *Spruill* v *Boyle-Midway*, 1962 (para. 5.13). In *Moran* v *Faberge*, 1975, a teenager poured perfume over a lighted candle. The contents of the bottle ignited and injured another young person. The manufacturer was found at fault in not warning against flammability. To the contrary is *Landrine* v *Mego Corp.*, 1983, where a child swallowed an uninflated balloon attached to a toy. This extract from the judgment explains the distinction between the cases:

> No duty to warn exists where the intended or foreseeable use of the product is not hazardous ... Digestion of a balloon is not an intended use, and to the

extent it is a foreseeable one, it is a misuse of the product for which the guardian of children must be wary.

In *Winnett* v *Winnett*, 1974, it was held that a manufacturer could not have foreseen that a 4-year-old child would be allowed near an operating farm forage wagon.

Adults likewise are at risk from careless or stupid handling of products. In *Haberly* v *Reardon*, 1958, a painter who suffered an eye injury from drops of paint succeeded in his claim that he was not adequately warned of the dangers of the chemicals in the paint. But there are limits. In *Canifax* v *Hercules Powder*, 1965, a manufacturer of dynamite fuses escaped liability for failing to warn of the short burning time of the fuses.

The ordinary consumer is expected to have the knowledge common in society as to the qualities of the goods in question.

> For example, sugar is unwholesome to diabetics. Ice cream and butter may contain sufficient cholesterol to be unwholesome to persons with high blood pressure and heart trouble. Whiskey is unwholesome to alcoholics. Diabetics who eat sugar, heart cases who cannot resist ice cream or butter, and alcoholics who drink too much whiskey know that the strict warranty of wholesomeness puts no money in the banks for them.
>
> (*Lartigue* v *Reynolds Tobacco*, 1965)

This argument has been used in the past to defeat claims by long-term smokers against tobacco companies, but as the dangers of addiction become clearer it seems manufacturers now prefer to settle such claims.

A car manufacturer will not be blamed if his product, otherwise reasonably safe, is driven at excessive speed, nor if a tyre comes off after an exceptional impact: *Schemel* v *General Motors*, 1967; *Heaton* v *Ford Motors*, 1967. On the other hand again, if a car is meant to be driven at high speed, it may be necessary to warn against driving at speeds which make it unsafe: *Le Boeuf* v *Goodyear Tyre Co.*, 1980. In *Le Boeuf* neither the drunkenness of the driver nor the fact he was exceeding the speed limit were any defence for the manufacturer.

The probability of injury from careless or reckless use of motor vehicles has led American courts to develop the concept of 'crashworthiness'. Crashes are such likely events that whatever precautions are practicable must be taken to reduce the resulting injuries. If a collision injury can be proved to have been made worse by a design failure such as a rigid steering wheel or the absence of a roll bar, or externally mounted fuel tanks, the manufacturer's liability will be greatly increased: *Huff* v *White Motor Co.*, 1977. So far as is known, the issue of crashworthiness has not yet been discussed in English courts, but see para 5.5 for a Canadian ruling.

7.7 OBVIOUS DANGERS

It is particularly difficult to say whether or when a manufacturer will be held liable for defects or dangers which are or should be immediately obvious to the user. On the one hand a court may say that a product which is patently dangerous should not be on the market, or should not be available in that particular form, or at least without some appropriate warning. On the other hand, it may hold that the user has only himself to blame for his injuries. Cases illustrating these contrasting points of view, each decided very much on its own merits, include *Murphy* v *Cory Pump Co.*, 1964, where a child had her leg mangled by the unfenced blade of a motor mower. The court held the manufacturer not liable, since 'no one was misled by its appearance'. The blade was clearly visible, and a warning given. A different view was taken in *Wright* v *Massey Harris*, 1969. Here an adult was injured while clearing corn ears jammed in the mechanism of a self-propelled corn picker. Despite the obviousness of the danger the judge held the manufacturer liable, because the design of the machine disregarded basic safety principles. See also para 5.10.

In *Vincer* v *Williams*, 1975, the court said there was no need for a safety gate in a rail round a swimming pool – though this would have stopped a child climbing down the ladder and falling in – and in *Berry* v *Eckhardt*, 1978, a claim that collision injuries were partly due to the fact that a car seat belt warning system did not work was rejected. The user should have known that it was dangerous not to wear a seat belt.

7.8 WEAR AND TEAR

American law has long since accepted that there is 'no duty on a manufacturer to furnish a machine that will not wear out': *Auld* v *Sears Roebuck*, 1942. Despite the principle of strict liability, therefore, producers should not be liable for injuries caused by fair wear and tear of their products. But difficulty may arise in deciding whether injury was in fact caused by gradual and inevitable deterioration of the product, or by repairs, modifications or misuse, or by some original, inherent defect. The length of time between production and accident is clearly relevant, but not conclusive.

The case of *Mickle* v *Blackmon and Ford Motor Co.*, 1969, concerned a car driver who suffered additional injury in a collision through being impaled on the gear stick, whose top broke in the collision. The judge said:

> We readily concede that the passage of thirteen years between the marketing

of a product and its injury-producing failure is a formidable obstacle to fastening liability upon the manufacturers ... But the important inquiry is not how long the knob lasted but what caused its failure. Mere passage of time should not excuse Ford if its negligence was the cause ... The jury could reasonably conclude that Ford's conduct, in manufacturing a needed safety device of a material which could not tolerate a frequently encountered aspect of the environment [sunlight] ... exposed many users of its product to unreasonably great risk of harm.

In theory English law should be capable of following the same lines of inquiry, but in practice it has been argued that the passage of time alone was sufficient to preclude any further investigation: *Evans* v *Triplex*, 1936.

7.9 DRUGS

Perhaps the single most vexed issue with regard to product liability is the way it might affect the manufacturers of drugs. As to new drugs in particular, the official commentary on para. 402A provides a partial exception to the rule by emphasising the risk/benefit test. So,

with the qualification that [the drugs] are properly prepared and marketed, and proper warning is given where the situation calls for it, [the supplier] is not to be held to strict liability for unfortunate consequences attending their use merely because he has undertaken to supply the public with an apparently useful and desirable product, attended with a known but apparently reasonable risk.

In practice therefore liability in many American drug cases has turned on the adequacy of testing, warnings, and the probability of injury, much in accordance with current English concepts of negligence. Blood and blood products are similarly treated[3].

7.10 SELLERS' LIABILITIES

Upon whom then should the burden of strict liability fall? Para. 402A refers to 'seller's' liabilities, but the courts say this expression is 'merely descriptive'. In theory at least anyone engaged in the production or distribution of goods may be held responsible for them. In practice, of course, most claims are made against manufacturers. The choice of defendant rests with the injured party, and seems to depend largely on questions of his 'reasonable availability', proximity, resources and the like: *Vandermark* v *Ford*, 1964. The courts may also take account of the relative blameworthiness of manufacturer and retailer, but there is as yet no express rule to that effect. The proposed Uniform Product Liability Act, however, sees strict liability as essentially a manufacturer's burden and holds that in the absence of contract retail sellers should be liable only for negligence, as under English law. This would almost certainly be the only basis on which sellers of used goods could be held liable: *Tillman* v *Vance*, 1979.

American courts are concerned to see that somewhere along the line there should be a defendant to answer an injured party's claim. Present freedom of choice has been justified on the grounds that: 'Strict liability on manufacturer and retailer alike affords maximum protection to the injured plaintiff and works no injustice to the defendants for they can adjust the cost of such protection between them in the course of their continuing relationship': *Vandermark*, above. On the same argument a manufacturer may be held liable for injuries caused by defective parts supplied by his sub-contractor, even though the defects could not have been discovered by any reasonable test or inspection by the manufacturer. This conclusion, as illustrated in *Ford* v *Mathis*, 1963, has now been adopted in the UK by the Consumer Protection Act.

7.11 SUCCESSOR LIABILITY

A further possible liability is that of the 'successor corporation'. As explained by the American Law Institute's report in 1996, where one business takes over another it may find itself held responsible by law for its predecessor's defective products. This position is justified by the courts in certain States by reference merely to the acquisition of the predecessor's goodwill and continuity of the product line or business – unless the interval between production and injury is so long as to absolve the new company from liability: *Ray* v *Alad*, 1977. In most States, however, successor corporation liability is imposed only exceptionally: *Chemical Design* v *American Standard*, 1993. Exceptions arise where the new company contracts to cover its predecessor's liabilities, or takes over all or most of its predecessor's assets, so depriving a plaintiff of any means of redress, or where there is fraud. The possibility of fraud is illustrated by *Schmoll* v *AC and S Inc.*, 1988, where the company was restructured in order to avoid otherwise inevitable liability to asbestos victims. An agreement to repair or service a predecessor's goods does not of itself lead to successor liability.

7.12   MARKET SHARE LIABILITY

Yet another principle of American case law so far without parallel in England is that of 'market share liability' – devised to meet the hardship of plaintiffs unable to identify the producers responsible for their injuries, for example because they were injured in the womb by drugs taken by their mothers to avoid miscarriages. The Supreme Court of California permitted such a plaintiff in *Sindell* v *Abbott*, 1980, to sue a group of independent drug manufacturers who between them controlled most of the relevant market. Each producer then had to pay a part of the award equivalent to his market share unless he could prove he had not made the drug which caused the injury. In *Sheffield* v *Ely Lilley*, 1983, it was held that this doctrine, which perhaps unduly favours those who cannot identify defendants against those who can, applied only to inherently defective drugs and not those negligently manufactured, and only where passage of time made identification impossible. The market share principle has not been widely adopted, though it was applied in *Smith* v *Cutter Biologicals*, 1992, a case on contaminated blood products.

7.13   SERVICES

Strict liability may extend beyond goods to services and land, as in *Schipper* v *Levitt*, 1965, where a mass developer of houses was held strictly liable for defective workmanship. The court said: 'An entrepreneur in the mass housing business should be subject to the same legal responsibility as a manufacturer or supplier of chattels.' It has subsequently been held that there is no significant difference between a builder developer and a builder contractor: *Moxley* v *Laramie Builders*, 1980.

But other professional services may be treated differently. The need for strict liability is not so great where there is no mass production of goods nor usually any great difficulty in tracing a defendant: *La Rossa* v *Scientific Design*, 1968. Medical services in particular have largely escaped strict liability, as for example, in *Magrine* v *Spector*, 1970; *Murphy* v *Squibb*, 1985. Basically it is a question of cost benefit again. In *Fluor* v *Jeppesen*, 1985, strict liability was imposed on the producers of an incorrect air navigation chart in view of the disastrous consequences[4].

7.14 ECONOMIC LOSS

A further – though remote – possibility under the American system is that of ordering compensation for purely economic loss. The references in para. 402A to 'personal injury' and 'physical harm', including under para. 402A damage to property, suggest, of course, that economic losses as such can not be compensated in this way. That is certainly the general rule of English law: para. 5.18.

There are, however, one or two American cases where 'physical harm' has been interpreted to include loss of use of property, without any pre-requisite of harm to the person. On this basis courts have held manufacturers liable for the cost of replacing or repairing defective or useless parts. The most important case is that of *Santor* v *Karagheusian*, 1965. Here the problem concerned a carpet sold in accordance with the manufacturer's representation as grade 1 but which through the manufacturing process had developed a fault making it worth considerably less. The retailer refused to put the matter right, and eventually went out of business in that State. The buyer then sued the manufacturer. The judge could have reached his decision in the buyer's favour by reference to the warranty rule in para. 402B, below, but chose instead to rely on the non-contractual elements of strict liability.

> From the standpoint of principle we perceive no sound reason why the implication of reasonable fitness should be ... actionable against the manufacturer where the defectively made product has caused personal injury, and not actionable when inadequate manufacture has put a worthless article in the hands of an innocent purchaser who has paid the required price for it ... If the article is defective and the defect is chargeable to the manufacturer, his must be the responsibility for the consequent damage or injury.

The damages were assessed at the difference between the retail price and actual value of the carpet, that is the loss of a bargain.

For the most part, however, the courts see damage to the product itself and resulting purely economic loss as questions of contractual rights. In *Seely* v *White Motor Co.*, 1965, for instance, a trader lost business when his truck was damaged because of a defective brake. His claim against the manufacturer of the brake was rejected; first, since he had not suffered any physical injury, and, second, because he had no contract with the manufacturer. Similar rulings have been given in other leading cases such as *East River Corp* v *Transamerica Delaval Inc.*, 1986, and *Bocie Leasing* v *General Motors*, 1995. In *Bocie* a helicopter was wrecked because of a defective engine. The owner sued the manufacturer for loss of the machine and resulting loss of profit in his business. The New York Court of Appeals explained at length its reasons for rejecting his claim:

> Tort recovery in strict products liability and negligence against a manufacturer should not be available to a downstream purchaser where the claim losses flow from damage to the property that is the subject of the contract. Transforming manufacturers into insurers, with the empty promise that they can guarantee perpetual and total public safety, by making them liable in tort for all commercial setbacks and adversities is not prudent or sound tort policy. In such instance, no directly related or commensurate public interest is served or protected by holding manufacturers liable. Tort law should not be bent so far out of its traditional progressive path and discipline by allowing tort lawsuits where the claims at issue are, fundamentally and in all relevant respects, essentially contractual, product failure controversies. Tort law is not the answer for this kind of loss of commercial bargain.

The Model Uniform Product Liability Act likewise rejects pure economic loss as a basis for compensation unless caused by breach of contract. One might predict nonetheless that the distinctions between economic and physical injuries will be eroded eventually, if only because they depend on the divisions between contract and tort which are themselves undermined by product liability. In Europe, the proposed Consumer Guarantee Directive moves towards making manufacturers liable for the fitness of their goods in the same way as retailers.

Subject to the rules we have outlined, anyone injured by a defect can sue. The plaintiff need not be the owner of the goods. He may be the user, or someone injured by goods in the hands of the user. So, for example, passers-by injured by vehicles with defective brakes will be protected: *Kuschy* v *Norris*, 1964. On general duty of care principles English law would presumably give the same extended meaning to 'user' or 'consumer': para. 5.4.

We observe finally that although producers' liabilities under para. 402A are partly contractual in origin they cannot be excluded by agreement. The commentary on the paragraph prohibits any exclusion or limitation of liability by contract or notice, emphasising that whatever the warranty theories used to justify its development, product liability is now essentially tort based.

7.15 WARRANTY LIABILITY

Para. 402A, then, is the most significant contribution of American law to the whole issue of product liability. But we take account also of para. 402B.

In effect this rule supplements para. 402A by holding suppliers bound by any express warranty they may give as to the fitness of their goods, whether directly to their buyers or to the world at large.

Para. 402B states:

> One engaged in the business of selling chattels who, by advertising, labels, or otherwise makes to the public a misrepresentation of a material fact concerning the character or quality of a chattel sold by him is subject to liability for physical harm to a consumer of the chattel caused by justifiable reliance upon the misrepresentation even though (a) it is not made fraudulently or negligently, and (b) the consumer has not bought the chattel from or entered into any contractual relation with the seller.

It will be seen that just as proof of negligence is generally unnecessary for the purposes of para. 402A, so proof of any contractual connection is unnecessary under para. 402B in order to enforce a manufacturer's warranty, at least in a case of physical injury. It is sufficient, for example, to show that a retailer has relied on the manufacturer's assurances, and not necessary to show that the ultimate buyer or user knew of them: *Westlye* v *Look Sports*, 1993. In *Brown* v *Neff*, 1993, a passenger in a truck which overturned because of a mechanical fault succeeded in his claim against the garage owner who had issued an inspection certificate, despite the owner knowing the vehicle had not passed the test. There was neither privity of contract nor reliance in this case, but that was not important: 'Liability for intentional or negligent misrepresentations which threaten harm is grounded upon a duty which is co-extensive with physical risk.' Other examples include *Klages* v *General Ordnance Equipment*, 1976 – a manufacturer who advertised a mace weapon as causing 'instantaneous incapacitation' of any attacker was held liable when it failed; and *Crocker* v *Winthrop Laboratories*, 1974 – the manufacturer was found liable for injury caused by a drug incorrectly advertised as non-addictive and harmless. From the consumer's point of view para. 402B compares very favourably with the present uncertainty in English law over the enforceability of manufactures' guarantees, as discussed in Chapter 1.

7.16 TRADING WITH AMERICA

We should remind ourselves again at this stage that while liability under American law is often strict, it is not absolute. Contrary to popular belief, in other words, it is not a system which imposes liability for any and every accident, however caused. Few if any goods are or could ever be completely safe, and the law does not expect them to be. A customer who ordered a meal of fish chowder, for example, could not complain of finding a fishbone there – even though it stuck in her throat: *Webster* v *Blue Ship*, 1964. In *Scholler* v *Wilson*, 1977, the American court reached the same conclusion on the inherent danger of raw pork as in the English case of *Heil* v *Hedges*, 1951 (para. 3.17). *Harris* v *Northwest Natural Gas*, 1979, denied liability for gas hazards on facts almost identical with those in *Pearson* v *NW Gas Board*, 1968 (para. 5.4), and for the same reasons. A patient suffering from altogether exceptional allergies could have no claim for injuries caused by drugs which were safe for everyone else: *Tayar* v *Roux Laboratories*, 1972 – effectively the same response as that given in the English case of *Griffiths* v *Conway*, 1939 (para. 3.17). Countless consumers in America still lose their claims for compensation for their injuries despite the rigour of the law.

But we must recognise nonetheless that the safety standards adopted in America pose very real difficulties for British companies trading there. Any 'minimum contact' with the USA, through the presence of representatives or agents, will enable a claim for injuries to be made in an American court. The risk of liability being imposed on the British exporter may, however, be reduced if the representative is established as a separate, independent company; not merely a subsidiary operating as directed by the parent company. Insurance cover may be extremely expensive, but for all practical purposes it is essential. Its availability and cost depend very largely on the exporter's ability to prove his technical proficiency and overt concern for consumers' safety. There must be no suggestion that he has sacrificed safety in the interests of economy. Particular thought should be given to the provision of comprehensive and conspicuous instructions as to use, and warnings against misuse. Advertisements should be factual and certainly should not make exaggerated safety claims. Records of research and notes of the resulting action and the reasons for it should be kept available for several years after production has ended.

7.17 PRODUCT LIABILITY IN THE EU AND OTHER COUNTRIES

It is fair to say that American product liability law presents more challenges than any other system for manufacturers and importers. It is true also that in the endless litigation and arguments it generates, it offers more answers than any other system – which is why it is such an instructive and interesting study. But we should not therefore overlook the answers given by other legal systems, even though, in the light of our earlier chapters, we need note them only briefly. The following summary refers only to the basic rules of law. Whether the rules actually work in any given country for the benefit of those who most need them – or are in fact nullified by costs or delays or other difficulties – we are not in a position to say.

So far as continental Europe is concerned, the rules of product liability are determined first and foremost by whether the country in question is one of the 15 Member States of the European Union. By 1997 all of these countries except France had harmonised their rules to the extent required by the Product Liability Directive of 1985. The basic principles in the 14 countries are therefore essentially the same as those set out in our account of the Consumer Protection Act 1987 in Chapter 6. The French difficulties with the Directive are said to derive from the fact that French law already imposes even stricter rules of liability upon producers. In all the EU countries civil law duties are supplemented by the criminal obligations imposed by the General Product Safety Directive described in the next chapter.

Within the Member States there are certain relatively minor variations in the application of the Product Liability Directive, as the Directive itself allows. As we saw in Chapter 6, currently a Member State can decide for itself whether or not to include agricultural produce within the law, whether to have a state of the art defence, and whether to set a limit on compensation. One or two other difficulties have arisen from translation. Germany, for example, has understood the compensation requirement to exclude awards for pain and suffering.

In addition to the Directive, each Member State has, of course, its own laws of contractual and non-contractual or tortious liability. The latter usually depend, as in Great Britain, on proof of negligence. Many countries, including France and Germany, have developed this branch of the law so as to require manufacturers to disprove negligence. In practice this reversed burden of proof leads to strict liability. On the vexed question of the adequacy of warnings, an interesting German case in 1992 on excessive sugar in baby food held that warnings must be aimed at the 'superficial, unsophisticated user'. A particularly important development in another Member State is the Dutch case of *Van Ballegooijen* v *Bayer Nederland*, 1994. This concerned a drug called Diethylstilbestrol (DES), designed to prevent miscarriages. Tragically the drug caused cancer among female babies still in their mothers' wombs. When the cancers became apparent some 20 years later, the 'DES daughters' had no means of knowing which of the 300 or so manufacturers of the drug had supplied the drug their mothers had taken. The Dutch Supreme Court held that since all the manufacturers were at fault in supplying this lethal product, all were jointly and severally liable, that is each was liable for all the harm done, but could claim contribution from the rest.

This answer to the problem of the unidentifiable defendant is notably different from the American 'market share' solution in the comparable case of *Sindell* v *Abbot Laboratories*, 1980 (para. 7.12). It is not at all clear what English courts would do in similar circumstances. The Consumer Protection Act would not apply because of the 10 year limit on bringing claims (para. 6.12), so it would be a question of proving negligence. But against whom? A judge might perhaps impose the burden of disproving negligence on each one of a number of defendants, or, equally possibly, reject the claim altogether because the defendant could not be precisely identified. There is in any case the difficulty that English law, unlike many other systems, has not yet fully developed procedures specifically designed for large groups of plaintiffs all with the same grievance – the so-called 'class action'.

Apart from its immediate effect within the European Union, the Product Liability Directive has also achieved a remarkable degree of harmonisation of the law in much of the rest of Europe and indeed across the world. Among many neighbouring European countries we find legislation in the same or similar terms. Examples include the Norwegian Product Liability Act 1988, the Swiss statute of 18 June 1993, and a Hungarian Act of 1994. Russia's Consumer Protection Act 1992 states general rules similar to the principles of the Directive. Israel's Defective Products (Liability) Law 1980 broadly expresses the Directive when still in draft form, conforming with the principle of strict liability.

Very much further afield, China (Acts of 1993 and 1994), Japan (1994), Taiwan (1994) and the Philippines (1992) have all adopted laws based more or less exactly on the Directive. India, Pakistan, Singapore and Malaysia thus far retain the traditional contract and tort remedies. We bear in mind that in many countries, and in these eastern countries in particular, there may be a very wide gap between what the law says and what happens in practice. The law provides a framework, but Asian custom and practice is to settle disputes by mediation and arbitration outside the court system. These informal procedures do not necessarily benefit consumers in the long run, although they are at least saved the trauma of litigation. Elsewhere again, comparability of national law with the Directive was achieved in Brazil by the Consumer Protection Code of 1990 and in Australia by a major amendment in 1994 of the Trade Practices Act 1974.

7.18 THE NEW ZEALAND ANSWER

If we look as far as New Zealand we may see that another, altogether different solution is possible. Since 1974, under what is now the Accident Rehabilitation and Insurance Compensation Act 1992, as amended, all claims for damages for personal injuries caused by accident in that country have been abolished. In their place is a state insurance system which, for all its deficiencies, is essentially rational, humane, efficient and economic. It is concerned with need, not fault (except for deliberate self-injury and injuries sustained in the course of crime). It asks only whether the claimant was injured by accident, including medical misadventure, and, if so, what continuing loss of earning capacity he or she has suffered thereby.

Very briefly, the New Zealand scheme works as follows. Since most accidents have very short-term consequences, the employer must make up 80 per cent of the victim's first week's loss of wages if injury arises out of employment. Losses from injuries not suffered at work, or suffered by the self-employed, must be borne by the victim for the first week. Claimants are then entitled to immediate payments of up to 80 per cent of lost earning capacity, within a statutory limit (in 1996) of NZ$1222.55 (nearly £500) per week. Weekly payments of $60 – an 'independence allowance' – may be made for permanent impairment resulting from an accident, in addition to any other social rehabilitation entitlements. The annual cost of the scheme, which includes medical and hospital expenses, and preventive and rehabilitation work, is currently some NZ$1 600 000 000 – approximately £650 million, or, very roughly, £220 per head of the population. It is funded by levies on employers, averaging about £2.60 for each £100 of payroll; on earners, at the rate of 70 cents for each $100 of earnings; on vehicle owners – currently $90 for a private car – plus a tax of 2 cents a litre on petrol. Less than 10 per cent of total expenditure goes on purely administrative costs, whereas in Britain for every £100 paid out in damages anything up to another £110 is paid in private insurance and legal costs,.

The New Zealand model of reform of personal injury litigation was examined and rejected by the Pearson Report in 1976, for reasons which remain debatable. In the present writer's view, for what it is worth, the certainty and efficiency of a reasonable and immediate insurance provision must be infinitely preferable to the speculative gains and losses of years of legal argument, and would undoubtedly serve to lower the overall cost of accidents. It might be objected that by abolishing claims for damages the New Zealand system removes the incentive to be careful, but that is not so. Insurance premiums can be loaded by way of deterrent, and the criminal law is still there to punish the worst offenders. The crucial point is that in

New Zealand a person's guilt or innocence does not decide the fate of the injured party, as it does in Britain. While the European Union's product liability reform has thus been generally welcomed for its own sake, perhaps its greatest significance may one day be seen as a step on the way to a much better solution.

7.19 SUMMARY

The developments in American product liability law in the 1950s and 1960s were among the main reasons for the more recent reforms in European law. Essentially these developments involved applying the familiar principle of sellers' strict contractual liabilities to the more distant relationship of manufacturers and the ultimate users of their products, where liability had previously turned on proof of negligence. The question of negligence has now become almost – though not completely – irrelevant in this context so far as the American courts are concerned.

Many novel and difficult questions have had to be resolved under the new regime. While transatlantic answers may not always be agreeable to UK producers, the fact remains that after the enactment of the Consumer Protection Act in 1987 they have become directly relevant and important to them. Hardly any of the questions confronted by the American courts have yet come before UK courts. As and when they do so, British courts are bound to be influenced by American arguments and rulings. Procedural differences, particularly as regards the use of juries, should nonetheless ensure that the notorious extremes of the American system are avoided.

Imposing strict liability upon producers greatly reduces the burden of proof and related difficulties of injured parties. It is now the rule in most industrialised countries. But it clearly does not guarantee redress, nor by any means end the need for legal proceedings and all the expense and delay inherent in them. Still less does it affect those whose injuries are not caused by defective products, but by road or industrial or other kinds of accident, where compensation remains dependent on proof of negligence. Only some kind of overall insurance system could meet the resulting needs efficiently and economically. New Zealand, unique in its attempts to develop such a system, may show the way.

NOTES

1. The Restatement (Third) of Torts: Products Liability, published mid-1998, broadly endorses case law developments discussed in this chapter. It imposes strict liability for manufacturing defects but upholds negligence as the test of liability for defective design and inadequate warning. Adoption of the Restatement is at the discretion of each State.
2. The Third Restatement, 1998, puts the onus of proving a reasonable alternative design upon the plaintiff.
3. The Third Restatement, 1998, expressly defines products as excluding blood and blood tissue.
4. The Third Restatement, 1998, expressly defines products as excluding services.

8 Suppliers' criminal liabilities

8.1 THE CRIMINAL LAW

Our previous chapters have all concerned suppliers' liabilities to compensate aggrieved or injured buyers or users of their products, on grounds either of breach of contract or negligence, or under rules of strict liability. In this final chapter we summarise the main provisions of the criminal law affecting commercial and industrial suppliers. These rules are not intended to compensate the individual victim – the province of civil law – but to protect society at large from harm and to punish the wrongdoer. The two functions may be combined if the criminal court is willing to exercise its power to make a compensation order, but this is not often done.

Most of the offences we shall mention are triable summarily in magistrates' courts, where the maximum penalty for any one offence may be as much as a £5000 fine and/or up to six months' imprisonment. Some offences are triable by judge and jury in the Crown Court, where the penalties may be very much heavier. Depending on the statute in question, certain breaches of the criminal law of themselves entitle victims of the wrongful acts to claim damages, but unless the criminal court makes a compensation order it is usually necessary to launch separate civil proceedings for this purpose. Evidence can be given in these proceedings of the wrongdoer's conviction. Such evidence does not necessarily prove that the wrongdoer is also civilly liable, but is clearly relevant to the claim.

The Acts of Parliament and regulations which create minor or relatively minor offences often impose strict liability. The effect, subject to any defences which may be specified, is to make the person who committed the crime guilty even though he or she might not have intended to commit it, and indeed might have done everything possible to try to avoid com-

163

mitting it. As regards more serious crimes, however, the law usually requires proof of intention – a 'guilty mind', or, in legal jargon, *'mens rea'*.

8.2 THE GENERAL PRODUCT SAFETY REGULATIONS

For present purposes, probably the most important of all the rules we mention here are those resulting from Britain's membership of the European Union. In 1992 the European Commission's long-standing concern with product safety resulted in Directive no. 92/59, which came into English law in the form of the General Product Safety Regulations 1994. These Regulations are in effect the criminal equivalent of Part I of the Consumer Protection Act (Chapter 6), though more limited in scope in that the Act affects all goods, while the Regulations apply only to consumer goods. Their purpose is essentially to stop unnecessarily dangerous goods from reaching the domestic market. Breach of the Regulations, which are enforceable by Trading Standards inspectors, may be punished by a fine of up to £5000 and/or imprisonment for up to three months.

Reflecting its continental origin, the main requirement of the Regulations is stated both very briefly and very widely. Regulation 7 says simply: 'No producer shall place a product on the market unless the product is a safe product.' This rule is called the 'general safety requirement'. The necessary explanations and qualifications are as follows. Regulation 2 defines a producer as the manufacturer, if established in the European Union, or the person appearing as manufacturer by adding his own name or mark to the product, or the person who reconditions the product. If the manufacturer is not established in the EU, his representative is responsible. If he has no representative, the importer is liable. Other professionals in the chain of supply may also be liable, if their activities affect the safety of a product.

The products in question are those supplied in the course of business and intended for or likely to be used by consumers, but not commercially. Examples of the difficulty of drawing the line between consumer use and commercial use might include electrical and electronic equipment, computers, etc., which could be used both domestically and for business purposes. If used solely for business purposes, the product is covered by the Regulations only at the time of supply, and thereafter by the Health & Safety at Work Act, below. No distinction is drawn by the Regulations between new, used and reconditioned goods, subject to Regulation 3, below.

Regulation 2 goes on to say, perhaps not very helpfully, that a dangerous product is one which is not safe. A safe product is then defined as one which in normal or reasonably foreseeable conditions of use creates no risk or only such minimum risks as are considered acceptable and consistent with a high level of protection of health and safety. The length of time a product may be intended to be used is a particularly important element in assessing its safety. The 'acceptability' of a risk depends on such factors as the basic characteristic of the product (e.g. the sharpness of a knife), its composition, packaging, instructions for assembly and maintenance, its effect on other products it is likely to be used with, the way it is presented or labelled, any instructions for use or disposal or other indication or information provided by the producer, and the types of consumer most at risk – especially children. The fact that a higher level of safety could be achieved, or that comparable but safer products are available, does not of itself prove a product unsafe.

Regulations 3 and 4 exclude certain goods from the scope of the Regulations. They do not apply to secondhand goods which are antiques, nor to goods supplied for repair or reconditioning before use. The consumer must, however, be told that repaired or reconditioned goods are not covered by the Regulations. Other products whose safety standards are already wholly regulated by law are also outside the Regulations. Regulations 5 and 6 avoid conflict with the provisions of s. 10 of the Consumer Protection Act which would otherwise apply.

8.3 SAFETY DUTIES

The rules following the general safety requirement in Regulation 7 explain in more detail what producers and distributors may have to do to fulfil their safety duties. Regulation 8 obliges producers to give consumers any information needed to enable them to guard against the normal and inherent risks of using the product, unless the risks are obvious. A light-hearted article in *The Times* in 1997 reported on the very real difficulties producers face in deciding how to fulfil this Regulation. The examples given suggested perhaps an excessively cautious or pessimistic approach. They included warnings such as: 'Take care – product will be hot after heating'; 'Do not iron clothes on body'; 'Contains nuts' (on a packet of peanuts). It was suggested that translation difficulties might explain the advice on a Korean kitchen knife: 'Warning – keep out of children'. A letter in the same newspaper said: 'To conform with the relevant British standard, we are obliged to stick labels on to the glass door cabinets we manufacture, stating: "Do not hit the glass with hard or sharp objects".' But no doubt it is better to be safe than sorry.

Another important obligation on producers is to keep themselves informed of the possible risks of their products and to take appropriate action, which might have to include withdrawing the product, to avoid such risks. It might therefore be necessary to mark products or batches for ease of identification. Other measures might include sample testing, investigating complaints and notifying distributors of the results.

Distributors have responsibilities under the Regulations as well as producers. By Regulation 9 they must take due care to comply with the general safety requirement, and must not supply goods which they know or ought to know are dangerous. This rule is most important as regards sales to children and young persons generally, where suppliers must do their best to predict and prevent misuse or abuse of their products, if need be by refusing to sell them. Within the limits of their activities, suppliers must also take part in monitoring product safety, pass on information as to risks and co-operate in action taken to avoid such risks. Breach of Regulation 9 is a criminal offence.

Regulation 10 says that products already complying with specific UK safety rules, such as those laid down in the regulations noted below, are presumed safe unless proved unsafe. If there are no specific rules about a particular product, its conformity with the general safety requirement will depend on compliance with any relevant standards or specifications, for example those of the British Standards Institute, or the lion symbol, the European safety mark, codes of practice, the state of the art, and the standard of safety which 'consumers may reasonably expect'. We note that the state of the art defence and the standard of reasonable expectation are key features also of the Consumer Protection Act, which we discussed in paras 6.7–8.

The remaining Regulations concern enforcement. Provisions of the Consumer Protection Act on prohibition notices, notices to warn, suspension notices and forfeiture, below, are applicable here also. Apart from liabilities under Regulations 7 and 9, producers and distributors are bound also by Regulation 13. This makes it a crime to offer or agree to put on the market any dangerous product, or to expose or possess any such product for that purpose, or to offer or agree to supply any dangerous product or expose or possess any such product for supply.

8.4 DEFENCES

Both producers and distributors may escape liability if they come within the terms of Regulation 14. A defendant is not liable for breach of the

Regulations if he can show he 'took all reasonable steps and exercised all due diligence' to avoid committing the offence. If the defendant says the offence was committed only because of the act or default of another person, or because he relied on information given by another person, he must give the prosecution notice of that defence and must be able to show it was reasonable to rely on the information. The court will wish to know what steps he took or could have taken to verify the information and whether he had any reason not to believe it.

Two cases in 1995, decided under identical provisions in the Consumer Protection Act, show how strictly the rules are applied. The defendants in *Coventry CC* v *Ackerman Group* imported and supplied egg boilers. There were no instructions on the boxes to say that the eggs should be broken into the boilers or their yolks pricked before being microwaved. When the defendants were alerted to the possible dangers to inexperienced microwave users they sent their retailers printed instructions which they recommended should be affixed to the boxes. Not all retailers did so. Following prosecution, it was held that a mere recommendation, leaving compliance to the retailer's discretion, was not enough to reduce the danger. The recommendation did not explain the risk, and could have been seen as merely an aid to better use. The defendants were liable for failure to exercise due diligence.

In *Balding* v *Lew-ways Ltd* a manufacturer was prosecuted for supplying unsafe tricycles. He claimed that since the tricycles conformed with BS5665, as required by the Toy Safety Regulations 1989, he must therefore have exercised all due diligence. But on this occasion the court rejected this argument, holding that compliance with a British Standard was not of itself proof of due diligence, because the Standards did not cover all the required areas of safety. Other examples of the working of the due diligence defence are noted below.

8.5 OTHER CONSUMER SAFETY REGULATIONS

Safety standards of many consumer goods are laid down in detail in regulations made by the Secretary of State for Trade under powers given by EU law or the Consumer Protection Act or previous Acts. The regulations may cover composition, contents, design, construction, finish or packing, or 'other matters relating to goods'. The Secretary can require goods to conform to particular standards and information to be given in appropriate ways to show conformity. He can regulate the testing or inspection of goods and require warnings or instructions to be marked on or to accompany goods. He can also exclude 'inappropriate information' which might mislead. The Secretary can prohibit anyone from supplying or possessing for supply goods he has found unsafe.

A person supplying goods in the course of business (excluding sales for export or for scrap or reconditioning) in breach of regulations under the Act may be fined up to £5000 and/or imprisoned for up to three months. Prosecutions are undertaken by local authority Trading Standards departments. No liability arises if the defendant can prove the offence was committed because of the act or default of some other person. Usually this 'other person' will be an independent third party but may possibly be an employee of the defendant, if and insofar as what he does is both contrary to orders and beyond the defendant's immediate control: *Tesco Supermarkets* v *Nattrass*, 1972. Another defence is that the defendant took all reasonable steps and exercised all due diligence to avoid committing the offence. That defence does not of itself enable a seller to rely without question on a manufacturer's advertisements or assurances: *Taylor* v *Fraser*, 1977. Breach of the regulations also gives rise to strict civil liability to anyone injured thereby, an unusual provision in our criminal law.

Safety regulations currently affect the following types of goods: aerosols; all-terrain vehicles; asbestos products; babies' dummies; benzene in toys; bunk beds; ceramic ware; children's clothing; cosmetics; electrical appliances; fabrics; fireworks; food imitations; furniture; gas appliances; heating appliances; imitation dummies; motor vehicle tyres; nightwear; pedal cycles; pencils; perambulators; plugs and sockets; scented erasers; tobacco products; toys; toy water snakes. Details can be found in, for example, Sweet and Maxwell's *Encyclopaedia of Consumer Law*.

Apart from the safety regulation aspect, the Consumer Protection Act gives other important powers to the Secretary of State. Under s. 13 he may issue prohibition orders forbidding supply of any type of goods he specifies as unsafe. The orders are of immediate and general effect, subject only to the requirement in Schedule 2 of advance warning and discussion with interested parties if practicable. He may serve prohibition notices or supervision notices on individuals, forbidding them to supply prescribed goods or permitting supply only on prescribed terms. The Secretary may also serve a 'notice to warn' on individual traders requiring them to publish at their own expense whatever warning he thinks necessary about unsafe goods they have already supplied. Again there must be prior notification and consultation if practicable. Goods apparently supplied in breach of the Act may be seized, but compensation is payable if no conviction follows.

8.6 THE HEALTH AND SAFETY AT WORK ACT

Apart from its application to employers and employees, the Act is very important also for all industrial suppliers, whether designers, manufacturers, distributors or installers. Section 6 obliges suppliers of articles and substances *for use at work* to ensure *so far as is reasonably practicable* that they can be used in safety. This phrase will have a familiar ring for readers of our earlier chapters. Taking precautions 'so far as reasonably practicable' under s. 6 involves basically the same standard of care, 'reasonable care', as that long since laid down by the common law and enforceable by claims for damages.

It follows that s. 6 does not create any new duties. Its effect is essentially to make punishable by the criminal law that which was already a civil wrong. To see what is meant by 'reasonably practicable' therefore we need only turn back to our discussions of likelihood and seriousness of risk, cost of precautions and the like in Chapter 5 and to the day-to-day illustrations given there of the working of the law.

There are nonetheless two significant differences between the criminal and civil versions of the duty of care, apart from the penalties imposed for breach. The Act reverses the burden of proof, so that suppliers must disprove the practicability of precautions – usually a very difficult task. Secondly, the precautions necessary under s. 6 relate to the proper use of products and not, as at common law, to likely misuse as well.

There is then nothing really new about s. 6 apart, again, from the possibility of unlimited fines and imprisonment up to two years, but the practical results of expressing the longstanding civil duty in criminal terms are very considerable. The object of the criminal law is as we have said to prevent injury. Section 6 seeks to do that in the industrial context by stopping dangerous machinery and other products getting onto the market in the first place. Health and Safety inspectors are empowered thereby to visit the places where articles and substances for use at work are made and if they do not seem reasonably safe to issue prohibition or improvement notices to stop them being made or to require further precautions. Appeals against such orders are made to employment tribunals, but breach is punishable in magistrates' courts or in Scotland in the Sheriff Court.

Looking now at the details of s. 6, we see it is concerned with the safe design and manufacture of articles and components for use at work in Great Britain, whether new or secondhand. It does not apply to articles used exclusively for consumer purposes, as to which, see the General

Product Safety Regulations, above, though this is, of course, a difficult line to draw. Articles intended primarily for consumer use may also be used at work, and in that case s. 6 applies. It affects also the liabilities of manufacturers, importers and suppliers of substances to be used at work, exclusively or otherwise. 'Substances' may be natural or artificial, solid or liquid, or in gas or vapour form.

The duty of care in relation to these products is explained by reference in particular to their testing and examination, provision of information as to the results of tests and safe use, research to eliminate or reduce risks and safe installation. Responsibility falls equally on designers, manufacturers, importers, suppliers, erectors and installers, on companies and their employees and on individuals in business insofar as the matter is one within the control of the company or person concerned. This proviso limits the liability of those who repair goods or deal in used goods. Employees as such are unlikely to be prosecuted unless they act with wilful disregard for others' safety. If articles or substances are supplied on credit responsibility falls upon the supplier and not the finance house, and if leased, upon the lessor.

Section 6(8) raises an interesting point of detail. On the face of it, it relieves the supplier of liability if his customer promises in writing to take all necessary steps to ensure that the article or substance provided will be safe for use at work. This provision recognises the limits on the supplier's liability to make his products equally safe for all the many different uses to which they may be put. It is doubtful, however, whether the scope of this defence is as wide as it appears. One might assume that it will not apply unless the supplier has already made the article or substance as safe as he can, otherwise he would be able to opt out of his duty simply by securing his customer's written permission to do so, which would seem to defeat the whole purpose of the Act.

Conversely a customer might make it a condition of purchase that the supplier gives a written undertaking of his own compliance with the Act. That of itself would not affect the supplier's liability (since the question is whether he took the precautions, not whether he said he did), and if and insofar as he has fulfilled his promise that might indicate that any subsequent accident is actually the customer's fault.

8.7 THE SUPPLY OF MACHINERY (SAFETY) REGULATIONS

The general terms of s. 6 of the Health & Safety at Work Act have been developed in great detail by the Supply of Machinery (Safety) Regulations

1992–4. These provisions derive from EEC Directive no. 89/392, the 'Machinery Directive', as amended.

The Regulations cover machinery and safety components. Machinery is defined as an assembly of linked parts, including at least one moving part, formed together for the processing, treatment, moving or packaging of a material, or as an integrated assembly of machines, or as interchangeable equipment, other than a spare part or tool, modifying the function of a machine. Safety components are those supplied to fulfil a safety function and whose failure or malfunction would endanger safety or health. Exemptions include machinery operated manually, apart from that used for lifting or lowering loads, machinery for medical use in direct contact with patients, means of transport, and miscellaneous other types of machinery covered by other regulations.

Broadly, the Regulations make it an offence for a 'responsible person' to supply a machine or safety component unless it meets the 'essential health and safety requirements', the appropriate conformity assessment or attestation has been carried out, an EC declaration of conformity or incorporation has been issued, CE marking affixed, and the product is in fact safe.

In more detail, the responsible person is either the manufacturer or an importer into the European Economic Area. If the manufacturer is outside the EEA, the importer must ensure compliance with the Regulations. 'Supply' includes offering to supply, but excludes exhibition of the goods at trade fairs and the like. A machine or component is safe when – properly installed, maintained and used – there is either no risk or only minimum risk of injury or damage. The practicability of precautions at the time of manufacture is taken into account.

The Regulations set out the essential health and safety requirements at length. They must be fulfilled so far as possible. By way of example, we report here on the principles of safety integration stated in the Regulations. Machinery must be so constructed as to be fit for its function, and capable of adjustment and maintenance without risk when these operations are undertaken in conditions foreseen by the manufacturer, including foreseeable abnormal situations.

Manufacturers must try to eliminate or reduce risks as far as possible, take protective measures against risks which cannot be eliminated, inform users of residual risks and state whether training and/or personal protective equipment is needed. Machinery must if possible be designed to prevent abnormal use if such use would be dangerous, failing which users must be warned against unsafe use. Design and construction must take account of the constraints of personal protective equipment. Machinery must be supplied with all necessary special equipment for adjustment, maintenance and use. The Regulations lay down other rules in similar terms on materials, lighting, handling of machinery, control systems, guards, noise, etc.

Proof of compliance with these requirements is on the responsible person. He or she must carry out all necessary tests and be able to provide a technical file for inspection by the Health & Safety Executive. The file comprises overall drawings of the machine and control circuits; detailed drawings showing compliance with the essential safety requirements; a list of such requirements used when the machine was designed and the methods adopted to meet them; a statement of conformity with any appropriate technical standards; and a copy of instructions for use. The responsible person must draw up an EC declaration of conformity, to be issued with the machine, stating his or her name and address and giving particulars of compliance with the Regulations. Alternatively he or she may make a declaration of incorporation, when the machine is to be incorporated in other machinery. Unless incorporation is intended, a CE mark, not less than 5 mm in height, must then be affixed to the machine. The mark is a form of self-certification. Sale of non-conforming machinery is forbidden. Breach of the Regulations is punishable by a fine of up to £5000 and/or three months' imprisonment. The Regulations provide a defence of due diligence: para. 8.4.

Further information on the above requirements is given in the Department of Trade's helpful guidance notes entitled *Product Standards – Machinery*. The Department also offers a list of independent safety consultants.

8.8 FOOD SAFETY

Problems with food safety represent a very significant part of the overall issue of product liability. Within the past few years there has been widespread public alarm over outbreaks of salmonella, listeria, BSE, etc. In 1997 about 100 000 incidents of food poisoning were reported – which were believed to be only about one-tenth of the number of incidents which could and should have been reported. In the same year some 200 people died because of food poisoning. In response to these concerns the government has proposed establishing an independent Food Standards Agency, to be responsible for maintenance of standards and for advising and educating on nutrition.

The legal framework is provided by the Food Safety Act 1990 and developed in great detail by the many UK and EU regulations on additives, contaminants, composition, packaging and labelling of food passed under this and other Acts. There are still grounds for criticism of the adequacy of the law. There is, for instance, no clear rule on the marking of genetically modified food, except for foods produced from genetically modified soya beans and maize. The Consumers' Association has pointed out that words such as 'environmentally-friendly', 'natural', 'organic' and 'low-fat' have no precise meaning, and may mislead. The Association has noted the absence of any rule preventing use of the word 'pure', in relation to food, merely as a brand name. Commenting in *Which?*, June 1997, on the accuracy and value of nutritional information, the Association said: 'We found that only 10 per cent of the foods we tested contained nutrients in the quantities stated on the label, and nearly 50 per cent were more than 10 per cent out.'

The 1990 Act creates four main offences. By s. 7 it is an offence to make food (including drink) intended for human consumption into a health hazard by adding any article or substance to it, or by using any article or substance as an ingredient in preparation, or by abstracting any constituent from it, or by any other process. The dangers in question may be immediate or cumulative. This section could be invoked to cover cases of sabotage, but sabotage would probably be dealt with by more serious charges. Section 8 forbids sale or offers for sale of food which does not comply with food safety requirements. Failure to comply with these requirements may result from an offence under s. 7, or because the food is unfit for human consumption, or is so contaminated that it would be unreasonable to use it for that purpose. Under s. 14 it is illegal to sell food not of the nature, substance or quality demanded by the purchaser. By s. 15 it is also an offence to label or display or advertise food falsely or in a way likely to mislead as to its nature, substance or quality.

The Act and accompanying regulations are enforced by local authorities. Their officers have power to inspect, seize and condemn food from business or other premises within the Act. They can prosecute for breach of the rules, and can also issue improvement and prohibition notices. A criminal court may impose a prohibition order where premises, plant, processes or individuals represent a threat to health.

A person prosecuted for breach of the Act or regulations may escape liability by establishing one or other of the defences provided by the Act. By s. 20 it is a defence to show the offence was committed because of the act or default of another person, possibly an employee of the defendant (see para. 8.13). Section 21 offers a defence of due diligence, under which the defendant must prove he or she took all reasonable precautions to avoid committing the offence. This may well require the defendant to prove adequate checks on foodstuffs and on any information about them given by third parties.

Smedleys v *Breed*, 1974, was an important House of Lords decision on the defences provided by the now repealed Food & Drugs Act, which would probably still be relevant to the operation of s. 21. The prosecution was based on the presence of caterpillar larvae found in a tin of peas despite the very elaborate precautions which were proved to have been taken to avoid any foreign matter. The defendants had produced some 3 500 000 tins of peas that season and had had only four complaints. 'The chances of it happening again were . . . 3 499 999 to 1'. As Lord Hailsham said after the consumer reported her discovery,

> the caterpillar achieved a sort of posthumous apotheosis. From local authority to the Dorchester magistrates, from the Dorchester magistrates to a Divisional Court presided over by the Lord Chief Justice of England, from the Lord Chief Justice to the House of Lords the immolated insect has at length plodded its methodical way to the highest tribunal in the land.

Their Lordships held that in order to establish a defence under s. 3 the defendants would have to show that the presence of the extraneous matter could not have been avoided by any human agency – which they were of course unable to do. At the same time the court emphasised that local authorities were not bound to prosecute in cases such as this where only very strictly speaking could it be said that an offence had been committed. They should keep a sense of proportion and consider whether prosecution was really necessary to protect the interests of consumers. Magistrates who thought prosecutions unnecessary were advised by their Lordships that they might find liability but nonetheless grant an absolute discharge.

Regulations and Orders have also been made prescribing the composition of numerous foodstuffs and forbidding the sale or labelling or advertisement of these products except in accordance with the regulations. The items in question include baking powder, bread, butter, canned meats, cheese, cocoa and chocolate products, coffee and coffee products, condensed milk cream, curry powder, dried milk, fish cakes, fish and meat spreads, flour, fruit juices, gelatine, ice cream, margarine, meat pies and sausage rolls, preserves, salad cream, sausages and other meat products, soft drinks, suet, sugar products and tomato ketchup. Restrictions are imposed on the sale and advertisement of goods with certain added antioxidants, colouring matter, stabilisers or emulsifiers, or other miscellaneous additives, preservatives and solvents.

Regulations forbid the sale or importation of food containing arsenic, fluorine, lead or mineral hydrocarbons beyond the prescribed amounts or other than in the natural forms specifically exempted. Another measure is an EEC Directive imposing strict controls on any material or article intended to come into contact with food and containing vinyl chloride. More general regulations require that packaging materials must not contaminate foodstuffs.

8.9 MEDICINAL PRODUCTS

So far as drugs and other medicines are concerned the matter is in the hands of the Committee on Safety of Medicines, an independent and expert licensing body created by the Medicines Act 1968, and the new Medicines Control Agency. It is a criminal offence to sell an unlicensed medicine. Issue of a licence now depends on proof of adequate staff and equipment and quality control facilities, the Committee's certificate that the drug in question has been appropriately tested on animals, and a product licence certifying the Committee's belief in the safety and quality of the drug. The Committee will refuse a licence unless satisfied of the positive value and safety and quality of the drug. For this purpose it relies on information supplied by the manufacturers and does not conduct its own trials or research. The Committee urges doctors to report adverse reactions, and manufacturers are required to keep a record of such information. The success of these requirements remains open to question.

The Medicines Act divides drugs into ethical products – those which can only be obtained on prescription – and proprietary medicines – those safe enough to be bought without prescription. Some of these are available from pharmacies only, others by general sale. Regulations require that proprietary medicines should be named, carry particulars of their ingredients, quantity, use, warnings as to side effects, expiry date, product licence, batch reference and manufacturer's licence. Not all of these particulars are necessary for prescribed drugs. Aspirin and paracetamol, among others, must be sold in 'childproof' containers.

8.10 MOTOR VEHICLES

One specific product whose safety and quality is outstandingly important to the consumer is the motor vehicle. This has been the subject of a great deal of highly specialised legislation. The main Act at present in force is the Road Traffic Act 1988. Various very detailed regulations have been made under this and previous Acts, notably the many Motor Vehicles

(Construction and Use) Regulations. The regulations specify what equipment must be fitted and the standards of fitness for numerous parts and accessories including tyres, brakes, mirrors, speedometers, seat belts, lights, etc. They also list the numerous EEC and EU Directives on vehicle design, construction and equipment to which vehicles must conform. Regulations have also been made on the design of motor-cycle helmets.

8.11 THE TRADE DESCRIPTIONS ACT

Despite its commercial importance we have left the law against deceptive advertising to the end, since it does not relate directly to questions of fitness or safety of goods. But there is still a connection. If advertised goods are unsuitable or dangerous they may thereby prove the advertisement untrue and the advertiser guilty. The criminal court can make a compensation order as well as imposing a fine or imprisonment. A conviction does not of itself affect the validity of any contract made with the advertiser.

It may be helpful therefore to conclude with a brief review of the main provisions of the Trade Descriptions Act 1968, the UK's most comprehensive attempt to control advertising standards. The Act concentrates on two problem areas: advertisements about goods and services. Deceptive pricing, formerly dealt with by this Act, is now regulated by Part III of the Consumer Protection Act.

The basic rules on goods are laid down in ss. 1 to 3. Section 1 creates the offence of 'applying a false trade description' to goods. Section 2 explains the meaning of trade description, and s. 3 that of falsehood. Their short effect is as follows. The Act only applies to statements or representations made in the course of trade or business, a phrase we discussed in Chapter 3. It is immaterial whether or not the false statement was made with the intention to deceive. The statement itself may be written or spoken, or appear in or on the goods, as, for example, the figure on a car's odometer. The cases suggest that the seller can only avoid making a statement of this kind by making another statement equally as 'bold, precise and compelling' – *R* v *Hammertons*, 1976 – disclaiming all responsibility for the accuracy of the reading. The disclaimer must be brought to the buyer's attention before sale. It should preferably be in the car, and the odometer itself taped over. The same level of precautions may not be necessary when selling to another dealer.

Section 2 defines a trade description as 'an indication, direct or indirect, and by whatever means given' relating to any of the following aspects of goods: their quantity, size or gauge; manufacture, production, processing or reconditioning; composition; fitness for purpose; strength, performance, behaviour or accuracy; other physical characteristics; testing and results; approval or type conformity; other history including previous ownership or use. A straightforward example of breach of this part of the Act was in the salesman's statement in *Robertson* v *Diciccio*, 1972, that the car was 'beautiful' when in fact it was in urgent need of repair. As regards previous ownership, *R* v *Inner London Justices*, 1983, shows that a half truth may be a lie. The advertisement claimed 'one previous owner', but did not say the owner had been a leasing company.

Statements affecting any other aspects of goods are not within the Act, and so even if made with intent to deceive attract no liability. Estimates of worth or value are largely matters of opinion, and correspondingly difficult for the law to deal with. The Act does not seek directly to control them. In *Cadbury* v *Halliday*, 1975, for example, there was no liability for a false statement of 'extra value'. But any facts or figures offered in support must be true. So an advertiser was liable for selling '£50 watches' for £4.99 when he could not prove that such watches were in fact generally available for £50: *MGN* v *Ritters*, 1997. Other statements outside the Act include assertions as to the availability of goods.

Under s. 3 the test is whether a trade description is 'false to a material degree', whether or not anyone is deceived by it. Small discrepancies might sometimes be both unavoidable and unimportant. So in *R* v *Ford*, 1974, it was held that whether a car could properly be sold as 'new' after the dealer had repaired it depended on the extent of the damage and quality of the repairs. But if a car has already been registered in the dealer's name it cannot be new: *R* v *Anderson*, 1987. No offence was committed in *Simmons* v *Ravenhill*, 1983, where a car was sold with a De Luxe badge though actually only a standard model car with certain De Luxe refinements. A trade description might also be illegal if simply 'misleading' as to one of the matters specified in s. 2, without actually being false. Similarly a statement which though not within s. 2 could be taken as such will result in liability if materially false.

The interesting and important problem of 'slackfill' should be noted in this context. Many goods are supplied in containers whose size bears little or no relation to their contents, and which seem designed to deceive the consumer. Sometimes containers have to state the weight of their contents, but even so it could surely be argued that the size of a container is 'an indication, direct or indirect and by whatever means given' as to the 'quantity, size or gauge' of the goods inside, and if unnecessarily large must be 'misleading'. Strangely enough, however, there appears to be no agreed policy on this matter, and there seems to have been only one successful reported prosecution.

8.12 SERVICES

As regards advertisements for services, s. 14 makes it an offence for anyone in the course of business knowingly or recklessly to make a false statement about any of the following, or any statement likely to be taken as such: the provision in the course of business of any services, accommodation or facilities; the nature of such services, etc., or the time at which or manner in which or person by whom they will be provided; their examination or approval; the location or amenities of any accommodation so provided. According to *MFI* v *Nattrass*, 1971, a false statement is made 'knowingly or recklessly' if made without certainty as to its truth. If every effort is made to correct a statement believed true but later found to be false, liability may be avoided: *Wings* v *Ellis*, 1983.

By listing different offences rather than creating one general offence the Act again leaves loopholes. It seems that 'services, accommodation or facilities' exclude sales of land, so many optimistic statements in builders' and estate agents' advertisements are beyond the reach of the Act – but may be dealt with by the Estate Agents Act 1979. A sale is not a 'facility', so no offence is committed when a dealer falsely advertises a 'closing down sale': *Westminster CC* v *Alan*, 1981. Various other statements which have slipped through the net include the promise of a free gift with every purchase, when the promise is fulfilled by increasing the purchase price: *Newell* v *Hicks*, 1983.

Perhaps the most difficult question regarding services is that posed by cases such as *Beckett* v *Cohen* and *R* v *Sunair Holidays*, both in 1973. In *Beckett* a builder promised to build a garage to a particular design and within an agreed time, knowing that he might be unable to finish the job and in the event failing to do so. On the face of it this was a promise within the terms of s. 14 (i) and (iii), but the court expressed reluctance to turn what was essentially a breach of contract into a crime. Accordingly in this and the *Sunair* case, where various hotel amenities were promised but not provided, it was held that a promise of future services could only be criminal if it could be *proved untrue at the time it was made*; a considerable reduction in the apparent scope of the Act. A travel agency could therefore be criminally liable for booking rooms in a hotel which had not been built, for example, but not for promising services which could have been provided but were not. A trader who tries to repudiate a promise, for example by denying his liability under a guarantee, might thereby indicate that the promise was false at the time he made it: *Banbury* v *Hounslow LBC*, 1971.

8.13 DEFENCES

The last main area of interest in the Trade Descriptions Act is in s. 24(i). This says that a person charged with breach of the rules discussed above can escape liability if he can prove:

> (a) that the commission of the offence was due to a mistake or to reliance on information supplied to him or to the act or default of another person, an accident or some other cause beyond his control; and (b) that he took all reasonable precautions and exercised all due diligence to avoid the commission of such an offence by himself or any person under his control [or] . . . that he did not know, and could not with reasonable diligence have ascertained, that the goods did not conform to the description or that the description had been applied to the goods.

Under paragraphs (a) and (b) the defendant must show that the wrong was someone else's fault and not his own fault. In *Tesco Supermarkets* v *Nattrass*, 1972, the House of Lords held that 'another person' could include the defendant's own employee, though the decision turned on the pre-cautions which head office proved it had in fact taken and on the very substantial size of the organisation. In smaller enterprises where personal supervision is possible, the *Tesco* ruling should not provide any defence.

Section 24(i)(b) above shows that it is not sufficient for the defendant just to accept another's word: he must make enquiries himself where practicable to test or confirm the truth of the matter. So where a trader advertised watches as 'waterproof' in reliance on the manufacturer's erroneous assurance to that effect the court held that he could and should have tested one himself: *Sherratt* v *Gerald*, 1970. Similarly a used car dealer may need to contact the previous owner of a trade-in vehicle or have it examined by experts if the mileage is in doubt: *Naish* v *Gore*, 1971.

8.14 MISLEADING ADVERTISEMENTS

In 1988 the perhaps excessively detailed rules of the Trade Descriptions Act were supplemented by the more general provisions of the Control of Misleading Advertisements Regulations, as required by European Com-mission Directive no. 84/450. The Regulations seek to prevent publication of 'misleading' advertisements – other than those for financial services or on TV or radio, which are supervised by other agencies. An advertisement is misleading if it is 'likely to deceive', to the detriment of consumers or the advertiser's competitors. It is not necessary to show that anyone was in fact misled or suffered loss.

The Regulations are intended as a 'long-stop' or 'fall-back' solution to problems of deceptive advertising which fall outside the Trade Descriptions Act, or cannot adequately be dealt with by that Act or other legislation, or by self-regulating bodies such as the Advertising Standards Authority. If other established means of dealing with a complaint have failed, the Director General of the Office of Fair Trading can ask an advertiser to withdraw the offending material voluntarily, or else he may apply to the High Court or Court of Session in Scotland for an injunction. An injunction can be given against anyone concerned with publication of the material to prevent further publication of it or of any similar matter. The Court may order the advertiser to prove the truth of any factual claims. The Regulations do not create any new criminal offences, but breach of an injunction is contempt of court, punishable by fine or imprisonment. Contracts made as a result of misleading advertising are not affected by the Regulations, but might give rise to claims for damages for breach or be set aside on grounds of misrepresentation.

The Office of Fair Trading currently receives over 100 complaints a year regarding deceptive advertising. Of those within its remit, most are resolved by voluntary undertakings. Injunctions have been sought and granted in cases concerning, for example, totally unrealistic claims as to profitability, 'quack' treatments (including in 1996 an alleged cure for baldness which involved nothing more than standing on one's head for a short period each day), and claims as to OFT endorsement of a product or service when such endorsement is never in fact given.

8.15 SUMMARY

'Product liability' usually refers only to the liabilities of manufacturers to compensate injured users of their goods. There are, however, circumstances in which the supply of dangerous goods may be a crime, whether or not anyone is injured thereby. The most far-reaching of these criminal provisions are the General Product Safety Regulations 1994, based on an EU Directive. The Regulations impose a 'general safety requirement', affecting almost all types of consumer goods. Producers, 'own-branders' and reconditioners are primarily responsible for ensuring the reasonable safety of goods supplied in the course of business. Distributors also may be liable for selling goods they know or ought to know are not safe.

More detailed requirements are laid down by regulations made under the Consumer Protection Act and other legislation. The regulations cover standards of design and construction, and instructions to users. Breach of the rules is a criminal offence, and anyone injured thereby is entitled to an award of damages. Miscellaneous other important rules concern food and drugs, packaging and labelling of dangerous substances, motor vehicle safety, etc.

As regards the safety of articles and substances for use at work, manufacturers and suppliers are bound by s. 6 of the Health & Safety at Work Act 1974 and the Supply of Machinery (Safety) Regulations 1992–94, another EU requirement, to ensure safety so far as reasonably practicable, and where appropriate to make a declaration of type conformity or incorporation, affix a CE mark and prepare a technical file.

Any person who supplies unfit or dangerous goods or services in the course of his or her business may commit a crime under the Trade Descriptions Act if by word or conduct he or she has advertised them as safe or suitable for a particular purpose. Many other specific forms of misdescription are punishable under the Act. It is generally immaterial whether or not the supplier intended to deceive.

Appendix 1 Sale of Goods Act 1979 [sections 11–20B, 34–35A only]
[Amendments are shown in brackets]
Reproduced by kind permission of Her Majesty's Stationery Office

11. When condition to be treated as warranty

[(1)   This section does not apply to Scotland.]

(2)   Where a contract of sale is subject to a condition to be fulfilled by the seller, the buyer may waive the condition, or may elect to treat the breach of the condition as a breach of warranty and not as a ground for treating the contract as repudiated.

(3)   Whether a stipulation in a contract of sale is a condition, the breach of which may give rise to a right to treat the contract as repudiated, or a warranty, the breach of which may give rise to a claim for damages but not to a right to reject the goods and treat the contract as repudiated, depends in each case on the construction of the contract; and a stipulation may be a condition, though called a warranty in the contract.

(4)   [Subject to section 35A below] Where a contract of sale is not severable and the buyer has accepted the goods or part of them, the breach of a condition to be fulfilled by the seller can only be treated as a breach of warranty, and not as a ground for rejecting the goods and treating the contract as repudiated, unless there is an express or implied term of the contract to that effect.

(6)   Nothing in this section affects a condition or warranty whose fulfilment is excused by law by reason of impossibility or otherwise.

(7)   Paragraph 2 of Schedule 1 below applies in relation to a contract

made before 22 April 1967 or (in the application of this Act to Northern Ireland) 28 July 1967.

12. Implied terms about title, etc.

(1)   In a contract of sale, other than one to which subsection (3) below applies, there is an implied [term] on the part of the seller that in the case of a sale he has a right to sell the goods, and in the case of an agreement to sell he will have such a right at the time when the property is to pass.

(2)   In a contract of sale, other than one to which subsection (3) below applies, there is also an implied [term] that—

(a)   the goods are free, and will remain free until the time when the property is to pass, from any charge or encumbrance not disclosed or known to the buyer before the contract is made, and

(b)   the buyer will enjoy quiet possession of the goods except so far as it may be disturbed by the owner or other person entitled to the benefit of any charge or encumbrance so disclosed or known.

(3)   This subsection applies to a contract of sale in the case of which there appears from the contract or is to be inferred from its circumstances an intention that the seller should transfer only such title as he or a third person may have.

(4)   In a contract to which subsection (3) above applies there is an implied [term] that all charges or encumbrances known to the seller and not known to the buyer have been disclosed to the buyer before the contract is made.

(5)   In a contract to which subsection (3) above applies there is also an implied [term] that none of the following will disturb the buyer's quiet possession of the goods, namely—

(a)   the seller;

(b)   in a case where the parties to the contract intend that the seller should transfer only such title as a third person may have, that person;

(c)   anyone claiming through or under the seller or that third person otherwise than under a charge or encumbrance disclosed or known to the buyer before the contract is made.

[(5A)   As regards England and Wales and Northern Ireland, the term implied by subsection (1) above is a condition and the terms implied by subsections (2), (4) and (5) above are warranties.]

(6)   Paragraph 3 of Schedule 1 below applies in relation to a contract made before 18 May 1973.

13. Sale by description

(1)   Where there is a contract for the sale of goods by description, there is an implied [term] that the goods will correspond with the description.

[(1A)   As regards England and Wales and Northern Ireland, the term implied by subsection (1) above is a condition.]

(2)   If the sale is by sample as well as by description it is not sufficient that the bulk of the goods corresponds with the sample if the goods do not also correspond with the description.

(3)   A sale of goods is not prevented from being a sale by description by reason only that, being exposed for sale or hire, they are selected by the buyer.

(4)   Paragraph 4 of Schedule 1 below applies in relation to a contract made before 18 May 1973.

14. Implied terms about quality or fitness

(1)   Except as provided by this section and section 15 below and subject to any other enactment, there is no implied [term] about the quality or fitness for any particular purpose of goods supplied under a contract of sale.

[(2)   Where the seller sells goods in the course of a business, there is an implied term that the goods supplied under the contract are of satisfactory quality.

(2A)   For the purposes of this Act, goods are of satisfactory quality if they meet the standard that a reasonable person would regard as satisfactory, taking account of any description of the goods, the price (if relevant) and all the other relevant circumstances.

(2B)   For the purposes of this Act, the quality of goods includes their state and condition and the following (among others) are in appropriate cases aspects of the quality of goods—

(a)   fitness for all the purposes for which goods of the kind in question are commonly supplied,

(b)   appearance and finish,

(c)   freedom from minor defects,

(d)   safety, and

(e)   durability.

(2C)   The term implied by subsection (2) above does not extend to any matter making the quality of goods unsatisfactory—

(a)   which is specifically drawn to the buyer's attention before the contract is made,

(b)   where the buyer examines the goods before the contract is made, which that examination ought to reveal, or

(c)   in the case of a contract for sale by sample, which would have been apparent on a reasonable examination of the sample.]

(3)   Where the seller sells goods in the course of a business and the buyer, expressly or by implication, makes known—

(a)   to the seller, or

(b)   where the purchase price of part of it is payable by instalments and the goods were previously sold by a credit-broker to the seller, to that credit-broker, any particular purpose for which the goods are being bought, there is an implied [term] that the goods supplied under the contract are reasonably fit for that purpose, whether or not that is a purpose for which such goods are commonly supplied, except where the circumstances show that the buyer does not rely, or that it is unreasonable for him to rely, on the skill or judgment of the seller or credit-broker.

(4)   An implied [term] about quality or fitness for a particular purpose may be annexed to a contract of sale by usage.

(5)   The preceding provisions of this section apply to a sale by a person who in the course of a business is acting as agent for another as they apply to a sale by a principal in the course of a business, except where that other is not selling in the course of a business and either the buyer knows that fact or reasonable steps are taken to bring it to the notice of the buyer before the contract is made.

[(6)   As regards England and Wales and Northern Ireland, the terms implied by subsections (2) and (3) above are conditions.]

(7)   Paragraph 5 of Schedule 1 below applies in relation to a contract made on or after 18 May 1973 and before the appointed day, and paragraph 6 in relation to one made before 18 May 1973.

(8)   In subsection (7) above and paragraph 5 of Schedule 1 below references to the appointed day are to the day appointed for the purposes of those provisions by an order of the Secretary of State made by statutory instrument.

Sale by sample

15.   Sale by sample

(1)   A contract of sale is a contract for sale by sample where there is an express or implied term to that effect in the contract.

(2)   In the case of a contract for sale by sample there is an implied [term]—

(a)   that the bulk will correspond with the sample in quality;

[. . .]

(c)   that the goods will be free from any defect, making their quality unsatisfactory, which would not be apparent on reasonable examination of the sample.

[(3)   As regards England and Wales and Northern Ireland, the term implied by subsection (2) above is a condition.]

(4)   Paragraph 7 of Schedule 1 below applies in relation to a contract made before 18 May 1973.

Miscellaneous

[15A.   Modification of remedies for breach of condition in non-consumer cases

(1)   Where in the case of a contract of sale—

(a)   the buyer would, apart from this subsection, have the right to reject goods by reason of a breach on the part of the seller of a term implied by section 13, 14 or 15 above, but

(b)   the breach is so slight that it would be unreasonable for him to reject them, then, if the buyer does not deal as consumer, the breach is not to be treated as a breach of condition but may be treated as a breach of warranty.

(2)   This section applies unless a contrary intention appears in, or is to be implied from, the contract.

(3)   It is for the seller to show that a breach fell within subsection (1)(b) above.

(4)   This section does not apply to Scotland.]

[15B.   Remedies for breach of contract as respects Scotland

(1)   Where in a contract of sale the seller is in breach of any term of the contract (express or implied), the buyer shall be entitled—

(a)   to claim damages, and

(b)   if the breach is material, to reject any goods delivered under the contract and treat it as repudiated.

(2)   Where a contract of sale is a consumer contract, then, for the purposes of subsection (1)(b) above, breach by the seller of any term (express or implied)—

(a)   as to the quality of the goods or their fitness for a purpose,

(b)   if the goods are, or are to be, sold by description, that the goods will correspond with the description,

(c)   if the goods are, or are to be, sold by reference to a sample, that the bulk will correspond with the sample in quality, shall be deemed to be a material breach.

(3)   This section applies to Scotland only.]

PART III
EFFECTS OF THE CONTRACT

Transfer of property as between seller and buyer

16.   Goods must be ascertained

[Subject to section 20A below] Where there is a contract for the sale of unascertained goods no property in the goods is transferred to the buyer unless and until the goods are ascertained.

17.   Property passes when intended to pass

(1)   Where there is a contract for the sale of specific or ascertained goods the property in them is transferred to the buyer at such time as the parties to the contract intend it to be transferred.

(2)   For the purpose of ascertaining the intention of the parties regard shall be had to the terms of the contract, the conduct of the parties and the circumstances of the case.

18.   Rules for ascertaining intention

Unless a different intention appears, the following are rules for ascertaining the intention of the parties as to the time at which the property in the goods is to pass to the buyer.

Rule 1.—Where there is an unconditional contract for the sale of specific goods in a deliverable state the property in the goods passes to the buyer when the contract is made, and it is immaterial whether the time of payment or the time of delivery, or both, be postponed.

Rule 2.—Where there is a contract for the sale of specific goods and the seller is bound to do something to the goods for the purpose of putting them into a deliverable state, the property does not pass until the thing is done and the buyer has notice that it has been done.

Rule 3.—Where there is a contract for the sale of specific goods in a deliverable state but the seller is bound to weigh, measure, test, or do some other act or thing with reference to the goods for the purpose of ascertaining the price, the property does not pass until the act or thing is done and the buyer has notice that it has been done.

Rule 4.—When goods are delivered to the buyer on approval or on sale or return or other similar terms the property in the goods passes to the buyer:—

(a)   when he signifies his approval or acceptance to the seller or does any other act adopting the transaction;

(b)   if he does not signify his approval or acceptance to the seller but retains the goods without giving notice of rejection, then, if a time has been fixed for the return of the goods, on the expiration of that time, and, if no time has been fixed, on the expiration of a reasonable time.

Rule 5.—(1) Where there is a contract for the sale of unascertained or future goods by description, and goods of that description and in a deliverable state are unconditionally appropriated to the contract, either by the seller with the assent of the buyer or by the buyer with the assent of the seller, the property in the goods then passes to the buyer; and the assent may be express or implied, and may be given either before of after the appropriation is made.

(2)   Where, in pursuance of the contract, the seller delivers the goods to the buyer or to a carrier or other bailee or custodier (whether named by the buyer or not) for the purpose of transmission to the buyer, and does not reserve the right of disposal, he is to be taken to have unconditionally appropriated the goods to the contract.

[(3)   Where there is a contract for the sale of a specified quantity of unascertained goods in a deliverable state forming part of a bulk which is identified either in the contract or by subsequent agreement between the parties and the bulk is reduced to (or to less than) that quantity, then, if the buyer under that contract is the only buyer to whom goods are then due out of the bulk—

(a)   the remaining goods are to be taken as appropriated to that contract at the time when the bulk is so reduced; and

(b)   the property in those goods then passes to that buyer.

(4)   Paragraph (3) above applies also (with the necessary modifications) where a bulk is reduced to (or to less than) the aggregate of the quantities due to a single buyer under separate contracts relating to that bulk and he is the only buyer to whom goods are then due out of that bulk.]

19.   Reservation of right of disposal

(1)   Where there is a contract for the sale of specific goods or where goods are subsequently appropriated to the contract, the seller may, by the terms of the contract or appropriation, reserve the right of disposal of the goods until certain conditions are fulfilled; and in such a case,

notwithstanding the delivery of the goods to the buyer, or to a carrier or other bailee or custodier for the purpose of transmission to the buyer, the property in the goods does not pass to the buyer until the conditions imposed by the seller are fulfilled.

(2)   Where goods are shipped, and by the bill of lading the goods are deliverable to the order of the seller or his agent, the seller is prima facie to be taken to reserve the right of disposal.

(3)   Where the seller of goods draws on the buyer for the price, and transmits the bill of exchange and bill of lading to the buyer together to secure acceptance or payment of the bill of exchange, the buyer is bound to return the bill of lading if he does not honour the bill of exchange, and if he wrongfully retains the bill of lading the property in the goods does not pass to him.

20.   Risk prima facie passes with property

(1)   Unless otherwise agreed, the goods remain at the seller's risk until the property in them is transferred to the buyer, but when the property in them is transferred to the buyer the goods are at the buyer's risk whether delivery has been made or not.

(2)   But where delivery has been delayed through the fault of either buyer or seller the goods are at the risk of the party at fault as regards any loss which might not have occurred but for such fault.

(3)   Nothing in this section affects the duties or liabilities of either seller or buyer as a bailee or custodier of the goods of the other party.

[20A.   Undivided shares in goods forming part of a bulk

(1)   This section applies to a contract for the sale of a specified quantity of unascertained goods if the following conditions are met—

(a)   the goods or some of them form part of a bulk which is identified either in the contract or by subsequent agreement between the parties; and

(b)   the buyer has paid the price for some or all of the goods which are the subject of the contract and which form part of the bulk.

(2)   Where this section applies, then (unless the parties agree otherwise), as soon as the conditions specified in paragraphs (a) and (b) of subsection (1) above are met or at such later time as the parties may agree—

(a)   property in an undivided share in the bulk is transferred to the buyer; and

(b)   the buyer becomes an owner in common of the bulk.

(3)   Subject to subsection (4) below, for the purposes of this section,

the undivided share of a buyer in a bulk at any time shall be such share as the quantity of goods paid for and due to the buyer out of the bulk bears to the quantity of goods in the bulk at that time.

(4)   Where the aggregate of the undivided shares of buyers in a bulk determined under subsection (3) above would at any time exceed the whole of the bulk at that time, the undivided share in the bulk of each buyer shall be reduced proportionately so that the aggregate of the undivided shares is equal to the whole bulk.

(5)   Where a buyer has paid the price for only some of the goods due to him out of a bulk, any delivery to the buyer out of the bulk shall, for the purposes of this section, be ascribed in the first place to the goods in respect of which payment has been made.

(6)   For the purpose of this section payment of part of the price for any goods shall be treated as payment for a corresponding part of the goods.]

[20B.   Deemed consent by co-owner to dealings in bulk goods

(1)   A person who has become an owner in common of a bulk by virtue of section 20A above shall be deemed to have consented to—

(a)   any delivery of goods out of the bulk to any other owner in common of the bulk, being goods which are due to him under his contract;

(b)   any removal, dealing with, delivery or disposal of goods in the bulk by any other person who is an owner in common of the bulk is so far as the goods fall within that co-owner's undivided share in the bulk at the time of the removal, dealing, delivery or disposal.

(2)   No cause of action shall accrue to anyone against a person by reason of that person having acted in accordance with paragraph (a) or (b) of subsection (1) above in reliance on any consent deemed to have been given under that subsection.

(3)   Nothing in this section or section 20A above shall—

(a)   impose an obligation on a buyer of goods out of a bulk to compensate any other buyer of goods out of that bulk for any shortfall in the goods received by that other buyer;

(b)   affects any contractual arrangement between buyers of goods out of a bulk for adjustments between themselves; or

(c)   affect the rights of any buyer under his contract.]

. . .

34.   Buyer's right of examining the goods

[Unless otherwise agreed, when the seller tenders delivery of goods to the buyer, he is bound on request to afford the buyer a reasonable opportunity of examining the goods for the purpose of ascertaining whether they are in conformity with the contract [and, in the case of a contract for sale by sample, of comparing the bulk with the sample.]

35. Acceptance

(1)   The buyer is deemed to have accepted the goods [subject to subsection (2) below—

(a)   when he intimates to the seller that he has accepted them, or

(b)   when the goods have been delivered to him and he does any act in relation to them which is inconsistent with the ownership of the seller.

(2)   Where goods are delivered to the buyer, and he has not previously examined them, he is not deemed to have accepted them under subsection (1) above until he has had a reasonable opportunity of examining them for the purpose—

(a)   of ascertaining whether they are in conformity with the contract, and

(b)   in the case of a contract for sale by sample, of comparing the bulk with the sample.

(3)   Where the buyer deals as consumer or (in Scotland) the contract of sale is a consumer contract, the buyer cannot lose his right to rely on subsection (2) above by agreement, waiver or otherwise.

(4)   The buyer is also deemed to have accepted the goods when after the lapse of a reasonable time he retains the goods without intimating to the seller that he has rejected them.

(5)   The questions that are material in determining for the purposes of subsection (4) above whether a reasonable time has elapsed include whether the buyer has had a reasonable opportunity of examining the goods for the purpose mentioned in subsection (2) above.

(6)   The buyer is not by virtue of this section deemed to have accepted the goods merely because—

(a)   he asks for, or agrees to, their repair by or under an arrangement with the seller, or

(b)   the goods are delivered to another under a sub-sale or other disposition.

(7)   Where the contract is for the sale of goods making one or more commercial units, a buyer accepting any goods included in a unit is deemed to have accepted all the goods making the unit; and in this subsection 'commercial unit' means a unit division of which would materially impair the value of the goods or the character of the unit.

(8)] Paragraph 10 of Schedule 1 below applies in relation to a contract made before 22 April 1967 or (in the application of this Act to Northern Ireland) 28 July 1967.

[35A. Right of partial rejection

(1) If the buyer—

(a) has the right to reject the goods by reason of a breach on the part of the seller that affects some or all of them, but

(b) accepts some of the goods, including, where there are any goods unaffected by the breach, all such goods,

he does not by accepting them lose his right to reject the rest.

(2) In the case of a buyer having the right to reject an instalment of goods, subsection (1) above applies as if references to the goods were references to the goods comprised in the instalment.

(3) For the purposes of subsection (1) above, goods are affected by a breach if by reason of the breach they are not in conformity with the contract.

(4) This section applies unless a contrary intention appears in, or is to be implied from, the contract.]

Appendix 2 Unfair Terms in Consumer Contracts Regulations 1994

(SI 1994, No. 3159)
Reproduced by kind permission of Her Majesty's Stationery Office

1.   Citation and commencement

These Regulations may be cited as the Unfair Terms in Consumer Contracts Regulations 1994 and shall come into force on 1st July 1995.

2.   Interpretation

(1)   In these Regulations—

'business' includes a trade or profession and the activities of any government department or local or public authority;

'the Community' means the European Economic Community and the other States in the European Economic Area;

'consumer' means a natural person who, in making a contract to which these Regulations apply, is acting for purposes which are outside his business;

'court' in relation to England and Wales and Northern Ireland means the High Court, and in relation to Scotland, the Court of Session;

'Director' means the Director General of Fair Trading;

'EEA Agreement' means the Agreement on the European Economic Area signed at Oporto on 2 May 1992 as adjusted by the Protocol signed at Brussels on 17 March 1993;

'member State' shall mean a State which is a contracting party to the EEA Agreement but until the EEA Agreement comes into force in relation to Liechtenstein does not include the State of Liechtenstein;

'seller' means a person who sells goods and who, in making a contract to which these Regulations apply, is acting for purposes relating to his business; and 'supplier' means a person who supplies goods or services and who, in making a contract to which these Regulations apply, is acting for purposes relating to his business.

3. Terms to which these Regulations apply

(1)   Subject to the provisions of Schedule 1, these Regulations apply to any term in a contract concluded between a seller or supplier and a consumer where the said term has not been individually negotiated.

(2)   In so far as it is in plain, intelligible language, no assessment shall be made of the fairness of any term which—

(a)   defines the main subject matter of the contract, or

(b)   concerns the adequacy of the price or remuneration, as against the goods or services sold or supplied.

(3)   For the purposes of these Regulations, a term shall always be regarded as not having been individually negotiated where it has been drafted in advance and the consumer has not been able to influence the substance of the term.

(4)   Notwithstanding that a specific term or certain aspects of it in a contract has been individually negotiated, these Regulations shall apply to the rest of a contract if an overall assessment of the contract indicates that it is a pre-formulated standard contract.

(5)   It shall be for any seller or supplier who claims that a term was individually negotiated to show that it was.

4. Unfair terms

(1)   In these Regulations, subject to paragraphs (2) and (3) below, 'unfair term' means any term which contrary to the requirement of good faith causes a significant imbalance in the parties' rights and obligations under the contract to the detriment of the consumer.

(2)   An assessment of the unfair nature of a term shall be made taking into account the nature of the goods or services for which the contract was concluded and referring, as at the time of the conclusion of the contract, to all circumstances attending the conclusion of the contract and to all the other terms of the contract or of another contract on which it is dependent.

(3)   In determining whether a term satisfies the requirement of good faith, regard shall be had in particular to the matters specified in Schedule 2 to these Regulations.

(4)   Schedule 3 to these Regulations contains an indicative and non-exhaustive list of the terms which may be regarded as unfair.

5. Consequence of inclusion of unfair terms in contracts

(1) An unfair term in a contract concluded with a consumer by a seller of [sic] supplier shall not be binding on the consumer.

(2) The contract shall continue to bind the parties if it is capable of continuing in existence without the unfair term.

6. Construction of written contracts

A seller or supplier shall ensure that any written term of a contract is expressed in plain, intelligible language, and if there is doubt about the meaning of a written term, the interpretation most favourable to the consumer shall prevail.

7. Choice of law clauses

These Regulations shall apply notwithstanding any contract term which applies or purports to apply the law of a non member State, if the contract has a close connection with the territory of the member States.

8. Prevention of continued use of unfair terms

(1) It shall be the duty of the Director to consider any complaint made to him that any contract term drawn up for general use is unfair, unless the complaint appears to the Director to be frivolous or vexatious.

(2) If having considered a complaint about any contract term pursuant to paragraph (1) above the Director considers that the contract term is unfair he may, if he considers it appropriate to do so, bring proceedings for an injunction (in which proceedings he may also apply for an interlocutory injunction) against any person appearing to him to be using or recommending use of such a term in contracts concluded with consumers.

(3) The Director may, if he considers it appropriate to do so, have regard to any undertakings given to him by or on behalf of any person as to the continued use of such a term in contracts concluded with consumers.

(4) The Director shall give reasons for his decision to apply or not to apply, as the case may be, for an injunction in relation to any complaint which these Regulations require him to consider.

(5) The court on an application by the Director may grant an injunction on such terms as it thinks fit.

(6) An injunction may relate not only to use of a particular contract term drawn up for general use but to any similar term, or a term having like effect, used or recommended for use by any party to the proceedings.

(7) The Director may arrange for the dissemination in such form and manner as he considers appropriate of such information and advice con-

cerning the operation of these Regulations as may appear to him to be expedient to give to the public and to all persons likely to be affected by these Regulations.

SCHEDULE 1
CONTRACTS AND PARTICULAR TERMS EXCLUDED FROM THE SCOPE OF THESE REGULATIONS

These Regulations do not apply to—

    (a)   any contract relating to employment;

    (b)   any contract relating to succession rights;

    (c)   any contract relating to rights under family law;

    (d)   any contract relating to the incorporation and organisation of companies or partnerships; and

    (e)   any term incorporated in order to comply with or which reflects—

        (i) statutory or regulatory provisions of the United Kingdom; or

        (ii) the provisions or principles of international conventions to which the member States or the Community are party.

Regulation 4(3)   ## SCHEDULE 2
ASSESSMENT OF GOOD FAITH

In making an assessment of good faith, regard shall be had in particular to—

    (a)   the strength of the bargaining positions of the parties;

    (b)   whether the consumer had an inducement to agree to the term;

    (c)   whether the goods or services were sold or supplied to the special order of the consumer, and

    (d)   the extent to which the seller or supplier has dealt fairly and equitably with the consumer.

Regulation 4(4)   ## SCHEDULE 3
INDICATIVE AND ILLUSTRATIVE LIST OF TERMS WHICH MAY BE REGARDED AS UNFAIR

  1. Terms which have the object or effect of—

    (a)   excluding or limiting the legal liability of a seller or supplier in the event of the death of a consumer or personal injury to the latter resulting from an act or omission of that seller or supplier;

    (b)   inappropriately excluding or limiting the legal rights of the consumer vis-à-vis the seller or supplier or another party in the event of total or partial non-performance or inadequate performance by the seller or supplier of any of the contractual obligations, including the option of offsetting a debt owed to the seller or supplier against any claim which the consumer may have against him;

(c) making an agreement binding on the consumer whereas provision of services by the seller or supplier is subject to a condition whose realisation depends on his own will alone;

(d) permitting the seller or supplier to retain sums paid by the consumer where the latter decides not to conclude or perform the contract, without providing for the consumer to receive compensation of an equivalent amount from the seller or supplier where the latter is the party cancelling the contract;

(e) requiring any consumer who fails to fulfil his obligation to pay a disproportionately high sum in compensation;

(f) authorising the seller or supplier to dissolve the contract on a discretionary basis where the same facility is not granted to the consumer, or permitting the seller or supplier to retain the sums paid for services not yet supplied by him where it is the seller or supplier himself who dissolves the contract;

(g) enabling the seller or supplier to terminate a contract of indeterminate duration without reasonable notice except where there are serious grounds for doing so;

(h) automatically extending a contract of fixed duration where the consumer does not indicate otherwise, when the deadline fixed for the consumer to express this desire not to extend the contract is unreasonably early;

(i) irrevocably binding the consumer to terms with which he had no real opportunity of becoming acquainted before the conclusion of the contract;

(j) enabling the seller or supplier to alter the terms of the contract unilaterally without a valid reason which is specified in the contract;

(k) enabling the seller or supplier to alter unilaterally without a valid reason any characteristics of the product or service to be provided;

(l) providing for the price of goods to be determined at the time of delivery or allowing a seller of goods or supplier of services to increase their price without in both cases giving the consumer the corresponding right to cancel the contract if the final price is too high in relation to the price agreed when the contract was concluded;

(m) giving the seller or supplier the right to determine whether the goods or services supplied are in conformity with the contract, or giving him the exclusive right to interpret any term of the contract;

(n) limiting the seller's or supplier's obligation to respect commitments undertaken by his agents or making his commitments subject to compliance with a particular formality;

(o) obliging the consumer to fulfil all his obligations where the seller or supplier does not perform his;

(p) giving the seller or supplier the possibility of transferring his rights and obligations under the contract, where this may serve to reduce the guarantees for the consumer, without the latter's agreement;

(q) excluding or hindering the consumer's right to take legal action or exercise any other legal remedy, particularly by requiring the consumer to take disputes exclusively to arbitration not covered by legal provisions, unduly restricting the evidence available to him or imposing on him a burden of proof which, according to the applicable law, should lie with another party to the contract.

2. Scope of subparagraphs 1(g), (j) and (l)

(a) Subparagraph 1(g) is without hindrance to terms by which a supplier of financial services reserves the right to terminate unilaterally a contract of indeterminate duration without notice where there is a valid reason, provided that the supplier is required to inform the other contracting party or parties thereof immediately.

(b) Subparagraph 1(j) is without hindrance to terms under which a supplier of financial services reserves the right to alter the rate of interest payable by the consumer or due to the latter, or the amount of other charges for financial services without notice where there is a valid reason, provided that the supplier is required to inform the other contracting party or parties thereof at the earliest opportunity and that the latter are free to dissolve the contract immediately. Subparagraph 1(j) is also without hindrance to terms under which a seller or supplier reserves the right to alter unilaterally the conditions of a contract of indeterminate duration, provided that he is required to inform the consumer with reasonable notice and that the consumer is free to dissolve the contract.

(c) Subparagraphs 1(g), (j) and (l) do not apply to:—
transactions in transferable securities, financial instruments and other products or services where the price is linked to fluctuations in a stock exchange quotation or index or a financial market rate that the seller or supplier does not control;
contracts for the purchase or sale of foreign currency, traveller's cheques or international money orders denominated in foreign currency;

(d) Subparagraph 1(l) is without hindrance to price indexation clauses, where lawful, provided that the method by which prices vary is explicitly described.

Appendix 3 Consumer Protection Act 1987

[sections 1–9 only]
Reproduced by kind permission of Her Majesty's Stationery Office

PART I

PRODUCT LIABILITY

1.—(1) This Part shall have effect for the purpose of making such provision as is necessary in order to comply with the product liability Directive and shall be construed accordingly.

(2) In this Part, except in so far as the context otherwise requires—
'agricultural produce' means any produce of the soil, of stock-farming or of fisheries;

'dependant' and 'relative' have the same meaning as they have in, respectively, the Fatal Accidents Act 1976 and the Damages (Scotland) Act 1976;

'producer', in relation to a product, means—

(a) the person who manufactured it;

(b) in the case of a substance which has not been manufactured but has been won or abstracted, the person who won or abstracted it;

(c) in the case of a product which has not been manufactured, won or abstracted but essential characteristics of which are attributable to an industrial or other process having been carried out (for example, in relation to agricultural produce), the person who carried out that process;

'product, means any goods or electricity and (subject to subsection (3) below) includes a product which is comprised in another product, whether by virtue of being a component part or raw material or otherwise; and 'the product liability Directive' means the Directive of the Council of the European Communities, dated 25th July 1985, (No.85/374/EEC) on the approximation of the laws, regulations and administrative provisions of the member States concerning liability for defective products.

(3)   For the purposes of this Part a person who supplies any product in which products are comprised, whether by virtue of being component parts or raw materials or otherwise, shall not be treated by reason only of his supply of that product as supplying any of the products so comprised.

2.—(1)   Subject to the following provisions of this Part, where any damage is caused wholly or partly by a defect in a product, every person to whom subsection (2) below applies shall be liable for the damage.

(2)   This subsection applies to—

(a)   the producer of the product;

(b)   any person who, by putting his name on the product or using a trade mark or other distinguishing mark in relation to the product, has held himself out to be the producer of the product;

(c)   any person who has imported the product into a member State from a place outside the member States in order, in the course of any business of his, to supply it to another.

(3)   Subject as aforesaid, where any damage is caused wholly or partly by a defect in a product, any person who supplied the product (whether to the person who suffered the damage, to the producer of any product in which the product in question is comprised or to any other person) shall be liable for the damage if—

(a)   the person who suffered the damage requests the supplier to identify one or more of the persons (whether still in existence or not) to whom subsection (2) above applies in relation to the product;

(b)   that request is made within a reasonable period after the damage occurs and at a time when it is not reasonably practicable for the person making the request to identify all those persons; and

(c)   the supplier fails, within a reasonable period after receiving the request, either to comply with the request or to identify the person who supplied the product to him.

(4)   Neither subsection (2) nor subsection (3) above shall apply to a person in respect of any defect in any game or agricultural produce if the only supply of the game or produce by that person to another was at a time when it had not undergone an industrial process.

(5)   Where two or more persons are liable by virtue of this Part for the same damage, their liability shall be joint and several.

(6)   This section shall be without prejudice to any liability arising otherwise than by virtue of this Part.

3.—(1)   Subject to the following provisions of this section, there is a defect in a product for the purposes of this Part if the safety of the product is not such as persons generally are entitled to expect; and for those purposes 'safety', in relation to a product, shall include safety with respect to products comprised in that product and safety in the context of risks of damage to property, as well as in the context of risks of death or personal injury.

(2)   In determining for the purposes of subsection (1) above what persons generally are entitled to expect in relation to a product all the circumstances shall be taken into account, including—

(a)   the manner in which, and purposes for which, the product has been marketed, its get-up, the use of any mark in relation to the product and any instructions for, or warnings with respect to, doing or refraining from doing anything with or in relation to the product;

(b)   what might reasonably be expected to be done with or in relation to the product; and

(c)   the time when the product was supplied by its producer to another;

and nothing in this section shall require a defect to be inferred from the fact alone that the safety of a product which is supplied after that time is greater than the safety of the product in question.

4.—(1)   In any civil proceedings by virtue of this Part against any person ('the person proceeded against') in respect of a defect in a product it shall be a defence for him to show—

(a)   that the defect is attributable to compliance with any requirement imposed by or under any enactment or with any Community obligation; or

(b)   that the person proceeded against did not at any time supply the product to another; or

(c)   that the following conditions are satisfied, that is to say—

(i)   that the only supply of the product to another by the person proceeded against was otherwise than in the course of a business of that person's; and

(ii)   that section 2(2) above does not apply to that person or applies to him by virtue only of things done otherwise than with a view to profit; or

(d)   that the defect did not exist in the product at the relevant time; or

(e)   that the state of scientific and technical knowledge at the relevant time was not such that a producer of products of the same description as the product in question might be expected to have discovered the defect if it had existed in his products while they were under his control; or

(f)   that the defect—

(i)   constituted a defect in a product ('the subsequent product') in which the product in question had been comprised; and

(ii)   was wholly attributable to the design of the subsequent product or to compliance by the producer of the product in question with instructions given by the producer of the subsequent product.

(2)   In this section 'the relevant time', in relation to electricity, means the time at which it was generated, being a time before it was transmitted or distributed, and in relation to any other product, means—

(a)   if the person proceeded against is a person to whom subsection (2) of section 2 above applies in relation to the product, the time when he supplied the product to another;

(b)   if that subsection does not apply to that person in relation to the product, the time when the product was last supplied by a person to whom that subsection does apply in relation to the product.

5.—(1)   Subject to the following provisions of this section, in this Part 'damage' means death or personal injury or any loss of or damage to any property (including land).

(2)   A person shall not be liable under section 2 above in respect of any defect in a product for the loss of or any damage to the product itself or for the loss of or any damage to the whole or any part of any product which has been supplied with the product in question comprised in it.

(3)   A person shall not be liable under section 2 above for any loss of or damage to any property which, at the time it is lost or damaged, is not—

(a)   of a description of property ordinarily intended for private use, occupation or consumption; and

(b)   intended by the person suffering the loss or damage mainly for his own private use, occupation or consumption.

(4)   No damages shall be awarded to any person by virtue of this Part in respect of any loss of or damage to any property if the amount which would fall to be so awarded to that person, apart from this subsection and any liability for interest, does not exceed £275.

(5)   In determining for the purposes of this Part who has suffered any loss of or damage to property and when any such loss or damage occurred, the loss or damage shall be regarded as having occurred at the earliest

time at which a person with an interest in the property had knowledge of the material facts about the loss or damage.

(6)   For the purposes of subsection (5) above the material facts about any loss of or damage to any property are such facts about the loss or damage as would lead a reasonable person with an interest in the property to consider the loss or damage sufficiently serious to justify his instituting proceedings for damages against a defendant who did not dispute liability and was able to satisfy a judgment.

(7)   For the purposes of subsection (5) above a person's knowledge includes knowledge which he might reasonably have been expected to acquire—

(a)   from facts observable or ascertainable by him; or

(b)   from facts ascertainable by him with the help of appropriate expert advice which it is reasonable for him to seek;

but a person shall not be taken by virtue of this subsection to have knowledge of a fact ascertainable by him only with the help of expert advice unless he has failed to take all reasonable steps to obtain (and, where appropriate, to act on) that advice.

(8)   Subsections (5) to (7) above shall not extend to Scotland.

6.—(1)   Any damage for which a person is liable under section 2 above shall be deemed to have been caused—

(a)   for the purposes of the Fatal Accidents Act 1976, by that person's wrongful act, neglect or default;

(b)   for the purposes of section 3 of the Law Reform (Miscellaneous Provisions) (Scotland) Act 1940 (contribution among joint wrongdoers), by that person's wrongful act or negligent act or omission;

(c)   for the purposes of section 1 of the Damages (Scotland) Act 1976 (rights of relatives of a deceased), by that person's act or omission; and

(d)   for the purposes of Part II of the Administration of Justice Act 1982 (damages for personal injuries, etc.—Scotland), by an act or omission giving rise to liability in that person to pay damages.

(2)   Where—

(a)   a person's death is caused wholly or partly by a defect in a product, or a person dies after suffering damage which has been so caused;

(b)   a request such as mentioned in paragraph (a) of subsection (3) of section 2 above is made to a supplier of the product by that person's personal representatives or, in the case of a person whose death is caused wholly or partly by the defect, by any dependant or relative of that person; and

(c)   the conditions specified in paragraphs (b) and (c) of that subsection are satisfied in relation to that request,

this Part shall have effect for the purposes of the Law Reform (Miscellaneous Provisions) Act 1934, the Fatal Accidents Act 1976 and the Damages (Scotland) Act 1976 as if liability of the supplier to that person under that subsection did not depend on that person having requested the supplier to identify certain persons or on the said conditions having been satisified in relation to a request made by that person.

(3)   Section 1 of the Congenital Disabilities (Civil Liability) Act 1976 shall have effect for the purposes of this Part as if—

(a)   a person were answerable to a child in respect of an occurrence caused wholly or partly by a defect in a product if he is or has been liable under section 2 above in respect of any effect of the occurrence on a parent of the child, or would be so liable if the occurrence caused a parent of the child to suffer damage;

(b)   the provisions of this Part relating to liability under section 2 above applied in relation to liability by virtue of paragraph (a) above under the said section 1; and

(c)   subsection (6) of the said section 1 (exclusion of liability) were omitted.

(4)   Where any damage is caused partly by a defect in a product and partly by the fault of the person suffering the damage, the Law Reform (Contributory Negligence) Act 1945 and section 5 of the Fatal Accidents Act 1976 (contributory negligence) shall have effect as if the defect were the fault of every person liable by virtue of this Part for the damage caused by the defect.

(5)   In subsection (4) above 'fault' has the same meaning as in the said Act of 1945.

(6)   Schedule 1 to this Act shall have effect for the purpose of amending the Limitation Act 1980 and the Prescription and Limitation (Scotland) Act 1973 in their application in relation to the bringing of actions by virtue of this Part.

(7)   It is hereby declared that liability by virtue of this Part is to be treated as liability in tort for the purposes of any enactment conferring jurisdiction on any court with respect to any matter.

(8)   Nothing in this Part shall prejudice the operation of section 12 of the Nuclear Installations Act 1965 (rights to compensation for certain breaches of duties confined to rights under that Act).

7. The liability of a person by virtue of this Part to a person who has suffered damage caused wholly or partly by a defect in a product, or to a dependant or relative of such a person, shall not be limited or excluded by any contract term, by any notice or by any other provision.

8.—(1) Her Majesty may by Order in Council make such modifications of this Part and of any other enactment (including an enactment contained in the following Parts of this Act, or in an Act passed after this Act) as appear to Her Majesty in Council to be necessary or expedient in consequence of any modification of the product liability Directive which is made at any time after the passing of this Act.

(2) An Order in Council under subsection (1) above shall not be submitted to Her Majesty in Council unless a draft of the Order has been laid before, and approved by a resolution of, each House of Parliament.

9.—(1) Subject to subjection (2) below, this Part shall bind the Crown.

(2) The Crown shall not, as regards the Crown's liability by virtue of this Part, be bound by this Part further than the Crown is made liable in tort or in reparation under the Crown Proceedings Act 1947, as that Act has effect from time to time.

Index

References are to paragraph numbers.

Leading the Sales Team

David Hillier

Leading the Sales Team is a sales management book with a difference. Hillier has spent years successfully leading sales teams - and this shows in the book's down-to-earth style and concern with real life. The emphasis throughout is on tried and tested, sales-oriented solutions that can be applied in actual, often adverse, business conditions.

The author begins by looking at the qualities of the effective sales leader. He shows how the organization, structure and motivation of the team are all critical to success and gives numerous examples of job descriptions, commission schemes, review systems and disciplinary procedures. There are separate sections on boosting sales, improving customer service, building team spirit, analysing performance, organizing the office, managing time, recruiting and retaining high performers and working with 'difficult' staff. The book ends with practical advice on troubleshooting, problem-solving and crisis management.

This is a hands-on guide to managing, motivating and inspiring the sales force which, with its companion volume *Training the Sales Team*, will be invaluable to any sales manager intent on achieving better results quickly.

Gower

Making Major Sales

Neil Rackham

This work is based on the most extensive research project ever undertaken in the area of selling skills. It determines the best ways of selling high value products or services. The author and his team observed and studied more than 35,000 sales calls made by 10,000 sales people in twenty-three different countries over a period of twelve years. Their analysis revealed that many of the methods developed for selling low value goods just don't work in the environment of today's major sale.

The findings, published for the first time in this revolutionary book, will overturn a whole collection of accepted sales truths. *Making Major Sales* provides a set of simple and practical techniques which have now been tried in many leading companies with dramatic improvements in sales performance. The ideas described by Neil Rackham have already helped thousands of people to become more successful with large sales.

Gower

Motivating Your Sales Force

John Lidstone

Motivating sales people always has been one of the most important, as well as perhaps the most difficult, of all the tasks facing the sales manager. Today's increasingly competitive business climate demands a higher degree of knowledge and skill than ever in motivating the sales force to achieve results.

John Lidstone's book represents a twofold contribution. First, it offers a framework of understanding about human behaviour and the factors that influence it. Secondly, it provides practical guidance on how to develop a realistic programme of motivation. After a brief summary of current motivation theory and an analysis of leadership styles, the bulk of the text examines the needs which modern research has found to be important to sales people, and describes ways of satisfying these needs while at the same time meeting planned objectives. The final chapter is designed to help the reader construct a programme for action in relation to his or her own sales force.

Gower

Sales Promotion in Postmodern Marketing

Alan Toop and Christian Petersen

In this challenging book the authors argue for a radical review of sales promotion practice. They point out that all the circumstances that led to the evolution of modern marketing have changed prodigiously. Consumer spending patterns are different. The mass markets of the 1960s and 1970s have fragmented. Less is being spent on advertising and more on sales promotion and direct mail. The shape of retailing has altered drastically. Marketing activity is increasingly constrained by legislation and lobbying. Above all, today's consumer is more individual, more assertive, more sceptical and less willing to be seen as part of an undifferentiated mass.

According to the authors these developments will make successful brands ever more valuable. But success will require a different approach to what actually constitutes a brand, and a more subtle and flexible use of a wide range of media and methods to communicate brand values. Much of the book is devoted to a searching examination of non-advertising sales promotion techniques. The media and the methods are reviewed in detail to show how each of them can be deployed to maximum effect, and in a final section the management implications are considered.

The text is designed to give practical guidance and is illustrated throughout by examples of successful campaigns drawn from several countries and a wide variety of businesses. The result is a treasure house of ideas and insights that will be of immense value to all concerned with advertising and sales promotion, and indeed with marketing generally.

Gower